The Logic of
SEXUATION

SUNY series in Psychoanalysis and Culture
Henry Sussman, editor

The Logic of
SEXUATION

From Aristotle to Lacan

ELLIE RAGLAND

State University of New York Press

Published by
State University of New York Press, Albany

© 2004 State University of New York

For information, address State University of New York Press,
90 State Street, Suite 700, Albany, New York 12207

Production, Dana Foote
Marketing, Anne M. Valentine

Library of Congress Cataloging-in-Publication Data

Ragland-Sullivan, Ellie, 1941–
    The logic of sexuation : from Aristotle to Lacan / Ellie Ragland.
        p. cm. — (SUNY series in psychoanalysis and culture)
    Includes bibliographical references and index.
    ISBN 0-7914-6077-0 (alk. paper) — ISBN 0-7914-6078-9 (pbk. : alk. paper)
    1. Sex (Psychology) 2. Lacan, Jacques, 1901–   I. Title. II. Series.

BF175.5.S48R34 2004
155.3—dc22   2004041706

10 9 8 7 6 5 4 3 2 1

Dedicated to my mother, Lucile Stowe Ragland, and my brother, Gene Ragland, with love and gratitude for their support and encouragement

CONTENTS

PREFACE AND ACKNOWLEDGMENTS

Jacques Lacan (1901–1981) may be considered the most important thinker in France since René Descartes and the most innovative and far-ranging thinker in Europe since Friedrich Nietzsche, Karl Marx, and Sigmund Freud. Lacan's formation was that of a psychiatrist and psychoanalyst in the Freudian school. His return to Freud's theories, however, and particularly his rethinking of Freud's early observations on symbols, language, and sexuality led him to a rereading of Freud's texts that is so comprehensive and so radical that it virtually constitutes a new vision of man. Lacan's further work on sexuality and sexuation links *jouissance* (libidinal enjoyment) to language in a way that redefines the two kinds of knowledge that constitute what we call mind, but with the mind depicted as inseparable from the body. He, thereby, makes sense of Freudian libido as mental/bodily energy that functions as the subject of desire and the object of enjoyment.

Lacan's teaching put an end to an era when it was possible to talk about the human subject without reference to the ethos of the language, desire, and jouissance that structure it and, hence, condition all conscious and unconscious perception. In this sense, Lacan's revolutionary theories in psychoanalysis have immediate relevance for philosophy, linguistics, literary theory, gender theory, and the wider disciplines in the human sciences and humanities. Traditional philosophical dilemmas regarding the nature of the perceiving subject and its relation to objects, the status of human knowledge, the way knowledge is constituted as a dialectic, the meaning of sexuation as a binding together of sexuality and culture in subjective sets of identifications of fantasy and unconscious memory, the structure of discourse, and the scope of freedom are all problematized and given a new meaning in startling fashion by Lacan's psychoanalytic teaching.

The purpose of this book is to lay out the complex and elusive ideas of Jacques Lacan regarding the meaning of the phallus, the sexual difference, feminine sexuality as different from masculine sexuality, and the place of the mother in Lacanian teaching. This is no small task because in redefining these terms Lacan constructed a new theory of what knowledge is, and an extensive theory of how jouissance forms a separate knowledge system, as powerful as the more familiar system of representations. At stake is a finding that surprises. The limit of rationality and freedom is psychosis. The logic in play is that the psychotic has never inscribed the signifier for sexual difference that causes the lack-in-being from which desire as a structural motivating principle is born. In this sense, psychosis becomes an empirical proof of Lacan's theories regarding the differential distinction of all subject positions as a response to the phallic signifier and to the lack-in-being that he names castration.

Lacan's theories require a three-dimensional logic to make sense. Conscious, typical binary thought simply obscures the structure of the unconscious, made up as it is of the symbolic, the imaginary, the real, and the symptom. Thus, any theory that grapples with Lacan's ideas by reducing them to one of his myriad thoughts risks not understanding the breadth and scope of this teaching. Lacan's claim that individuals make the world of their thought equal to their own conscious understanding of it is validated in such truncated readings of Lacan. The challenge for any reader is how to approach this dense thought and unfamiliar use of language to ascertain what Lacan meant. In this book I hope to have shed some light on this difficult aspect of Lacan's teaching such that psychological and philosophical studies that perplex over the referent and the cause of a given effect, for example, will have found answers to these age-old questions in Lacan's work.

My goal of rendering Lacan's theory of sexuation accessible to any study of his work presents a theory that broadens and deepens the study of gender, insofar as one's sexuation joins culture/language to mind/body by an interweaving of castration and the interpretation of sexual difference. Lacan argued that there is no signifier for gender in the unconscious. Given that there is no preordained male or female subject, there cannot be transgendered subjects either. Jacques-Alain Miller has offered the theory that biological boys and girls try to take their sexual identities from the Mother <> Father parental couple, while unaware that the Male <> Female sexual couple is not reducible to the parental couple. Lacan gives us the Masculine <> Feminine couple wherein the masculine has to do with identification within the symbolic order of language and social conventions while the feminine has to do with identification within the real order of the seemingly impossible to say or grasp. Masculine and feminine identifications are not, then, equatable with biological sex. While the material of the symbolic and the real will differ from culture to culture, one may find that males who are obsessionals in terms of desire are marked by feminine traits, while girls who are hysterics are marked by masculine identificatory traits.

The hope has been expressed that a chronological ordering of Lacan's teachings by historical periods will provide final clarity and insight. This is, certainly, a seductive idea and one that has been applied to Freud's texts. But such a tactic implies a linear progression in insight. Lacan taught that such a manner of reading Freud has led us to undervalue the majesty of Freud's scattered and elusive discoveries. Although one can, as Jacques-Alain Miller has demonstrated, trace clear periods of focus and development in Lacan's teachings, any periodization also follows Lacan's flight from institution to institution. This attests to the political, dangerous nature of Lacan's words. But what is truly gripping and unsettling is that Lacan often waits years to answer a question posed twenty years before. His pronouncements continually double back on themselves and consequently defy chronology. I have respected chronology in the sense that I have sought to show how Lacan's theories regarding the phallus, castration, femininity, masculinity, and the object make sense of Freud's own impasses in his study of feminine sexuality. I have started with Lacan's essay on "The Signification of the Phallus" (1958) and ended with his *Seminar IV* on *The Object Relation,* having studied his "Congress on Feminine Sexuality" (1958) and his *Seminar XX* (1972–1973): *Encore,* in between.

Finally, I should like to record here my gratitude to the University of Missouri for a year's sabbatical leave during which I wrote this book. I am also grateful to my mother, Lucile Stowe Ragland, for sharing her home with me and to my brother, Gene Ragland, for finding me office space in which to work. Thanks go, as well, to the Lacan Study Group with whom I have worked for two years for their suggestions and questions in reading portions of my manuscript. Thank you Gregg Hyder, Filip Kovacevic, Zak Watson, and Jack Stone. Further, I would like to thank the members of the Guild House at the University of Michigan in Ann Arbor for the super coffee they provided me while I was writing. I also appreciate help with typing up variations of my editings from Christy Houle and Vickie Thorp. Other friends and colleagues with whom I had discussions are too numerous to name. But I thank them one and all.

I

"On the Signification of the Phallus" (1958)
According to Lacan

Masculine (Symbolic)	Feminine (Real)

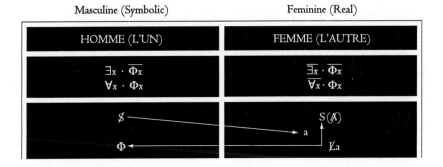

The idea that either Freud or Lacan can contribute anything new to an understanding of the sexual difference has been rejected by many American feminists and psychoanalysts as well. By retracing the history of one small disagreement, we shall try to put that view into perspective with the hope of redressing a balance that advances the study of psychoanalysis as a theory of how mind is constituted and linked to the body. In his return to Freud, Lacan maintained that not only does conscious thought emanate from unconscious thought, moreover, it bifurcates into four different ways of thinking depending on how the sexual difference is interpreted: (1) the "normative" masquerade, (2) the neuroses (obsession and hysteria), (3) perversion, and (4) the psychoses. These are structurations of desire that join mind to body, and are not meant here as pathologies or descriptions of varying sexual behaviors.

One of Lacan's principle theses is that while there is a sexual rapport in the animal world that seems to be based on instinct, humans have never had such a rapport because of the perturbations caused by the linkage of fantasy and language to the phallus (Φ) and castration ($-\phi$), as well as to the objects that first cause desire. Thus, each person's most basic partner is his or her own unconscious Other, not the other of the relationship. Lacanian scholar and analyst Geneviève Morel goes so far as to call this an equation and principle thesis in Lacan: "'Sexual non-rapport' is an equivalent of the 'phallus.'"[1] Contrary to Freud, Lacan stressed that the "meaning of the phallus" is linked to the fact that the penis is not the phallus.

The psychoanalytic debates of the twenties and thirties among Karl Abraham, Karl Jung, Karen Horney, Hélène Deutsch, Ernest Jones, Melanie Klein, Hannah Segal, and other post-Freudians could not make sense anymore than could Freud, of his theories on feminine sexuality and the phallus. Each analyst had a different theory of how feminine sexuality differed from masculine sexuality, and what the stakes truly were in what Freud called *Realität* (psychic reality). Although these debates were passionate, they never derived a thesis that elaborated a logic of psychoanalysis, not in Freud's essays such as "Some Psychic Consequences on the Anatomical Distinction between the Sexes" (1925), "Female Sexuality" (1931), and "Femininity" (1932), nor in those written by his colleagues.[2] Since those days, psychology, sociology and poststructuralism, among others of the "social sciences," have taken up the question of the meaning of the sexual difference, but have not evolved a logic such as Lacan's. Lacan sought to make "scientific" sense of the *sexual difference* itself, not only within the field of psychoanalysis but by borrowing from other fields and, thereby, extending the meaning and scope of psychoanalysis, logic, epistemology, and science, among other areas of study.

The three Freud essays just mentioned bring up the question that bothers many readers of Lacan. Why would he return to, or retain, Freud's use of the provocative word *phallus*? If we scrutinize some of the disagreements regarding the term *phallus*, starting with Lacan's differing from Freud over the meaning of the word itself, perhaps we can shed light on why some contemporary feminist thinkers such as Luce Irigaray and others have (mis-)taken Lacan for Freud, arguing that he equated the word *phallus* with the biological male organ, as Freud generally did. Lacan maintained that, from early childhood on, individuals distinguish among the penis as a real organ, the phallus as an imaginary object, and the phallic function of "no" as causative of a lack-in-being (or castration). So far-ranging is Lacan's thinking here that he gradually equates the early perception—within the first few months—of the sexual difference with the construction of a dialectical base of "mind": The latter emanates, strangely enough, from the structuration of desire between losing an object and wanting its return. Paradoxically, gender-based "essentialist" misreadings of Lacan's thought remain closer to Freud's biological reductionisms than to Freud's continual efforts to separate psychic reality from biological realities and exterior sensory data.

In this regard, Ernest Jones wrote: "I think that the Viennese could reproach us [Freud and his followers] with too high an evaluation of primordial fantasy life, at the expense of exterior reality. To that we will answer that no serious danger exists that analysts will neglect exterior reality insofar as it is always possible for them to underestimate Freudian doctrine on the importance of psychic reality."[3] In that multiple issues are raised in any consideration of what links psychic reality to the body, Lacan followed Freud's own efforts to decipher the meaning of the phallus. But Lacan's attention to Freud here is also merely a touchstone for another investigation—for answering the question of what constitutes "reality." Lacan points out that even for Freud the concept of reality remained simplistically split between exterior reality of sense data (*Wirklichkeit*) and interior psychic reality (*Realität*).[4]

Freud first made this distinction in *The Project* for a scientific psychology in 1895.[5] By 1889 he had put together the idea of a contrasted pair: *Realität* versus the wish or dream. Equating *Realität* with the *objective* psychic reality that accomplishes a desire or wish, he agreed that human psychism emanates from there. Lacan argued that one sees in Freud's equation of psychic reality with a fulfilled wish the incipient notion of a reality-based ego that marks Freud's second topology; there the ego serves as the mediator between the id and the superego. Be it as a wish or an interceding ego, Freud maintained that the nature of psychic *Realität* is specified in its being constituted by the realization of a desire (Westerhausen, p. 34). Moreover, the wish or dream accomplishes an objective concerning the *Realität*. But in what would the realization of dream desire consist? Freud admits in *Traumdeutung* (*The Interpretation of Dreams*) that he does not know.[6]

But Freud had another notion of reality as well, one following a "master discourse" kind of logic. He believed that the observable objects of the world bore the "reality" of the interpretation(s) he attributed to them. For example, he did not doubt that the "ideal couple" was derived from the oneness or unity of the mother and infant dyad and was, indeed, an objective reality. In this, he was a kind of phenomenological "empiricist" who took his own observations and interpretations to be positive facts, although he continually emended his interpretations in footnotes, addenda, and through an essay style of constant correction of his own erroneous views.

From the start of his teaching, Lacan began to restructure Freud's binary splits between reality and fantasy, (biology and psyche, and so on). This culminated in his own equation of fantasy with reality, wherein he proposed that unities of "natural" rapport between mother and infant only exists at the level of imaginary fantasy. So strong is this fantasy, Lacan insisted, that it eventually becomes the pervasive myth of a totalized essential Woman—a kind of Ur-mother—who is thought (in Kleinian fashion) to contain the object(s) that Lacan says cause desire—the gaze, the breast, the urinary flow, the feces, the voice, the (imaginary) phallus, the nothing, and the phoneme. The mother's constant temporal comings and goings are experienced by her infant, not so much as organ losses, but as a fading away of the grounding whose force field is the surface of the infant's own skin. The infant takes its body to be an imaginary consistency or a surface cut into by the real of the holes created by maternal absences and disappearances.

Jeanne Lafont refers to this simple topology of the one-dimensional border (or edge) and the hole as being written like this:

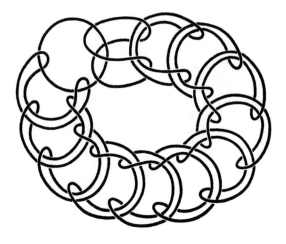

The hole and its edge are the base grammar of the real. In other words, the real is the "reality principle" which one is always pushed to retrieve, refind, and expel because it "ex-sists" outside the pleasures of imaginary bodily consistency and is felt as a rupture of well-being and homogeneous comfort.[7] Because the real was first created by the traumatic effects of loss, it must continually be mastered in that it is the central structure of being. Thus, its first form is that of a central void ($\emptyset$) that continually shatters or, at least, perturbs an incipient ego's sense of consistency and continuity. Insofar as language gradually fills the holes, as well as being disrupted by them, it contains its own material referent in the "letter" (*l'être*) of being, as opposed to the signifier of language. No pregiven metalanguage serves as the source of thought and memory, then. Rather than emanating from deep thought, language ties itself to the unary traits of imaginary identifications, real affects, symbolic conventions, and symptomatic sublimations of an ideal "Father's Name" linked to a mother's enigmatic desire and jouissance—Lacan's formulae for the "Oedipus complex."

The Lacanian phallus is an imaginary copula, then, seeming to join the two sexes for reproduction and/or love. But in the unconscious, the phallus is not inscribed as a link to language. It is, rather, an effect of difference. Patients of Freud's attested, in fact, to its imaginary properties of semblance or fantasy, Lacan taught. But they did not conceptualize the phallus as lying behind the masks that make the visible seem to be itself, and behind the words that try to name the real, while, instead, they repress, deny, repudiate, or foreclose it. For this reason alone, Lacan denounced Aristotle for basing logic on the grammar of language (Morel, pp. 97–98). The reality of language lies in its duplicity, not in its truth. In the late fifties Lacan portrayed the phallus as a mask, and "normative" sexual prescriptions of a given culture as a comic masquerade. One sees why he would claim that we see the masquerade at work more clearly in Greek and Roman art, or in Rabelais in the French Renaissance, than in contemporary Western art where the Father's Name signifier has come unhooked from the law, thus forestall-ing comedy at its own expense (Morel, p. 21). Such comedy is to be found, nonetheless, in television sitcoms and in other genres as well.

Later, we will return to the importance of Freud's efforts to distinguish between a truly *real* psychic reality (*Realität*) and one that accounts in a radically different way for external reality (*Wirklichkeit*). He makes the distinction precisely on the issue of the phallic phase. Indeed, Freud's claims regarding the phallus are responsible for the furor regarding such a notion that raged within the psychoanalytic movement of his day. For the moment, we will leave aside what Lacan called Freud's connections of desire to reality, to focus, rather, on Freud's first mentions of the phallus in 1923, 1924, and 1925 when he added the idea of a new libidinal stage of evolution he called the *phallic phase*, common to both sexes. In the heated debates that took place among analysts from 1920 to 1935 regarding the phallic phase, the key issue was their attempt to understand the true nature of the phallus in relation to the action of accomplishing a desire. As we know, the disagreements were wide flung: Karl Abraham and Melanie Klein viewed the phallus as an imaginary part-object that could just as easily be symbolized by the breast as by any other organ; Karen Horney, Ernest Jones, and Karl Jung argued for equal and equivalent principles of male womb envy and female penis envy, the Elektra complex equaling the Oedipus complex, and so on.

Lacan returned to these biologically oriented debates to note that the organ was always erroneously taken to be the-thing-in-itself. He argued that this phenomenologi-cal view kept the analysts in question from answering their own queries. Approaching the question of the sexual difference, not from the viewpoint of organ reality, but as something to be understood from the representational and libidinal registers of the imaginary, the symbolic, and the real, Lacan, nonetheless, paid honor to Freud for having seen and articulated the idea that unconscious phenomena are at issue in the enigmatic meaning of the sexual difference. Beyond serving as a mask over the sexual difference, or as an abstract signifier that marks it—that is, as a propositional function—the "meaning of the phallus" is also a real sexual genital jouissance ($\Phi+$) that links the body to conscious acts and thoughts via an everflowing unconscious language of fantasy and desire.

However, Lacan's linking of the body to language by way of unconscious fantasy, is never a light-hearted notion. He calls the fantasy a "canker" that appears in the guise of enjoying the body—enjoying the Other as body, as well—in such a way as to disorganize one's experience of one's own body. This is a very different idea of the body as fantasized (imaginary body) from Descartes's concept of it as a *res extensa* imagined in a pregiven space. For Descartes's whole body, Lacan substitutes a body that necessitates another kind of space: a topological space that is not limited to the three dimensions of the imaginary, symbolic, and the real (Morel, pp. 22–23.)

Stressing that Freud never clarified his many thoughts on the phallus, Lacan points to "The Infantile Genital Organization: An Interpolation into Theory of

Sexuality" (1923) where Freud called the phallus an imaginary object. Throughout all his texts commenting on the phallus, Freud alternated between describing it as illusory—an imaginary object or illusory psychic reality—and as the masculine genital organ. Like Elizabeth Grosz and others, psychoanalytic theorist Anne Berman has, somewhat accusatorily, suggested that it was Lacan—not Freud—who introduced the distinction between the penis and the phallus.[8] Indeed, in many English mistranslations of Freud's precise terms, one would not necessarily know that the distinction is Freud's own. In his article "The Infantile Genital Organization" (1923), for instance, one easily sees that Lacan's literal and correct reading of Freud's German would never have resulted in his claiming to introduce contrasts between the penis and the phallus if they had not already been clearly present in Freud.[9]

However, it was Lacan who added the proposition that the phallus orients "sexuality"—and, thereby, mentality—in a minimal number of interpretations of the sexual difference that are based on how a child identifies with the signifier and "agency" of the Father's Name, as transmitted by the mother's unconscious desire. This proposition claims that one's sexual identity has a (phallic) basis in terms of which the sexual difference has been interpreted as a castration to be repressed, denied, repudiated, or foreclosed. For example, the obsessional (neurotic) takes knowledge as his master signifier—S_2 reduced to S_1—as the phallic mark of his power. The hysteric (neurotic) identifies with her father, or a very close replica of him, in an equation of identity, knowledge, and "being" with sexuation: $\cancel{S} \rightarrow S_1$. The "normative" subject of a given social order takes the values and masquerades of the reigning symbolic Other as the "phallus" to please, or to be: $\varnothing/\Phi$. The perverse subject identifies with being the object (a) that would fill the Other's lack, which he equates with bringing jouissance to The Woman, or her feminine stand-in: $\varnothing/a$. The psychotic forecloses the phallic "no" which imposes a lack-in-being on other subjects, resulting in the identification of a whole subject with a whole Other: $S \cong O$.

These are the different pathways desire may take vis-à-vis the castrating "no" pronounced by the real father of jouissance, thereby dividing the sexes by placing an incest taboo on the infant/mother dyad. In his later seminars Lacan argues that the "no" creates holes in the symbolic, placing gaps or impasses between signifiers, and "cuts" in(to) the supposed consistency of the imaginary body, cuts whose effects create erogenous zones of desire at the surface of the real of flesh.[10] In other words, the losses of the primary object-cause-of-desire bring together the "psychic" operations of the desire to replace a lost trait or pleasure and the construction of the field of the partial drives (the invocatory, oral, and anal drives), all referred to the primary scopic one.[11] The second-level effect of the phallic interdiction is a "no" to being All One sex, an androgyn.

The result of the anatomical difference is interpreted in the imaginary and symbolic such that neither sex "has" the phallus, and neither sex "is" it. The masculine/feminine opposition is not a binary difference then. Rather, a subtle dialectic of desire organizes itself around the phallic signifier whose effects are primary, but which functions subsequently as a third term: a signifier without a signified Lacan says $(\Phi)/-$. Moreover, the third-term effect produces a quadrature, mathematically speaking. That is, three cannot cohere topologically at the place or site where the third category (the real) "ek-sists" on the inverse side of a cross-cap

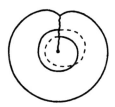

or Moebius strip [8] without making a kind of hole *and* knot at the point of the twist or turn. Lafont says:

> The cross-cap is a Moebius Strip where the hole would be reduced to a point, ignored and invisible. It is also the adjunction to a Moebius strip of a particular stopper, named [(*a*)] by Lacan, and which has the particularity of being bilateral itself both in carrying, not only the central point which structures the cross-cap, but also the double buckle of a Moebius strip. That is to say that it is at the center of this dialectic between the hole and its edges. (*Topologie lacanienne* . . . , pp. 18–19)

Indeed, any male or female may well *pretend* not to have "it" ("phallic" power or its desirability) even though one has "it"—be it as a corporation president or the mother in the kitchen running it (Morel, p. 26). In this sense, the phallus is commensurate with the master signifier (S_1). By reading on the obverse of the power/desire dialectic, by aiming askew, one sees the Freudian distinction between the penis meaning a biological organ and the phallus taken as a psychic reality. Lacan first valorized this concept of the phallus, not realizing, perhaps, that it would lead him to found a new concept of the phallus. Lacan's reconceptualization occurs, paradoxically, not at the point where the terms *penis* or *phallus* are used interchangeably, but at the points where Freud used the terms interchangeably in trying unsuccessfully to distinguish between *Realität* and *Wirklichkeit*.

Freud's concept of *Realität*, Lacan argues, shows the phallus to be an imaginary representation of an object of desire—the penis, the father himself, or a baby—and in *Wirklichkeit*, the phallus is a datum of biological reality in the sense of an organ that enjoys: that is, the penis itself. Lacan argued that Ernest Jones's errors were good examples of how all the post-Freudians of the twenties and thirties made egregious mistakes in proposing their own imaginary delineations. Indeed, their interpretations reduced psychoanalysis to the positivistic study we now call psychology.[12]

Jones, Lacan said, simply could not figure out how to give a symbolic status to the phallus. For Lacan, "symbolic status" always implied a logic of the signifier as that which implies lack ($) by representing a subject for another signifier. Going back to Aristotle's logic of class and attribute, Lacan argues that language remained insufficient and an obstacle to explaining the questions Aristotle raised. Lacan stressed, rather, Gottlieb Frege's, Ludwig Wittgenstein's, and Ferdinand de Saussure's findings: That the signifier always differs from itself—(a ≠ a); "a" does not equal "a". "I" does not equal itself from one speech act to the next: Frege, for example, was discontent with the linguistic expression "subject attribute." Lacan returned to Freud's laws of the unconscious—condensation and displacement—and Jakobson's discovery of metaphor and metonymy as the two principle axes of language, to demonstrate that the laws of the signifier *are* those of metaphor and metonymy. This means, as Geneviève Morel puts it, that "according to its context, the signifier can take on any value" (Morel, pp. 29–31). By exchanging the logical terms *function, argument, agent* for the grammatical ones, *subject, verb, attribute*, Lacan also borrowed "arms" from Frege for showing how logic unsticks itself from grammar. In this context, in the 1970s, Lacan proposed the phallus as a function of a sexuated subject (Φ) where "x" represents the subject (Morel, p. 31).

By not imagining the quadratic complexity of psychic reality, Jones claimed one can reconcile the irreconcilable: One could easily join *Realität* to *Wirklichkeit* in a simplistic, analogical reductionism. In his articles on feminine sexuality, for example, Jones takes the phallus to be a penis and reduces the function of the organ to penetration. Desire —conceived of as the accomplishment of a reality or a wish as Freud implied in describing *Realität*—was relegated by his followers to the level of a real (as in factual reality) or natural satisfaction. Thus, Jones's concept of wish as desire has nothing to do with the unconscious desire Lacan intuited in Freud, and defined as the gap or splitting between the need for satisfaction and the demand for love in "The Signification. . .".[13] Lacan wrote in 1958:

> By a reversal that is not simply a negation of the negation, the power of pure loss emerges from the residue of an obliteration. For the unconditional element of demand, desire substitutes the "absolute" condition: this condition unties the knot of that element in the proof that love is resistant to the satisfaction of a need. Thus desire is neither the appetite for satisfaction, nor the demand for love, but the difference that results from the subtraction of the first from the second, the phenomenon of their splitting.

Indeed, the unique constitutive reference for unconscious desire is that language be oriented by the primordial objects-cause-of-desire whose symbol—the *a*—lies at the heart of the three jouissances whose logic Lacan formalized in the Borromean knot where orders of the real, symbolic, and imaginary intersect. Between the symbolic and the real, he placed the symbolic phallus (Φ), equated with the language and concepts of reality given by a local/universal order. Between orders of the symbolic and imaginary, he placed the imaginary phallus ($-\phi$) by which he marked castration as a gap between a thing and its name, thereby representing a point of lack in the subject that gives rise to a "sense" (*sens*) beyond signification ($\cancel{S}$). And between the imaginary and the real, he situated the Other jouissance, sometimes marking the primary real of chaos and fragmentation, with a void at its center ($\varnothing$):[14]

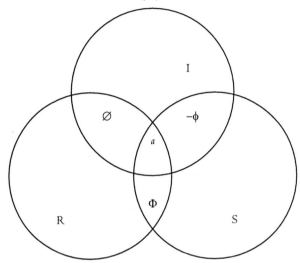

In the 1950s, desire becomes the unconscious question in the mother's discourse that refers itself to the signifier of the Father's Name, in reference to the third part of this dialectic: The child as phallus, or object of desire. In his last formula for the paternal metaphor (or Oedipal complex), Lacan rewrote Freud's Oedipus complex to argue that one "identity" solution to the lack-of-being-whole, created by the sexual divide, is to seek to fill the void left in its wake by simulacra of the lost object (a) through identifications.[15] The object (a) is proximate to unary traits (S_I)—indivisible, single strokes of identification—taken from the real, imaginary, and symbolic orders. Thus, the unary trait's own absolute density is a coalescence of traits from each of these orders, with a preponderance of emphasis given to the "force field" of which every drive is in ascendance over another.

And the drives emanate from what Lacan, in 1960, described as the first eight objects-cause-of-desire, which are both constituitive of an Ur-lining of the subject and without specularity or alterity. In *"Le sinthome: un mixte de symptôme et fantasme,"* Miller describes the barred subject as a void: One goes from the hole made by the perception of the sexual difference, the imaginary $-\phi$, to the subject emptied of enjoyment ($\cancel{S}$); that is, one goes from the hole made by the loss of the object a to the lack of enjoyment (from $\varnothing$ to $\cancel{S}$), insofar as its absence reflects traits of a positivized identity, but without representation.[16] In his Seminars on James Joyce, Lacan maintained that Joyce sought to fill the void by making the real voice suture all the crevices in being and body: $\varnothing/a$.[17]

Indeed, the object a in the center of the Borromean unit articulates, as well, the Φ; the $-\phi$; and the $\varnothing$: three castrations or negations. These are the three holes connected to each of the three jouissance(s). Lacan's innovation lies in his showing that the hole of the unconscious is inserted by the symbolic, which leaves positivized traces at the site of the object. Giving radically new meaning to any "materialist" theory of language, Lacan argues that the hole made by the phallic divide is one no imaginary fantasy can ever repair. The split between the sexes—$\Phi/—$—makes the "object" itself only ever "partial"—the negativized phallus is imaginary $(-\phi)$; the word can never equal the voice or the "letter" in saying it all in the symbolic; the hole in the Other $(\varnothing)$—the Other not existing as such—acquires a pseudoexistence of alienation, given that language names affects, images, and concepts (Lafont, p. 116).

Ernest Jones depicted the phallus as an imaginary object, structured in the same mode as any other object. Thus, Jones's "phallus" has no properties of lack in the image $(-\phi)$; in what the word depicts $(S_I \rightarrow S_2)$, nor in some supersexual libidinal phallic function $(\Phi x;\exists x;\Phi)$. Lacan gives three meanings of lack to the phallus, meanings on which its privilege depends. In this sense, Jones's "imaginary" is not Lacan's: Symbolizing the lack in the image I(mage) $(\sqrt{I})$ by the *square root of the negative*, Lacan makes the image that which only partly represents what it is trying to incarnate. This matheme states the proposition that part of its meaning is always lacking in the image.[18] While Jones opened the door wide to object-relations theories by making of the phallus a positivized partial object—the-things-in-itself, marked by moral attributes, both external and internal, and good or bad—Lacan argued that such an inside/outside distinction is always a subjective imaginary modeled on a false image of the body. The body's seeming wholeness is divided by the image of an outside and inside, giving one the idea of volume, of the container and the contained. "In their complexity," Lacan writes in 1973, "knots are well-designed to make us relativize the supposed three dimensions of space, founded solely on the translation we give for our body in a solid volume."[19] Lacan pointed out that the place of the object (a) is not *in* the mother's body, as object-relations theories claim, but *in* the fantasy. Jones's error, paradoxically, is that of any critique that attributes to the phallus qua penis the *function* of properties equatable with character attributes. Lacan accorded the phallus a function, proposing for it the status of the key signifier by which both sexes interpret their sexuality as lacking (or not) in reference to the mother's unconscious desire regarding her own sexual difference.

Giving new meaning to Freud's "The Ego and the Id" (1923), Lacan also redefines Freud's invention of an imaginary order by equating its formation with that of the ego. He follows Freud in viewing the ego as first and foremost a bodily ego. Unlike Freud, however, he argues that the ego is not merely a surface "entity," but is itself the projection of a surface.[20] Lacan's rethinking here is of a piece with his explanation for why we see the body in a solid body form. Although anatomy lends itself to such an interpretation, the body actually takes on that form "for the sake of our gaze" (*S. XX*, p. 133). By that he means that we see the body as whole in order to avoid seeing it as lacking, lack, paradoxically, being precisely that which the gaze shows. In "Painting,"

Gérard Wajcman writes that thought and space are, indeed, coherent and homogeneous in that both are extensions that cannot be thought outside of thought. Thus, space measures thought at the level of geometry, equating proof with the visible and the quantifiable.

Even though Descartes, like Irwin Panofsky, later, uproots the object from its representation by proposing that all space is homogeneous, Lacan removes the logical flaws from Descartes's *partes extra partes* proposal that all parts are identical, even in being different. In 1966, Lacan introduced the notion of value which can suppose an imaginary identity that is actually a measurable equality. But thought does not introduce measure—conceived of as separating things—into space. Rather, thought constitutes and builds space. But what are geometry's measures, Wajcman asks, answering that the body is its own image given meaning: Spatial extensions and thought are reducible to the imaginary/symbolic body—to its space. Descartes's impasse lay in his reducing visual structure to a metrical geometry that made it impossible for him to think the opposition between the desiring subject and the world of objects, enveloped as they are in the seemingly unified "clothing" of skin. Descartes's "Body," thought of as extended space, is as imaginary as Ernest Jones's phallus.

Jacques Derrida's poststructuralism imputes to Lacan a teaching based on phallo-phono-logo-centric principles. From this premise, Derrida views the Lacanian phallus, not as a part of the body which is, in turn, re-presented in perception, but as a privileged signifier whose function would be transcendental; a nondetermined metaphysical element among heterogeneous elements. For Derrida, the phallic function would be that of ending the eternal sliding of the phonemic signifier. We know, of course, that words do not continually slide arbitrarily into one another, either as proper nouns, verbs, adjectives, and so on, nor as phonemes. Words anchor sound in points of fixity in the imaginary, symbolic, real, and the symptom, fixities that constitute the meanings one lives from. They organize the "serial" (a,b,c; 1,2,3) that Lacan calls "the serious." Indeed, where there is fixity, Lacan argues, one finds the real.

Beyond merely communicating, or, more often, miscommunicating, words also seek to decipher the ineffable object (*a*), the enigmatic essence of one's own being which language seeks to cover, discover, conceal, or reveal as one's "true allure," one' desirability. The phallus is not the transcendental signifier Derrida calls it, but a key organizing signifier whose functions are manifold. It masks the real of sexuality and trauma by linking language to the law of difference—not only insofar as one sound or one meaning always differs from another—but also insofar as phallic "law," by delineating this from that, the masculine from the feminine, for example, orients desire. In this sense, the phallus can be said to construct the *Realität* Freud sought to describe, a psychic reality whose laws also have the formal properties of the already formalized functions of language.

Thus, the phallus's referents differ from the sense-data realities of biological life. Put another way, the phallus functions to structure biological realities by the processes of identification that govern desire. The form of the imaginary body, Lacan proposes, is composed of a set of identifications with mirror-stage other(s) in all three orders. It becomes a symbolic body by incorporating language as the Ideal ego construct Lacan places at the base of his *che vuoi* graph.[21] In "Group Psychology and the Analysis of the Ego" (1921), Freud called the Ideal ego a primordial identification.[22] Lacan interpreted Freud to mean that the primordial identification of a child is to difference or Otherness whose referents are symbolic-order signifiers.

The *phallic* signifier, in turn, orients the Other as a corpus of Language that interprets the imaginary body as the real desires of the mother referred to the Father's Name. This is the sense in which Lacan equated difference with language. Language, when taken as a signifier for the "father," becomes *the name* of that which divides the mother and infant, by substituting a name for an image or an effect that produces lack; that is, metaphor. Meanwhile, the mother is identified by the infant with the real body, which enjoys, not the Cartesian body that thinks. In Morel's phrasing, the Cartesian symbolic body thinks, and is, indeed, an equivalent of thinking against the real (Morel, "*La différence des sexes,*" p. 28).

Beyond orienting the drives within thought, Lacan's concept of the phallic function answers the question Freud posed concerning the difference between the accomplishment of a reality and the accomplishment of a dream desire: "The phallus as a signifier gives the reason of desire," Lacan wrote, "an image whose reality is its incompleteness ("The Signification . . .," p. 273). The word qua word (*parole*) describes an image of something whose dynamic is that of the *Fort! Da!* movement of the "Here"/ "There"—the gap, the lack—of the bobbin reel, rather than the imaginary stasis of an organ reality. Later, Lacan will describe speaking as an act that creates its own signifieds, while the interlocutor forgets the real trenchency of the act: *dire (saying)/dit (said)*. And this is not John Austin's speech act, or Judith Butler's performative. It is the act of speech as real. This idea of the phallus moves us from figuration to abstraction, to a logic of lack(s). Freud could never explain the link between *Realität* and dreams in his effort to join dream desire to sexual desire. So, he dropped his efforts to prove an unconscious, opting, rather, to attribute psychic cause to biological organs and to propose genetic developmental stages (oral, anal, and genital) as explicative of that in the human which is opaque and enigmatic.

But even though Freud made biology a first-cause mover of psychic *Realität,* he, nonetheless, vacillated throughout his career in his various efforts to explain what causes human sexual identification along lines that are not gender specific. He advanced several theories in trying to figure out how children could imaginarily attribute the penis to the mother in ways that refused the evidence of sexual difference. Elizabeth Grosz wonders why Freud did not simply stick with the idea of a psychic *Realität* which would equate penis=phallus=sociologically-powerful-or-culturally-successful man.[23]

What truly baffled Freud was the ineffable effect of the presence or absence of an organ, taken as a basis for assessing superiority or inferiority, and activity and passivity. Lacan turned Freud's concern into a problematic concerning "having" or "being."[24] Insofar as "having" phallic attributes simply means being associated with power—a family name, a career, and so on—such identifications are not gender or organ specific, Lacan stressed. One believes oneself to be powerful based on "what" a given society values, which becomes an equivalent of "who" one "is." Again, the issue is not the phallus as organ, but as a referent of the meaning attributed to a person at the level of identity in terms of where he or she is thought to "be" within the Other's gaze.

Luce Irigaray misconstrues the early Lacanian idea of a mirror-phase, logically deducible moment, in which the imaginary ego identity is constituted by the images of the first body parts with which one identifies. These are assumed from the introjective-projective mirror of the human form, as if one "put them on." The first forms refer to the primary caretaker, usually the mother. Irigaray confuses Lacan with Freud, arguing that Lacan viewed the mother's body as depreciated because it "lacks" a phallus. Indeed, Freud described the way his patients viewed the sexual difference, while himself maintaining an air of surprise and shock at their prejudices against women, and against the mother in particular, prejudices manifested by both sexes. Irigaray also clings to an object-relations theory, assigning judgmental capacities of good or bad to the infant as a kind of innate knowledge possessed long before he or she has the language that will let him or her discern whether he or she "has/is" the symbolic phallus (or not); this is an interpretative judgment bequeathed in an acquired descriptive (imaginary) language. Irigaray, thus, misunderstands that Lacan's theory of the mirror stage refers to the structural moment in "normative" or typical physical/mental development when a child integrates its own inchoate (pre-mirror fragmentation) body parts into a *seeming* unity, modeled on identifying with the perceived whole body image of another: The infant takes on its sense of being one in reference to another; or two. The small child's first sense of being whole is identified with the mother counterpart who, as a seemingly whole body, becomes the paradigm for an *imaginary* unity, applicable to boys and girls alike.[25]

At the point where Lacan seeks to explain why Freud might have imagined a voracious phallic mother, he encounters Freud's own inability to see the mother as lacking anything. Despite the evidence of what his analysands said to him, Freud could not envision the mother as *imaginarily* lacking an organ. Still, he was always certain that this was an *illusion* children extrapolated from their discovery of the sexual difference, each in reference to the same-sex parent.

Freud's theory here is far from Lacan's idea that a *repudiation* of the sexual difference links epistemology to the fetish, while *foreclosure* of the difference results in psychosis that produces delusions and hallucinations. Simply stated, every child will not interpret the meaning of the sexual difference in the same way, despite the gender difference. Put in other terms, no set (as in mathematical set theory) contains all the answers within itself. Thus, Freud's symmetrical argument could seem to fall within the incompleteness theorem (Gödel's, for example) implied by set theory. Lacan pointed out that, logically speaking, mathematicians uncovered the same functional principle as Freud in discovering that a null set in number set theory grounds the next number, which denotes the absence of number: the 0. Zero, in turn, is bracketed—[0] to distinquish it from the null set. The next number will be the first countable number, either 1 or 0 bracketed twice. Set theory continues by a series of ever-expanding bracketed zeroes. But the null set is designated by a barred zero. (Frege's $\emptyset$).[26]

Closer to Gottlieb Frege than to Freud, Lacan's discovery of the functionality of asymmetries differed from set theorists in his find that every set does not include the previous one. Frege's successor relation theory "is a minimal logic in which are given those pieces only which are necessary to assure it a progression reduced to a linear movement": Zero grounds one plus one more $0[1+n]$. But the "n" splits, inferring a gap or lack following "1," when taken as a natural number.[27]

Additionally, Lacan picked up on Georg Cantor's notion that one could not rethink space topologically via whole numbers, for they are countable. Rather, an infinite continuum can be made via countable fractions, which are transfinite or irrational. Equating the unary traits of identification (Freud's *Einiger Züge*) with the real and symbolic (the $+1$ of countable traits), Lacan emphasized that such traits can be added to the unthinkable imaginary number—$-\phi \rightarrow \sqrt{-1}$—but without producing sense. Rather, real numbers $(S[\emptyset])$ that decomplete a set allow subtraction, which gives rise to the -1 as negative and absent, albeit intrinsic to an ensemble of signifiers. Thus, Lacan wrote the unary trait (S_I) as $\sqrt{-1} + 1$ where nonsensical being ($[]$) which decompletes a set allows subtraction, which gives rise to the -1 as negative and absent, albeit intrinsic to an ensemble of signifiers. Thus, the unary trait (S_I) coalesces with the real and symbolic of thinking: $-1/\sqrt{-1}$ comes from $S(\emptyset)/-\phi$. That is, the paradigm of the detachment of the image from the word that creates a gap in meaning is precisely the $-\phi$, or negativized image of the phallus interpreted as a separable body part.[28]

Like Freud, Irigaray leaves out the negative grounding of thought, which is, then, derived from the body. She positivizes what Lacan interpreted as the child's *imaginary* representing of an organ evaluated in reference to loss. In Lacan's thinking, the *imaginary* problem concerns grappling with a difference between a cosimultaneous presence and absence in image, word, and real effect. This logic works from quite another "logic" than biology. While biology classifies species and assigns attributes according to the positive traits of visible having or not having, Lacan symbolized the particular problem of the null set or split "number" by the negative *phi* $(-\phi)$ meaning imaginary castration. The cut is between a specular image of an imaginary phallus that is there, and, then, potentially, not there because the little girl—the boy's counterpart—does not have it. Freud believed that little boys look in the mirror of identification and see that they have a visible organ the mother does not have; they impute sexual difference to themselves, or sexual sameness, if they identify with the mother. In Freud's interpretation of the words of his female patients, when little girls understand that the mother is like themselves, without the male genital organ, each one interprets this difference in terms of loss $(-\phi)$ which is, in turn, filtered through substitutive fantasy.

Jacques-Alain Miller reminds us that fantasy is imaginary and that once one has crossed the plane of identification, fantasy becomes pure drive ("Le *sinthome* . . .," p. 12). When the unary trait links up with its "being" of jouissance in the Ideal ego (I), one can see under or behind the fantasy that generally masks the real of the drive.

Indeed, one can go so far as to say the structure of the transference implies the identificatory unary traits, not the object (*a*) (p. 13).

Paradoxically, Irigarary argues that her picture of the sexual difference critiques Lacan's theories, while she actually follows Freud's theories of biological reductions to organs, ending up in a logical bind that has led critics to describe her as a biological essentialist. Irigaray does not depict the Freud who finally decided that the only explanation he could find for what he called "wounded narcissism" lay in the experience of having undergone a psychic trauma.

In "The Germs of Empires," Tim Dean distinguishes between physical and psychic trauma. In his delineation, the former ruptures the body's surface, while the latter ruptures the ego's boundaries. Stressing the links among sexuality and retroactive relation of prepubertal sexuality to postpubertal fantasy, Dean writes that "trauma names *the absent cause of history*, the force of the real in any symbolic network (cf. Althusser, 189),"[29] Cathy Caruth writes that "traumatic experience, beyond the psychological dimension of suffering it involves suggests a certain paradox: That the most direct seeing of a violent event may occur as an absolute inability to know it; that immediacy, paradoxically, may take the form of belatedness.[30]

Lacan's depiction of the body as an imaginary constellation first incorporated from the Other, then returned into the symbolic as a projection of ego identifications, can be brought together with Dean and Caruth to describe different aspects of the psychic trauma, which Lacan considered as a splitting that occurs when an imaginary consistency of Oneness is broken. Lacan argued that this is not the trauma Freud was seeking to understand. Rather, Lacan, "translated" Freud's "phallic phase"—common to both sexes—into a logic of phallic signification that sets up an asymmetry between the sexes, and whose referent is the phallus, taken as a propositional function. Lacan hypothesized that the sexual asymmetry concerns, not one's libidinal "object" choice, but submission (or not) to the (phallic) law of difference. The symbolic order is represented by the signifiers of "ideal" Father's Names on the masculine side of sexuation from which males and females take their identity: $\exists x \overline{\Phi x} / \forall x \Phi x$.

Insofar as a male identifies primarily with another male—not with the mother—he will achieve this identification by supposing an abstraction: A male who incarnates the law while being an exception to it, be he "Daddy," some omnipotent river spirit, the mother's brother, the signifier for "the stranger," or some other. Since girls are not required to identify away from the first Other, they have the freedom to ignore or subvert this phallic injunction to difference, this "no" to being all One sex: $\overline{\exists x \, \overline{\Phi x}} / \overline{\forall x \Phi x}$. The male identifies with a logic of accepting to be *all* under the law of the Ur-father, exception to the law which also grounds it, while the female identifies a part of herself as *not* [being] *all* under the law of a conventional reality one might describe as patriarchal/phallic/symbolic "law."

Sexuality is clearly affected by the degree to which male jouissance is fettered by the "law" of what Lacan called the obscene superego. Insofar as a man is *all* under the symbolic law, his guilt for any transgressions will be the inverse face of his trying to obey social-symbolic order (superego) demands. This particularly male burden is placed at the intersection of thought and enjoyment, as is male dependence on the unary character of his genitality. Guilt joins the compulsion-to-enjoy with yet another control or castration placed on the meaning(s) of the phallus that structure male sexuation. Moreover, the requirement of erective performance places an additional castration on men that women do not have. That feminine sexuality is *not all* under symbolic (phallic) injunctions, means that women are less enslaved to the Other's superego dicta. Lacan's explanation of the female superego makes more sense than Freud's deduction that women have weaker superegos than men and are, thereby, characterologically inferior. What Freud considered male superego superiority is what Lacan calls the enslavement to a master discourse logic wherein reality and language are "measurable" as clear communications made within conscious meaning.

In the last paragraph of her article on the phallus in *Feminism and Psychoanalysis*, Elizabeth Grosz says: "Freud and Lacan have been strongly defended by a number of feminists, most notable Juliet Mitchell and Ellie Ragland-Sullivan, who claim that psychoanalysis merely describes rather than participates in the social subordination of women. For both, it is the anchoring term which 'saves' the subject from psychosis by granting it a social position outside the incestual web of desire in the nuclear family. However, the phallus cannot be a neutral signifier, as Ragland-Sullivan and Mitchell claim; the relation between the penis and the phallus is not arbitrary, but is clearly socially and politically motivated" (*Feminism and . . .* , p. 322).

One might respond to Grosz in several ways. First, that such a relation would be politically and socially motivated does not per force make the relation arbitrary. Lacan's concern was to discern the difference between cause and effect in the larger ramifications of the sexual difference. Secondly, in the common biological sense, the etymology of the word *phallus* is taken from the Greek *exllos*, which associates the penis with the phallus, referred to as the biological organ. But at the level where meanings of the phallus are interpretations or representations that give rise to symbol and structure as themselves first causes (rather than organs), they determine the particularity of sexuality and subjectivity by constructing fantasy as a relation of signifiers ($S_1 \rightarrow S_2$) and jouissance (a) that fill the lack ($\emptyset$) in the subject.

In "*Le sinthome: un mixte de symptôme et fantasme*," Miller describes the symptom as that which resists knowledge in that its jouissance and truth are linked to *Thanatos*, to fixities of repetition (-compulsion). The symptom resides in the real of "what does not cease writing itself . . . [as] the way each one enjoys his or her unconscious insofar as the unconscious determines him or her" (pp. 16–17). In other words, the symptom is a mode of enjoyment at the level of the master signifier—(S_1 ;Φ)—that represents the symbolic order by elements one can measure or count.

Miller's formula is an advance over Lacan's early descriptions of the phallus as having the status of a simulacrum or a representation. Insofar as one of the meanings of the phallus is that it designates or stands in for something else—be it object of value or desired child—its first effect is, even then, to introduce the reality of difference into the seemingly holistic rapport between a meaning and an (immediately visible) object. Any effort to interpret this difference gives rise to questions that assume answers that become "fixed" representational meanings.

We see that Lacan's definition of the signifier as that which represents a subject for another signifier quickly becomes inadequate to define the subject as *sinthome*. After thinking of the subject's ($\cancel{S}$) first value—that which is represented by a signifier for another one: $S_I \rightarrow S_2$—one can assess its second value. Minus the unary traits (S_I) and the jouissance (a) that fill it, the subject appears, both in language and affects, as emptied of enjoyment: $\cancel{S};\varnothing$. That is, the *sinthome* localizes the subject as a barred subject distinct from the field of language and representations while still being made up of language (S_I, S_2). One can then see that S_I, (a), and S_2 (or the Ideal ego) are formations of the unconscious that place themselves *in* the gap made by lack. This dynamic shows that the subject "is [exists] only as represented" (Miller, p. 11). That is, it doubles itself.

If someone argues literally, as Ernest Jones, Karen Horney, and others in the twenties and thirties, or as some theorists do today, that any disparity resulting from the discovery of the sexual difference is a simple matter of corrective education that can only produce a final equality and equivalence between the biological sexes, such theorists will fail to admit to the radical difference of images and body experience that confronts boys and girls in their first efforts to ground identity in bodily realities. And this occurs long before conscious awareness of the sexual difference becomes something to interpret. Little girls know that their genital sexual parts are hidden or enclosed within the folds of their skin—clitoris, vagina, labia lips—in imaginary comparison between themselves and little boys. And these parts are not experienced as breaks or cuts, but as parts of a whole that relate to jouissance. Rather, what is "natural" to one becomes an image of the measurable or visible as a standard for the norm, that, in turn, is equated with social reality.

In mathematical terms, one could describe imaginary awareness of the sexual difference as having the weight or dimension of the line, whose topological density is that of an absolute real, a unary trait, or unbroken line. Yet, paradoxically, it takes an infinite number of extensionless points (i.e., 0) to add up to a infinite distance, such as that of a real number whose value is exactly 1.4. This is, indeed, Zeno's fifth paradox of plurality, which allows us to deduce the reason Descartes failed to solve the mind/body problem with his theory of the body as an "extended thing": An extended body consists of a number of parts that have no extension, as does distance (or it would be infinitesimally small). Yet, Descartes's idea presupposes the infinite as macrocosmic. Zeno, Descartes, Kant, and Freud are some of the thinkers who have tried to solve problems of how to quantify difference and distance by means of visible reductions to size. Zeno gives us Achilles and the tortoise who will never be congruent, thus suggesting a limit within infinity, just as Descartes's notion of extension implies something in reference to which a body would be extended. Kant adheres to the notion of macrocosm and microcosm in his *Third Critique* where one finds his aesthetic of the beautiful in his distinguishing the beautiful from the sublime.[31]

Freud argued that precisely such imaginary effects produce the real of trauma for the female who compares her genital structure to the male's. Lacan argued, rather, that each sex takes the penis as a phallus, a representation of what can be lost. He also argued that each sex takes his or her organ(s) as the standard for what is "natural" in the imaginary and real. Moreover, the girl has recourse, within Lacanian topology, to less anxiety regarding the sexual difference than the male. Insofar as the feminine genitalia constitute many marks on a plane—the border (of the vaginal split or the labia) seen or felt at the surface of the skin (and so on), she thinks of her sexuality in terms of a profundity, or as the backdrop of a base against which a thing is seen as "other" in reference to something else.

The boy, by contrast, has one overtly visible and moving apparatus made of three parts. The penis and testicles are assessed as susceptible to loss because the boys has imaginary proof that half the human race does not have the same organ, with its visible obviousness, its exposure. This alone would account for Freud's patients' efforts to equate "difference" with visible size. In "The Signification of the Phallus" (1958), Lacan had already stressed that the phallus does not become an index of power as such on the basis of turgidity, detumescence, or reproductive capacity. Later, in 1960, he placed the (imaginary) phallus in the list of eight objects susceptible to the (seeming or perceptible) cut of separability from the body, giving all eight a *Fort! Da!* quality.

Jeanne Lafont advances the topological mark as the complement of the hole; the point of an enigma. Within the psychoanalytic logic of forms that goes from figuration to abstraction, Lafont gives this definition: These operations "are to be found in the linking of the symbolic with the imaginary [that produces the gap between a word and an image $(-\phi)$]. They transform the symbolic into the imaginary . . . in the measure that they are formulated by figures which put perception [itself] into play. The topological objects in fact, like the sphere, the torus, the cross-cap, the Klein bottle, even the Moebius strip, are considered here as representations of the operations [they perform]. Between the real of the clinic, and the symbolic pertience of a word, there is an imaginary space of the transference, the obstruction of a reality [by interpretation wherein, for example, an image can serve as an unconscious knot or impasse]. The topological operations situate themselves at this dialectical point" (*Topologie lacanienne*, p. 30).

In the essay drawn from its course *Ce qui fait insigne* (1986–1987),[32] Jacques-Alain Miller focuses on the symbolic/imaginary properties of the concrete identificatory nature of the unary trait (S_1) as the basis for the structure of the transference. It is not the object (a) that represents the analyst, he maintains, but, rather, a positivization of absolute "traits" (unbroken lines) without representation (*"Le sinthome . . . ,"* pp. 11 and 13). In other words, it is not topological objects themselves that put representations into play, but, rather, that the *representations represent the operations they configure—*

starting with the constructions of any empty space or hole that is, in turn, filled by objects and master signifiers. At the level of perceptual effect, the Moebius strip represents the gaze, which subtends the other drives as that into which one is already born. One does not gaze. One is gazed at, unconsciously seeing onself as being seen. Things that present themselves as having mysterious properties are the signifiers of objects hidden in the overlap of the two sides of the Moebius band,

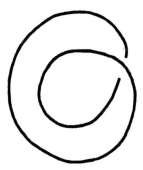

both sides constituting a surface. Lacan compares the twist in the Moebius form to the twist in thought that allows one to drop ideas or associations into the memory bank of the unconscious where knowledge remains hidden. In the gaze elicited by the female genitalia, feelings of desire and jouissance are at play in the space that opens onto the erotogenic field of the apertures and slits on the body's skin surface ("Subversion . . . ," p. 315).

Lacan reminds us of this in his interpretation of the burning child dream first narrated by Freud. Only after his son is dead and his shrouded body burning from the candle that had fallen onto it, does the dead boy's father grasp unconsciously that his son's words—"Father, don't you see I'm burning?"—could mean something about his *sexual desire* when he was living. For the father does not know consciously that his son's bandages are on fire. This "Other" knowledge has been occulted in the overlap of the Moebius strip.[33] This topological form replicates the gaze, one might say, as uncastrated: The real is showing, but not seen. Lacan also called this phenomenon of consciousness a scotoma (a mental blind spot) in *Seminar XI*. A problematic example of such a "reading" of sexuality as one's hidden (unconscious) desire, is exemplified by Hélène Cixous's description of Dora's mother, her governess, and Dora as loving a man, loving difference and disfiguration.[34] The penis, represented as phallus, is "disfigured" in *Cixous's* picture of it, in her picture of desire. "Desire is for an organ," Lacan said, "while love is for a name."

This is a radically different notion of the *cut* from the feminist equation of Lacan's concept of *castration* with a literal cutting of the female genitalia as put forth by Laura Mulvey, Elizaberth Bronfen, and others. Throughout his teaching, Lacan raises the biological Freud to the realm of signifying systems where the phallus, as well as other notions, take on different meanings. Although Lacan's equation of the phallus with language has been widely assimilated, we have seen that he meant many other things as well by "phallus." He also referred to the phallus as the imaginary object of frustration; the real object of privation; and the symbolic object of castration (lack or debt).[35] Indeed, to construct the concept of the phallus, these three registers are required. Thus, early in his teaching, Lacan departed from equating the phallus with language, in the simple sense of the word's naming a thing. The function of naming is attributed to the signifier of the Father's Name. Rather, he depicts the alienated word as residing at one remove from the real. And long before he developed his topological logic, he stressed the fact that a symbol or a figure always stands in for something else, something opaque.

In his essay "Painting" ["*Tableau*"], Gerard Wajcman writes that Lacan the toponymist, the topographer, became a topologist because the unconscious itself is topological. "Things are situated there." But the "things" in question are the "objects" (*a*) that cause desire for symbolic goods, or lure us in the imaginary, or catalyze the drive for enjoyment in the real. Lacan tried to situate this logic with his graphs that inscribe place and correspond to symbolic space, his schema that figure imaginary space and, thus, stratify the planes of the image with the surface prevailing there. As for real space, its representation supposes that one promote, along with the graphs and schemas, a *picture* that represents *sites*, or pure real places. For Lacan, Wajcman argued, topology is not a metaphor that represents the subject as signified or figured. It presents the structure or site where the subject emerges as effect of the trifunctionality of thought.[36]

The *imaginary* phallus becomes an object-cause-of-desire, not at the level of organ per se, but insofar as it denotes perceptual separability or the part that lacks-in-an-image. We remember that Lacan first named this operation negative castration ($-\phi$): Its cause is the real father of jouissance, whose function is to create lack by a symbolic castration of imposing "no" on the infant's thought. Miller points out that this gap later becomes the empty subject ($\emptyset$). Lacan's way of saying this was that the phallic signifier has no signified, only effects that evolve. These are clarified by Miller as the S_1, the $\emptyset$, and the (*a*). The signified or referent of the phallus, in other words, is the imaginary lack ($\sqrt{-1}$) around which fantasy organizes the S_1 (or unary trait), the $\emptyset$, and the (*a*). Miller relates symptoms and fantasy thus: "The relation of the symptom is not simply of a meaning, but of a meaning [given] to signifying structure—the fantasy—where there is a rapport of the subject to jouissance (*"Le sinthome: Un Mixte . . .,"* pp. 14–15).

To summarize briefly, Lacan argued as early as 1958 against Freud's thesis that biology causes sexuality, stressing that the phallus is not the real organ, the penis, neither (1) in its role of copulation, nor (2) in its typographical sense as an equivalent of the logical copula, nor (3) by virtue of its turgidity, as the image of the vital flow as transmitted in generation (*"Signification . . .,"* pp. 289–90). Rather, the phallus is the abstract signifier of difference whose function—and this is crucial—is to give a person access to others via the fantasmatic constitution of desire whose lack pushes one to reach out to the other across the solipsistic wall of one's own desirous Other.

Lacan's categories of the symbolic, imaginary, and real come into play in his arguments here insofar as logical orderings of the object (*a*), present in each category, make of structure topological structure—that is truth-functional by paradoxical contradictions—not by linguistic or mythic structure. Insofar as the three orders cohere, it is because they are interlinked by the fourth order Lacan named the knot or the symptom (Σ). These four orders coalesce to constitute the signifying chain we, in turn, call "mind." Miller describes the functioning of the chain as the automatism of repetition plus the symptom (the linking of jouissance to master signifiers) (p. 16) in reference to the knot that guarantees one's "self" image by positive and/or negative identifications referred to a particular Father's Name signifier. One's oedipal interpretation of the phallus and castration in childhood fixes one's language, enjoyment, and lack-in-being along four possible axes for the development of desire as it commands language and sexuality from a point halfway between language and repetition. The differential axes of the Lacanian clinic—the masquerade, the neuroses, the *père-version*, the psychoses—delineate the structure(s) of mind as a minimal number of interpretations of the sexual difference: its repression in the masquerade, its foreclosure in psychosis, its repudiation in perversion, and its denial in the neuroses.

If the mother's unconscious desire is for a given child to belong to the most popular social group, to accept the sexual "norms" of the masquerade of a given cultural moment, her child will try to please the Other whose gaze establishes the superegolike terms of the Ideal ego unconscious formation. Rather than an enlightenment developmental view of human sexuality, one has the masquerade that cultures have always used to camouflage sexual desire and the nonrapport at its center, whose insignia are the real traits that encircle a void ($\varnothing$). Insofar as sexuality is imposed on an infant from the outside world—in the imaginary order of identification with the breast, the feces, the gaze and the voice; in the real order where loss of such objects inscribes a symbolic unary trait susceptible of transformation from Eros to Thanatos and back; in the symbolic order of nomination by which one elaborates a belief system he or she takes to be right and true; and in the order of the symptom where it is invested with the jouissance that elevates it to a sublimated symptom (Σ) where one finds oneself in the Ideal—sexuality is a system of meaning that includes negative elements of uncertainty about one's value as an object, as well as a positive slope of pleasure and orgasmic fulfillment.

Lacan linked both functions to the phallus in terms of jouissance and castration, denoted respectively by a "plus" (+) or "minus" (−), the plus depending on the minus. That is, jouissance is correlated with lack that makes it always a diminution or transgression of the "law," lack thereby placing a limit on the excess (+). Geneviève Morel (p. 33) writes the phallic correlation to jouissance and castration thus:

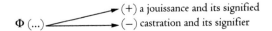

$\Phi\ (\ldots)$ $\longrightarrow$ $(+)$ a jouissance and its signified
$(-)$ castration and its signifier

Lacan was at pains to stress that neither sexual behavior nor "object choice" are the point, but, rather, that all sexuality emanates from the particularity of fantasy. Fantasy, moreover, is fundamentally perverse, Lacan argued, based as it is on turning away from superego dicta and veering, rather, toward transgressions that emanate from the real of object traits magnetized to fill the gap that is the subject ($\$ <> a$). Sexuality is itself the father version, the *père-vers*. To distance himself from the mother, from the feminine, the male aims at the (a) as a passive object in an effort to replicate lost objects of desire with traits retained in fantasy. Later, the effort to incorporate the partner as beloved will be a masculine drive, whether it emanates from a male or female. Real traits of desire become the necessary investment in the fetish that marks (perverse) sexuality by dramatic scenes, as in David Lynch's "Blue Velvet" where the fetish creates a masochistic kind of Eros.

The first difference that impinges on a child's conscious perception in his or her construction of an identity of being—a logic of separation—is the absolutism of the cut. The second is the perception of sexual difference, which creates dialectical thought. Thus, masculine and feminine distinctions are determined not by "psychic" essence or behavior, nor by any pregiven active or passive behavior(s) or attitude(s), including homosexual or heterosexual "postures," but as gender nonspecific identifications as lover (active) or beloved (passive). These point, rather, to rhythms and desires transformed into drives once the cut established in the mother/infant paradigm makes a space between the object and the desiring subject, rather than between a supposedly natural male or female behavior.

By *phallic* effort, Lacan means nothing other than the capacity for thinking dialectically, which can happen only insofar as an infant takes a distance from the object (a)-cause-of-desire embodied by the mother in the order of the real. Identifying with the *phallic signifier*, in this sense, means that the infant's capacity to learn or differentiate—that is, introject the Other—requires him or her to break off totalizing identifications with the mirror-stage mother's desire. Charles Pyle writes in "Lacan's Theory of Language: The Symbolic Gap" that Lacan uses the bar in violation of the normal assumptions of well-formedness in logic and math. Going to the root of the logic of the bar in Lacan's theory of language, Pyle comments on Lacan's frequent assertions that the bar represents the phallus.[37] At the level where imaginary identificatory fusions or conjunctions are known only as an effect of the bar—that is, as an effect of loss or the "cut"—which can also be taken as a phallic effect of separation by "no," one can readily characterize the effect of loss on an imaginary unity as real and traumatic. Losses of identification with parts of the mother—attached to a fantasy of her as whole—are traumatic losses of the imaginary illusions of a consistency of body and being that rupture a *mental* identification with something "outside" that produces effects of sameness and oneness.

Object-relations theorists or cognitive psychologists talk about this period of constructing an elemental mentality as the developmental stage of *individuation* when the infant breaks away from the mother between about six and eighteen months of age.[38] Such theorists generally represent this as a stage of consequence in terms of a developmental (neuropsychically based) norm. Lacan, following Freud, showed, rather, how secondary process symbolic material of the Other constructs primary-process thought in each of the three orders, thereby serving as a memory-mind storehouse of reminiscences from the start of life. Consequently unconscious memory will forever after enter conscious language, more like Proust's "privileged moments" of associative grasp, than as a "supposed" retrieval of (distorted) narratives, or scant rememorations. The unconscious enters the conscious realm as a negative dialectic between loss and the object(s) that cause desire: $\varnothing/a$. Primary process, created by secondary process, reenters language as an interpretation of the sexual difference and as an awareness of lost objects. One might write the structure of lack in a formula for symbolic castration:

Insofar as symbolic castration is the form of the incest taboo that takes as its referent the real father's "no" to a oneness between the mother's lack and the infant as filler of that lack, what occurs at the level of imaginary castration is that one confronts the logic of the cut between the imaginary and the question of sexual difference. This question is first posed for the boy as the threat of actual organ loss. But, in his assumption of sexuality cum "identity," one cannot specify the age or period as to choice of jouissance:

Moreover, such choices change throughout life. Morel comments on Lacan's enigmatic sentence: "the common error does not see that the signifier is *jouissance* and that the phallus is only its signified." ("Signification . . . ," p. 37).

Lacan's decades of working with the criminally insane enabled him to hypothesize the *Realität* of the psychotic, male or female, as the empirical variable against which the other structures can be measured. In that the psychotic remains one with the primordial mother's desire throughout life, he or she retains only one set of narcissistic identifications. These are rigidly tailored to the mother's jouissance. Such petrification of jouissance is, indeed, the antithesis of the social masquerade where desire is paradoxically "rigid" only in the sense that it is ever changing with the winds of trend. Within the logic of psychosis, instead of the exchange and freedom of movement manifested in the "normative" metaphorical substitutions of one thing for another, as long as one pleases the social Other, metonymic master signifiers speak from *la lalangue* of the real.

In the Schreber case, Lacan quipped, President Schreber's delusional transsexualism denounced the common "phallic" error of attributing an ordering by a "law" of difference of the sexes. The "error" consists in defining one's psychic sexuality—for which there is no signifier in the unconscious—by translating the penis into the phallus, and classifying oneself as a boy or a girl. One sees the Catch-22. No Derridean language game or sociological role change will make the stakes of the sexual difference disappear, those stakes being the "immortal" (desiring) terms that one is unconsciously bound to seek again and to repeat.

Although one can only agree with Elizabeth Grosz that the issue of the phallus is political, it is to a politics of ultimate being and suffering that Lacan points, not to the politics of altering the male patriarchy as a sociological entity by good will or law. There is always a politics of desire at issue in Lacan's theory that the feminine is an identificatory position of "passivity" vis-à-vis the phallus, whether one is male or female; rather, one is masculine or feminine.

As an abstraction, then, the phallic signifier represents sexual difference, not only as a signification of itself, signifying what it is to be a man for a woman or a woman for a man, a lover for a beloved or vice versa, more importantly, it serves as the bar that makes such a division the mark of the human over the animal. Choices arise out of jouissance conditions, not instincts. That men or women can substitute one meaning for another—based on substituting one love object for another—enables the human creature to think with mental complexity, rather than in terms of the strict behavioral semiotics to which even the most sophisticated ape is restricted. This is the sense in which the phallic pivot paradoxically separates and connects knowledge to sexuality, making it possible for meaning to function as a dialectical system of social exchanges of signifiers (S_1) and jouissance objects (a) that fill one's lack $(\$)$, while still communicating something to the other.

In the "Rome Discourse" (1953) ("The Function and Field of Speech and Language in Psychoanalysis") Lacan points out that the symbol only means pact; it is not the content of the gift per se that counts, but the exchange signified as an act (p. 50). Analogously, the phallus is a symbol of desire's ratio or desire's cause, Lacan says, because a relation of identity—a pretended twoness made out of one—is not a relation of desire. In desire, lacking and wanting imply one another. The "error" in male logic leads to the idea that two are one. the woman supposedly exists as an essence that enables man to deny that anything lacks in his being: $\$ \diagdown a \longrightarrow \Phi \longrightarrow S(\emptyset)$. Both fantasy and ideology enable men to deny that The Woman as essence does not exist.

One will recognize the logic of the impossible real in such negations. From this, a paradox follows: Man is man only insofar as he retains a false belief regarding Woman, a belief that surprisingly belongs to the feminine side of sexuation where the real, unconscious, and contingent prevail. This contradiction leads Lacan to the "feminist" proposition that the masculinist illusion of wholeness is based on a fantasy essentialization of the woman (who exists), such that some myth of the whole, essential, primordial mother continues to serve the male, unconsciously, as a guarantee to a stable, logical dependable universe.

Such essentialization differs, however, for men and women, and is further broken down depending on the desiring structure on which a person's thinking depends. While a "normative" or obsessional male may divide women between categories of mother or whore, for example, a psychotic male makes of "his" woman the woman who combines all the properties of mother and sexual woman. When Derrida argues that the sexual difference makes no difference, or when Hélène Cixous argues that the *écriture féminine* is a foil to the phallic signifier, one wonders how their totalizing arguments go beyond Jones, Horney, Deutsch, or other theories of a symmetry between the sexes advanced in Freud's day. How do they move forward the debate regarding what the sexual difference is, and why so much is at stake on that question?

In the 1950s, Lacan argued that the phallus no longer poses a question bearing only "on having" an *imaginary* organ; but *also* a question concerning "being." Being and having intersect in the visible world of the mask or appearance, where one believes one *is* what one *has:* With what objects will one identify? What partial traits, Freud's *Einzeger Züge,* translated by Lacan as unary traits, will build up particular chains of jouissance? What counts is that their dialectical interplay—loss and refinding—construct the particular conditions of jouissance surrounding the "object" one loves, the "object" referring not to a person or a whole person, but imaginary identifications, real traces, and symbolic naming, glued to the primordial object residues that first elevated desire to the demand in drive. The drive is itself an agent alongside desire: Together, they compose the unconscious subject of lack ($\bar{\$}$) and the object he or she seeks in jouissance (a) via the structure of fantasy ($\bar{\$} <> a$).

One seeks a replica or semblance of something lost in the first place: the (imaginary) phallus, the urinary flow, the feces, the breast, the voice, the gaze, the phoneme, the nothing, around which constellations of meaning build up. We "think" with our lost primary objects. We are ourselves made up of those *identificatory* (symbolic/imaginary) traits, as well as the real of the marks they left behind as indices of their loss. In this sense, memories or *recollections* are the continual return of a series or collage of single strokes, organized around varying partial objects that cause desire.

Freud's *Einziger Züge* refer to Dora's memory of the image of Frau K's beautiful white body, or her sensory recollection of her father's cigar smoke. What counts is not Freudian wish fulfillment, taken as a way to define psychic reality, but one's *being* as the phallus—as an *object* of desire—who is valued as *something* particular, rather than as nothing in particular. In that the Other's desire determines one's place within the social gaze, one's emptiness as a subject encounters suspension, anticipation—the time of desire that is the subject ($\bar{\$}$)—and a horrible dependence qua individual awaiting the response granted him or her in the other's gaze.

By submitting one's lack-in-being to the symbolic Other which incarnates social law as phallic, as purveyed by a given master discourse, both men and women who take language at face value follow the reality principle of a local universal symbolic order that, paradoxically, bespeaks a lack-in-(its)-being. In losing a part of one's Ideal being by *being* (or acting) for others (the Other), the subject can be defined as an "act." In Slavoj Zizek's terms, the *act* has the structure of a symbolic castration at the level of a lack-in-being. For Lacan, loss is a paradoxical because one must live in society by the sacrifices and exchanges that enable one to recuperate parts of one's Ideal ego. Sadly, one must concede a great deal to the Other if its illusions of consistency, harmony, and wholeness are to be retained. Even then, one pays a price for what is repressed in the real because the real returns in other forms to repeat the material of a trauma.

Metaphor or synecdoche—rhetoric—are not at issue in the relation of the penis to the phallus, then, but the way one is inscribed (or not) for sexual difference. "Having" and "being" do not concern having or lacking the penis, but the *being* one has evolved as a response to the signifier for the Father's Name, functioning in reference to the mother's unconscious desire. One may conclude from this logic that the link between the penis and the phallus is not so much hidden as it is obvious. Freud refers to the ancient meaning of the phallus as a simulacrum. But Lacan figured out something else. Through his own decades of analytic work with patients, he came to see that the question Freud was really trying to answer was why the sexual difference bore on the constitution of identity in the first place. What beyond the biological sense perceptions that govern organ reality had sexual reality (*Wirklichkeit*) to do with psychic reality (*Realität*)? In Lacan's terms, sense data is itself inscribed for and by meaning.

Lacan first discovered the absence of an inscription for sexual difference in psychosis. Gradually, he realized that sexuality is not foreclosed at the level of biological behavior or function (in psychosis), but as an identificatory inscription for being as masculine or feminine. Yet, symbolic and imaginary meanings name one in a "self" myth of an Ideal ego, which gives most people the necessary distance from the primordial mother to separate and create their own psychic reality beyond hers. Only in psychosis is this not true. Schreber went as far as becoming God's wife to retain his primary identification with his own mother as The Woman who exists, Schreber living from one single identity for being.[39]

The imaginary phallus would be opposed to the laws of the symbolic, then, in the sense that symbolic equals culture. For a child is given *being* as an object of its mother's desire, which is deflected imaginarily by the lack intrinsic in it. The mother's unconscious desire is usually turned outward, toward the symbolic-order phallic signifier(s) that symbolize difference and authority for her, insofar as difference constitutes a nonidentitarian principle. Thus, the penis as an organ can never be thought of merely as a fact of nature, insofar as it is always already interpreted—inscribed for meaning—as a fact of difference and as a symbol of desire.

Although Lacan did not replace Freud's terms, it should be clear that he gave them entirely new meanings. Jacques-Alain Miller asked him why in *Television:* Why use *unconscious* [*Unbewusste*] since it was such a negative term and since Lacan did not mean by it what Freud did at all?[40] Lacan answered that Freud had not found a better word to try to describe what he was getting at, so why go back on it? One can propose a similar logic in keeping the term *phallus* by which Freud sought to distinguish between biology and mentality.

Moreover, In Lacan, the masculine is not opposed to the feminine but, rather, is defined as being asymmetrical to the feminine, this asymmetry itself functioning as a signifier that constructs the way desire evolves within language. In hysteria, for example, the structure of being organizes itself around the question of the split in identification between identifying oneself as a woman, while privileging the identification with the father over that with the mother. That sexual identifications structure themselves around a (biologically) "unnatural" split—which is interpreted—is what Lacan called sexuation.

The imaginary phallus is *signified* by the phallic *signifier*, which Lacan also called the master signifier (S_1) that enunciates one's principle identity theme in the symptom (Σ). In the real, the phallus signifies positivized jouissance, while it stands for reality, or the prevailing local universal view of reality (taken as truth), in the symbolic. At this level, Lacan equated it with (secondary-process) language and called it the signifier of the Father's Name. While Lacan speaks of an "ethics of psychoanalysis" that concerns desire, wherein desire is the ratio of phallus, Irigaray, and others have misunderstood Lacan's theory here, imaginarizing (or essentializing) it by reducing it to the penis.[41]

On the masculine side of the sexuation graph, identification with the phallus is with its *Fort! Da!* movement of presence/absence, not with the some superior organ properties that mark "character" or power. This is one meaning of castration: $\Phi/-\phi$. First, the (*imaginary*) phallus is there, and then it is lacking in reference to the sex who does not have it. This early childhood drama, whose meaning is that of "representational" trauma, enables one to understand the source of male narcissistic identification with the phallus as a response to the double castration that marks him: Boys are defined as boys, first, insofar as they construct their identities away from the mother qua feminine (or "same as"); secondly, insofar as their identities are directed toward masculinity, which is itself an abstraction.

Thus, by defining masculinity as the imposition of difference onto sameness, the cultural Other produces the effect of castration as an *imaginary* difference—the cut between the image of the phallus and the naming of that image. Giving voice to this experience places a narrative within the unconscious, a narrative woven around fantasies that push the male to account for himself by assigning the phallus some meaning beyond its organ reality. This particular cut between an image, a name, and the real of effects shows that a minimal difference not only produces a maximal effect on each man, but also defines culture over nature in terms of sexual difference.

It is hardly surprising that the small phi ($-\phi$) denotes the first form of the subject of unconscious desire that Lacan later writes as a barred S ($\slashed{S}$) and calls the lack-in-being, the inverse face of desire. Lacan's arguments, demonstrating that the logic of gender is not biological per se, show an equation of "desire" and jouissance with psychic reality (Freud's *Realität*). Gender is structured for and by meaning, from beginning to end, not as the biological reality of a cause whose effects are a blind, instinctual push or urge toward reproduction, or toward some anonymous other, or toward some "super" gene.

The basis of psychoanalysis, as redefined by Lacan, is that there is no sexual rapport of harmony between the sexes because the first taboo is against incest or a

Oneness of jouissance with the mother. The taboo itself creates desire as the mark of castration that causes repression, as well as the quest to fill up the concrete lack with every "object" at one's disposal. Castration—or $\not S$—is, thus, the sign that the primordial objects must evaporate bit by bit in order that a sense of "self" or *being* can be assumed as a difference. Even though cultures mythologize this "no" into a Oneness, pretending that each person is always, already whole, even the concept of a whole self has the same logic as that which establishes a logical basis for law ($\exists x \overline{\Phi x}$). In the second masculine formula for sexuation, one has a logic of culture as possible ($\forall x \Phi x$) as long as castration (or lack) has been accepted.

The minimal structure of the social becomes the third term of the Father's no, or the phallic signifier as that which divides the psychic rapport between mother and infant. Each self or ego is made out of two individuals referring to a third "term."[42] This structural reality places the character of a split and paradox at heart of the social. Not only is sexuality not biologically caused, it is a constellation of responses (or images, words, and affects) that unveil the phallus and castration at the base of that which orients desire as neurotic, normative, perverse, or psychotic relations to the object (*a*). Insofar as one's *being* is never far from the sexuality one *has* or *is*, being is not just an identity state, then, but emanates from its own roots in fantasy, desire and jouissance. One *is* insofar as one responds to the Other to (re-)create the unconscious as sexuality at the point where desire and jouissance are constituted as a primary-process language (*la lalangue*) that returns into the secondary-process language that created it in the first place to speak a *parole* that goes beyond grammar.

A child must lose the primoridal objects that constitute his or her psychic *Realität* as a meaning apart from *Wirlichkeit*, Lacan concluded. This occurs, not only as a response to the mother's love, but also in the attachment of the child's being to the mother's unconscious desire and jouissance, the bases to psychic reality which construct The Woman as the grounding (mythical) figure who predominates over any "reality" one might call phallic, and over any terror linked to lack and named castration; or to the loss Lacan referred as the void ($\varnothing$) created by the first separations or cuts away from a seeming Oneness with the mother's "gifts" of satisfaction or dissatisfaction.[43]

2

Freud's "Female Sexuality" (1931) and "Femininity" (1932)
Oedipus Revisited via the Lacanian Pre-Oedipus

Before considering what Lacan finds in his return to Freud that further illuminates the enigma of female sexuality, let us again take up the question of what Lacan meant by sexuality. One could argue that Lacan discovered the link Freud sought—but never found—between the pleasure and the reality principles. Having desexualized the reality principle, Freud could never place libido in it, any more than he could locate the signifier in *Es* or Id. Lacan postulated that the ego is itself libidinized by its own identifications (or narcissistic investments), and that what Freud called ego resistance is the equivalent of any person's refusal to question the *Weltanschauung* of his or her unconscious knowledge. Lacan equated ego narcissism with the closures of the master discourse—punning on master, "to be me," which is homophonic in French with *maître/m'être*—by which any person negotiates relations with others, ego to ego in a pseudodialectic of exchange.

There is more than one catch to Lacan's theory of a "whole" ego's resisting. Why, one asks, would an ego tailor its speech and language to resist "hearing" what the other is saying? Lacan's answer is that the ego is inherently unstable. Constituted by the words and demands of an outside Other and by identifications with the others of one's surroundings, from infancy on, the ego is constructed as divided among the social Other, the others Freud called ego ideals, and the Ideal ego unconscious formation that stands at a pivotal point between the imaginary and symbolic orders. Lacan's innovation was to have grasped that the ego is not only not a whole agent, mediator between id and superego as Freud thought, nor is it whole within itself.[1] In Lacan's teaching, the (Ideal) ego is created as a symbolic order constellation, itself divided between the imaginary identifications imposed on an infant by the primary ego ideals of others, as well as the social expectations and conventions forced upon the infant. Both come from the outside world. In this sense, any ego that is not psychotic will be formed as a conflictual structure. It seeks to please the others and the Other who will hopefully love "it" and, thus, verify it as Ideal, a preformed Ideal.

Yet, given one's mirror-structure dependence on others for validation and valor-ization, one ends up caught in the crossfires of love/hate, jealousy/aggresstivity, com-petition, manipulation, and duplicity. The ego shows its true colors as a bric-a-brac fabric of aspirations, lies, and misrecognitions. Its resistances, then, bear the structure of a protest against any cut into its own fragile, imaginary vulnerabilities, based on idealized images of "self." Underlying ego duplicities, Lacan shows a further catch. Sexuality is not only *not* commensurate with the pleasure principle—a principle of ego constancy or entropy in Freud's thought—but responds, rather, to the reality principle, or the superego; that is, required conventions of a preexisting Other.

Freud's theory of a commensurable maturation between ego and libido is false. We remember Freud's postulation of a regressive pre-oedipal oral stage of develop-ment, followed by an anal retentive or acquisitive stage, marked in behavior by pos-sessiveness and control. His final—or ideal—stage of genital maturity is distinguished by reciprocity and giving. Lacan did not agree with this developmental model of the ego. Insofar as the ego is not a whole agency of mind that can manifest stages of maturation, developmental sophistications, or even defense and mediating properties, it is, rather, a constellation of identifications whose tendency is toward fixity and repeti-tions rooted in an unconscious formation of Ideal(s). In other words, the ego is split off from how others truly see "it."

This is quite a different view of the ego from Freud's dialectical agency, suscepti-ble to learning, changing, mastering, and mediating. Lacan, emphasized, rather, the subject of desire whose subjective knowledge eddies up from the unconscious real. While symbolic order conventions are the equivalent of social requirements and imag-inary identifications are misrecognitions of who one is, the real of jouissance or suffering does not lie. Nor do the concrete affects surrounding lack and loss, or the repeated enigmata of symptoms, all of which bring discontinuities, cuts, and aporia into illusory ego consistencies and tenuous well-formed narratives.

In "Phobia and Perversion," Daniel Machado writes: "The Study of Little Hans means that the subject as child could be in analysis—he had a symptom which could be analyzed. Hans was witness to the existence of sexuality in children—because sexuality means suffering and *jouissance*. It has nothing to do with sexology. Sexuality in psycho-analysis is only a condition for neurosis. That a child could suffer from sexuality to the point of making a neurosis is what Hans teaches Freud."[2]

Sexuality is not sexology, in Lacanian teaching, but rather suffering and jouis-sance: Lacan locates the "discontent" or *malaise* that Freud found in civilization in the "disturbance" of human sexuality where each person is subject to the mysterious desires of his or her own Other. In Freud's day, it is generally thought, jouissance was forbidden, or not socially tolerated by the Other of upper-class symbolic rules and laws, to the point that individuals in this social milieu sacrificed their sexual jouissance to superego moralities. Morever, while Freud's theory of sexuality was based on the myth that love and sex can join in a harmonious sexual relation with one another if one has "developed" a genital (i.e., generous, giving) character, the model Freud gives for such a relationship is the ideally harmonious parental couple of mother and father, and prior to that, mother and child. Object-relations theorists later refined this parental dyad into the ideal harmony of mother and infant. Life, literature, and clinical data prove the opposite. Love does not lead to the Oneness of harmony in sexual relations, nor in those between spouses, or between parent and child. Rather, as Jacques-Alain Miller argues, the mother/father couple does not automatically give children an example of sexual beings. The parental couple of Mother <> Father is not the sexual couple of Male <> Female.[3]

But to appreciate Lacan's innovations in rethinking the linkage of sexuality and anatomical gender to epistemology, one must grasp the logic of his formulas of sexuation. Although he evolved four, his first two were the *all* (Φ), and the *not all* ($\varnothing$): These delineate an asymmetrical opposition between man and woman concerning how knowledge functions for each. Indeed, from *Le séminaire, livre IX: L'identification* (1960–1961) on,[4] Lacan began to elaborate a logic of the *not all* based on an Aristotelian notion. Aristotle's negation was a simple division between a subject and its attributes.

Lacan's functional proposition replaced Aristotle's subject-copula-attribute by the hole or empty set, which gave him a way to represent the subject of the unconscious outside any known attribute.[5] Although, in feminine sexuation, Lacan seems to use the Aristotelian universal quantificator, negated for him, ($\overline{\forall x}$), the universal can only be inscribed outside itself and, thus, has no actual existence (Morel, p. 166). When Lacan concludes that there is no universal thinkable on the side of Woman—not even the proposition of "there may be" as is plausible on the masculine side—he speaks of the logic of discordential grammar which passes, not through the body, but results from a logical exigency in the word (Morel, p. 108). Thus, Woman as already *pastoute:* has access to the phallus (Morel, p. 172).

$$\overline{\forall x} \; \Big\langle \; \begin{array}{c} S(\varnothing) \\[6pt] \Phi \end{array}$$

Gradually Lacan took up the problem in his formulas of a logical slippage between Aristotle and Frege (Morel, p. 59). Even earlier, in chapter 14 ("The Signifier, as Such, Signifies Nothing") of *The Seminar, Book III* (1955–1956): *The Psychoses,*[6] he had opposed the notion of a totality to that of the *ensemble*, arguing that since a totality supposes a relation to a correspondent whose structure is solidary, one is within the enclosure of the *all* while, in truth, the *ensemble* differs from the totality by evoking an open relation based on supplementarity, not correspondence (Morel, p. 60). There is no *all*, Lacan says, except as empty, or as a propositional function of contingency. The logic by which one inscribes oneself in the phallic function is as the *all* of a sham, a masquerade, or the *not all* that brings on the real: One is *all* enclosed in the logic of difference from the mother (the male signified by the Φ); or *not all* enclosed within such logic (the female signified by the $\varnothing$). Lacan goes even further in connecting *male* sexuality to the *all* of identifying with the penis, while the more global bodily eroticism of the woman has the logic of the *not all*, a supplemental relation to the unary genital orgasm (Morel, p. 60).

That Lacan gives philosophical value to the ways one thinks or moves in language as functions of an interpretation of the lack or negativity inscribed by the sexual difference is an entirely original theory. Morel adds a word of caution, however, concerning Lacan's use of mathematics: Because Lacan's mathemes do not function in other writing(s), nor form a system of their own that one can elaborate or deduce new formulas from, they are not "mathematics proper" (p. 60). That is not to say, however, that they are not of the real. Nor that they cannot be used in other writings.

Freud's essay on "Female Sexuality" was completed in the summer of 1931,[7] restating many of his findings from the 1925 essay on "Some Psychical Consequences of the Anatomical Difference between the Sexes." Indeed, Freud's return to the topic was probably caused by repercussions that that particular essay had produced among analysts, particularly the English, for at the end of it, Freud critiqued several of their papers, an unusual practice in his writings. He reproached the analytic authors as if each paper had arisen spontaneously, rather than as a series of reactions to his own, at the time, revolutionary article. Even though "Female Sexuality" enlarges upon the 1925 essay, particularly in its fresh clinical material regarding the intensity and long duration of the little girl's pre-oedipal attachment to her mother, he adds that this is an element he finds characteristic of male or female femininity in general; the interest in the mother.

In the 1931 essay, Freud retains his view of the "normal" Oedipus complex: Tender attachment to the opposite-sex parent and hostile feelings toward the same-sex parent describe the way male sexuality is linked to thought and behavior. But, for the first time, he examines in detail the idea he had advanced in "Some Psychic Consequences . . ." (1925) in which female sexuality, which he had called "a dark continent," is constructed along different lines from the "normal Oedipus complex." Two problems face the girl that do not face the boy: She has to give up her first love object—the mother—in exchange for a male partner; and she must renounce the clitoral zone of genital pleasure in favor of the vagina if she is to become a feminine woman, a suitable partner for a man.

Lacan does not address this picture at the level of organ reality. Rather, he critiques such an ideal of the One, or the harmonious heterosexual couple. Not only is the Oneness toward which love aims an impossibility—for heterosexual or homosexual couples—love itself proves that the most basic partner of each person is his or her unconscious Other, not the other or beloved.[8] By stressing that problems and conflict issue from the nonrapport, Lacan argues that Freud's genitally mature happy couple is an impossibility given the asymmetrical development of the male and female at the level of identification and relation to a logic of the *all* or the *not all*. Moreover, Freud's "happy couple" incidentally reveals that the evolution of the sexual difference is not based on a difference in organ pleasure per se, given his discovery that clitoris equals penis in childhood masturbatory pleasure.

Lacan deduced something quite different from Freud. He postulated that children learn the sexual difference in reference to imaginary ideals of masculine and feminine in a given symbolic order. In *Seminar IV*, Lacan began to describe the real as an order of trauma constituted, in part, by the infant's taking on sexual difference as an experience of castration, or the forbidding of the pleasurable infinity of a continuous Oneness between mother and child. The one who teaches sexual difference, then, is the "real Father" who desires the mother sexually. Such desire works as a function of psychic separation or castration for the infant who begins to be tormented, not only by the intermittent losses of the corporal objects that cause desire, but also by the incipient assumption of identity based on lack, the father's "no" communicating "she's not all yours, you are not one with her." Such a split—between mother and infant—has radically different consequences for each sex, however.[9]

Such a "no," a first experience of the incest taboo, founds society on the laws of separation, difference, substitution, and exchange. Rather than deduce, as did Freud, that a cultural superego construct is individually formed and must, later, be modified as to its repressive influences, or decide, as did Herbert Marcuse (among others) that one can liberate society at large by a "free love/free sex" removal of superego repressions, Lacan argued in 1972 in "*L'étourdit*"[10] that the equation of "phallic" (genital) enjoyment with the phallus as an imaginary object of desire is fallacious. The value given the infant qua imaginary phallus is derived from a particular mother's unconscious desire vis-à-vis the symbolic phallus and her own lack-in-being. One cannot logically equate[11] the nonrapport between the sexes, with the symbolic father, taken as language, and successfully argue that language prohibitions cause the division, or the inverse.

Nor can solutions to the traumatizing effects of "no" be arrived at by deconstructing language so as to build a new real (Morel, p. 19). The link that must first be to Woman is made, rather, at the level of the *dire* (or saying) that comes to take the place of the real in an analytic discourse where the unconscious speaks in substitutive metaphors and displaced metonymies that bear on the signifiers in terms of which one exists (or not) as an object of the Other's desire. Morel points out that the zero level of the object-cause-of-desire is representable for the unconscious as symbolized by the subject on the basis of lack, while the number one is given by the Freudian second identification that Lacan called the unary trait (S_I). But the number two cannot be symbolized in the unconscious because it is a real number, denoting the impossibility of a sexual rapport of oneness between two (Morel, p. 112). The unconscious does not "speak" of harmonies, then. And consciousness covers up the impasses in real jouissance. The social (or phallic) interdiction to Oneness creates a mask of semblances, Lacan maintained, that divides the sexes.

This places difference or division at the elevated level of the unary trait of difference that has social value—the masculine—(whether it describes a woman or a man), because it is equatable with language and the law of differentiation. The feminine marks the site of a sexual masquerade that fetishizes the body or body parts, not only because they bring unary traits of jouissance into fantasy, but also because they are on the slope of the interdictions (excesses) that place the primary objects that cause desire on the real slope of primordial repression. This leads Lacan to speak of the problem of the "feminine" as being equivalent to the truth of metonymy, or the *dit* (the signified of the sayings [*dire*]), which tries to re-present the unconscious subject by the modalities of grammar and demand. Here the subject is actually an equivalent of the evanescent object (*a*), which is topologically closed off from language. As a nonbeing, the small (*a*) is absolute and nondialectical, its only residual traces being the excesses of jouissance— or *sinthomes*—by which one interprets one's own absent unconscious *dits* in the real through the truths uttered in socially inappropriate words, in (true) lies, in bodily symptoms, and so on (Stone trans., "*L'étourdit*," pp. 20–21).

More germane to a contemporary study of sexuality (and sexuation) than Freud's notion of a necessary heterosexual resolution of the sexual difference is his elaboration of the early female attachment to her mother at a pre-oedipal moment. So compelling is this period, Freud argued, that *he retracts his theory that the Oedipus complex is the cause of neurosis*, adding: "We have long given up any expectation of a neat parallelism between male and female sexual development." Further on he writes: "Our insight into this early, pre-oedipus phase in the little girl's development comes to us as a surprise, comparable in another field with the effect of the discovery of the Minoan-Mycenaean civilization behind that of Greece" (Freud, "Female Sexuality," p. 226). In this same passage, he describes this phase as, "elusive, lost in a past so dim and shadowy, so hard to resuscitate" and without any apparent awareness. Lacan stressed that no one can remember something that happens before they have the language by which to describe that experience to themselves. Since then, linguistics has taught us that no one possesses a minimal grammar adequate to describe the world to himself before age five or six, the age Freud marks as beginning the oedipal period of identifications as masculine or feminine.

Lacan's "topological structural" solution to Freud's impasse in understanding at this point is founded on a blockage in Aristotle's own logic; that is, Aristotle never separated logic from language. Although, his propositions regarding what is particular (Σ) or universal ($\forall$)—such as: Every man is mortal; thus no man is immortal— contain a negative function, they presuppose it positivistically. Lacan's solution to Aristotle's inability to explain this negative part of his logic was to approach the negative/positive division as residing in language itself and, furthermore, to view the divide as constructed on the basis of the traumatic assimilation of difference, whose Ur-paradigm is the sexual difference. In 1958 Lacan spoke of differences in love and desire between men and women. In 1960, he introduced the "forms of desire" as the object (*a*).[12] In 1971 he put forth a logic of *the pas tout* (the *not all*) as a basis of feminine sexuality in "*D'un discours qui ne serait pas du semblant*"[13] and elaborated his formulas of sexuation, first in *L'étourdit* (1972), and then in *Encore* (1972–1973).

The previous chapter developed Lacan's theory of the phallic signifier as a crucial reference in the construction of sexual identity. In Lacan's *écrit* "On a Question Preliminary to Any Possible Treatment of Psychosis" (1957–1958),[14] he equated the universality of the phallic signifier with language itself in the sense that the symbolic is always present before any infant's birth into what he than called the social Other. Not only does the symbolic order of language give an infant his or her identity by structuring her subjectivity, it also creates in her the unconscious fantasies and desires—a history—others impose on her.

The error of supposing that a child can consciously remember events that happened to her before she has developed a sufficient grammar for describing the world in terms by which she interprets what has been presented to her, does not even touch on the question of the source of the unconscious roots of those word memories. But the error has been repeated by object-relations theorists of the stature of Melanie Klein, and others as well. Such a mistake is based on the assumption that phonemes are an innate biological set of cognitive tools, "hard-wired" into the brain, and readily available to anyone for remembering the primary fantasy material of early infant life, and even prior, before birth. In such theories, memory would function like a kind of prehensile language organ.

But Freud recognized something else: the primordial mother as object, not as subject. Delving even deeper into the problems caused by the early attachment of a girl to her mother, Freud suggested in 1931 that female dependence on the mother is at the root of the specifically feminine neurosis, hysteria, which he characterized as a dread of being devoured by the mother (p. 227). What Freud described as an "immaturity of the psychical organization" characterized by projection (blaming the other) is as such not neurosis. Lacan depicted this "immaturity" as the "normal narcissism" of the master discourse.

While Freud suggested that the hysteric is hostile to an overly invasive mother, Lacan, unlike Freud or contemporary object-relations theorists, for whom the category borderline resonates, made a radical distinction between (neurotic) hysteria and the psychoses (schizophrenia and paranoia). Moreover, he valorized a kind of normal paranoia as the condition of the subject's being divided in the imaginary realm of the ego between an Ideal image of self and the splitting effects on that Ideal caused by the gaze of others (ego ideals) and the power of the symbolic Other to valorize those Ideals (or not).[15]

But, Lacan does not examine the hysteric's relations to her mother. His emphasis is, rather, on the manifestation of hysteria in the daughter's efforts to keep others from seeing that her father lacks anything, even to the point of her identifying with her father's castration and impotence, as did Dora. In trying to answer her existential question What is a woman? an hysteric seeks to know what her father wants unconsciously. Lacan added that the strong attachment of "certain women" to their fathers, noted by Freud in the analytic clinic, finds its root cause in the lack of a clear signifier for gender—that is, a set of associations that would add up to a preponderantly feminine identity emanating from the earliest installation of the Ideal ego unconscious formation—that would answer what a woman is in a particular symbolic order. The identification with the father that separates female hysteria from the normative (even obsessional) woman is one "resolution" of the oedipal assumption for "gender," taken as a set of identifications that define one as sexuated.

We remember that Lacan first rewrote the Freudian Oedipus complex ("On a Question . . . ," pp. 199–200) from which one takes on sexuation as Father's Name/Mother's Desire · Mother's Desire/? → Father's Name (Other)/(Phallus) In emphasizing that the mother's desire is unknown—that is, unconscious—Lacan focused in 1958 on the language of the Other that assigns meaning to a child's sexuality via identifications with culturally defined concepts of the masculine or feminine in macrocosm, and within a given family in microcosm. In that the "Father's Name" meant language at that point in Lacan's teaching and the mother's desire remained enigmatic as to her own unconscious resolution of the division between the sexes, one cannot know what symptom the child will become within the family.

By the 1970s, Lacan had understood that the object (a) continually introduces the stoppages of jouissance into language, placing discontinuities and inconsistencies in being, body, and language. Based on his acknowledgment of a radical inconsistency in the Other ($\emptyset$), Lacan rethought sexuality and sexuation once more. At the point where a person identifies with one or more object traits, repressed as *dits* and *sinthomes* in the real, individuals seek to fill the primordial void by making an equivalence of their Ideal ego with a form of the object (a)—such as the "voice" of authority, the queen of the gaze, the nurturer whose base identification is with the all-satisfying breast. Or, Like Rabelais, one may elevate the feces to the point where words, things, and goods become coequivalents that in and of themselves—as knowledge (S_2)—seem capable of suturing the hole in the Other.

An hysteric might be unconsciously identified with the (imaginary) phallus that she supposes can escape castration. In this sense, she imagines herself as strong enough to sustain her father, her fantasy being that *she* can both fill his lack *and* help him escape his castration. Lacan writes the hysteric's fantasy thus: $a/\$ <> 0$ (S. IV). In this sense, she identifies herself as castrated object with the uncastrated Woman who could possibly exist and create a whole Other (S. IV, cf. chs. 6 and 10). Identified with the "lack of being the father" in male sexuation—$\$$—rather than with women who define themselves as castrated and, thus, must join in the masquerade around the sexual difference, the hysteric's jouissance identification is as an object (a) that will try to fill the void in the Other ($\emptyset$), rather than with the a that would be fantasy partner to the lover's lack-in-being ($\$$).

Serena Smith distinguishes between normal hysteria and pathogenic hysteria in "The Structure of Hysteria—Discussion of Three Elements." If however, hysteria is a structure, not a sliding scale of behavior, the distinction to be made is between a "normative" woman who, in accepting the lack-in-being ($\$$) speaks a master discourse ($S_1 \rightarrow S_2$) that represses castration, and the hysteric. Paradoxically, the woman in the master logic has assimilated it as a structural reality. She thus identifies with, or as, a master (phallic) signifier (Φ), or superego. In discourse structure terms, she speaks from the position of agent or authority in the master discourse: $S_1 \rightarrow S_2 / \cancel{S} \leftarrow a$.[16]

The two new details Freud adds in this essay of 1931 are the discovery that the mother is as important to the girl as her father, and that the pre-oedipal attachment disappears from the language of conscious memory. Lacan taught us that the attachment disappears in memory, although it remains present in the structure of language—in the *dires* and *sinthomes*. Nonetheless, Lacan's early description of the imaginary as a virtual real, and his increasing awareness, that the real is constituted from the beginning of life as a base ordering of radically repressed traumata that cause symptoms, obviated his earlier theories that stressed the signifier. In these he focused on the lack-in-being created by alienation behind the words of language. But even in 1957 in "On a Question Preliminary to Any Possible Treatment of Psychosis" (1957–1958) (*Ecrits*, pp. 197–98), he substituted the word *pregenital* for *pre-oedipal*, inferring the infant's dependence on the object (a)—on desire as causal—as well as on the mother's love.

Insofar as the infant first identifies with the mother via the objects that cause desire—that is, with corporal parts: the breast, the feces, the urinary flow, the (imaginary) phallus, the voice, the phoneme, the gaze, and the sense of being nothing (that arises, for example, at the moment of the mother's disappearance)—the loss of a particular object (a) that grounds the infant in the illusion of being (whole)—is shocking. It is not surprising that Lacan will place Woman on the side of the (a) in sexuation. Moreover, he adds to Freud's comments on bisexuality that the bisexual disposition is stronger in women than in men who have usually eroticized only one sexual organ. In that the object (a) evolves more diffuse properties of being in corporal jouissance(s) than the penis, it is logical that Lacan locate it on the feminine side of his sexuation graph. There, the object (a) is proximate to the real void which touches on the object as loss, or as unary trait.

Freud used the word *object* (love object, etc.), which has been understood phenomenologically by object-relations psychoanalysts to mean a person, actual thing, or an organ one valorizes as a replacement for the mother. Lacan, typically, retained Freud's word *object*, but gave it new meaning. While individuals love others and things by investing jouissance in them, thus forging concrete attachments, it is not the person or thing in itself that Lacan stressed, but the links or unary traits left over from loss of the primordial objects that first caused the infant to desire something or someone. In this sense, the object (a) is the pointillism of everyday life: a particular scent, or a lilt of the voice, that elicit desire in the infant's effort to retrieve a part of the lost object. But from the start, there is this paradox: The *object* that causes desire is not the actual thing the infant—and later the adult—wants. The traits are real, but the objects sought are symbolic or imaginary lure objects. Whether infant or adult, one desires the particularity of the conditions of enjoyment that initially linked the subject as a subject of desire ($\cancel{S}$) to the fantasy objects he or she later imagines can fill his lack and confer on him or her the homeostatic constancy of Oneness.

Such objects become dynamic in the fields of the partial drives Lacan called the oral, anal, scopic, and invocatory, where constellations of meaning surround the object field that acts *in and upon* language. This occurs in "The Viscissitudes of the Drives" as Freud argued in 1915, by repression (of fantasy), sublimation (of the drives), reversal into its opposite of projection, and turning around upon the subject's own self in masochism.[17] Images, signifiers, and real impasses attenuate the subject's encounter with his own lack by sublimation, repression, projective denial, and sadomasochism.[18]

Even though nothing in Freud would lead one to link his concept of female sexuality directly to Lacan's idea of *object*-cause-of-desire, insofar as Lacan's distinction between masculine sexuality and feminine sexuality is not based on gender but on four possible interpretations of the phallus and castration, the new element Lacan stresses in the phallic function is that the real organ "enjoys"—(+)—and desires an object (*a*) that will cause its pleasure. The real phallus is sexual, by contrast with the imaginary phallus whose "signifiers" culminate in the macho graffitis that try to account for the nonsensical gap between erection and detumescence. The imaginary phallus's "sense" (the "meaning" of *Sinn*, as opposed to the "meaning" of *Bedeutung*) concerns being and power, not information or pleasure. The jouissance phallus contrasts, as well, with the symbolic phallus whose meaning is the negative of lack or castration—(−ϕ)—which makes desire possible, enabling it to function as an evanescent wanting, rather than a libidinal demand.

On the feminine side, Lacan calls the object (*a*) the "plus-de-jouir," or the excess *cause* in desire, whose uniquely positive enjoyment is present under many guises in all the objects sought in the drive. Gilles Chatenay describes this excess as "the real, of [one's] enjoyment."[19] Even though the objects that substitute for the lost object (*a*) appear and disappear, as Freud's *Fort! Da!* paradigm indicates, the object (*a*), nonetheless, radiates a diffuse jouissance that contains real remnants of unary traits that serve as the literal edges that bind themselves to make a hole, as well as the symbolic scars (S_I) left over from the cuts of losses (cf. p. 7, ch. I). The traits cannot, then, be undone or deconstructed in analysis, nor can the losses be repaired, but a "fantasy" ($\text{\$} <> a$) can be traversed: What is traversed is not the subject, however, who is pure absence, nor the object aspect of pure positivity, but the dialectic played out around the (+,−) of the phallic function of having, losing, and (re)finding (Morel, pp. 33–34).

In Lacan's teaching, "feminine" sexuality undergoes all the vicissitudes of jouissance—the real of genital pleasure (Φ), the wants inferred by lack (desire) ($\text{\$}$), and the encounters with the void of pure anxiety at the heart of real losses ($\varnothing$). Yet, even though the phallus has a positive side of jouissance, it is the real of any primordial object as it functions in fantasy, correlated with the drives, that gives rise to the denials, myths, and quests that determine the myriad treatments of Woman insofar as she is reminiscent of an excess to the phallic "norm."

One might equate The Woman with the (*a*) that tries to join the couple as two + *a*, or One + *a*. Functioning as an irrational number (#3), the (*a*) does not support the two, or the couple, as One. Rather, it is founded on the fact that it cannot support the two, for between mother and infant there is always the One plus the Other, as well. Yet the Other can never be taken as One. Lacan's larger point here is that there is no couple, for each person in the couple intervenes as a ternary, as an object (a), as a gaze conferred by others (S. XX, p. 49). A feminine man may, for example, evoke the social discomfort enshrouding the evanescent Woman, unveiling, as he does, the phallic lie that pretends to be a symbolic whole. Stepping, like the mystics of old, into the place of Woman, bedecked in enigma and mystery, such a man—for example, Socrates who remains an enigma for his students—unveils the real. A decidedly masculine woman may also push askew the social masks of the unified masquerade, unveil its lie by embodying unexpected forms of the (a) that perforate imaginary wholes and social facades with the truths of the real that turn Kantian beauty into the psychoanalytic sublime of unboundedness.

Lacan gives Freud credit for seeing a structural logic here. The logic of the two sexes is not analogous. There is no "Electra complex," no symmetry of the sexes. In other words, Freud ascertained that the difference between the sexes would not exist if the difference did not make a difference. The logic of this "find" has the same structure as Lacan's understanding that the postulation of a supreme being, exception to human law, gives grounding to the law, just as Zeno of old understood that the concept of limit is made possible only in reference to infinity.

Stuck in biology, Freud did not think in terms of a logic implicit in his discoveries. Rather, he retained reductionist ideas of the Oedipus complex as typical only of male children who love their mothers and feel negativity, even hatred, toward the father, whom they view as a rival. In trying to figure out the larger ramifications of how males ever get cured of their violence toward each other enough to work together in a social body, he advanced another simplistic biological answer: Males see the female genital, judge women as castrated, and, thus, as corporally deficient or lacking (in the Lacanian imaginary), and, perforce, bond together. In other words, Freud equated the logic of structure—which lies outside the world of the visible—with the visible in the world. In this, he was an empiricist before his time.

Lacan's more sophisticated account of the Oedipus complex, based on a reconceptualization of *Totem and Taboo* (1912–1913),[20] depicts the Ur-father of the primal hoarde as Freud's mythic effort to designate a real father of jouissance. Leonardo Rodriguez writes: "It was to the subjective impact of the universal cultural law prohibiting incest that Freud gave the name of the Oedipus complex."[21] Lacan, as we have already said, gave the name "real father" to the manifestation in the family of the "father's" sexual desire for the mother—be it imaginary Daddy, an uncle, a lesbian partner, and so on—and the name "symbolic father" to the function of castration, or the effect of the interdiction of incest *between the mother and the infant* (S. IV, p. 269).

Now, this gives a radically new meaning to the incest taboo, as well as to Freud's discovery of a pre-oedipal period. Insofar as incest is usually attributed to a prohibition of sexual relations between father (uncle, brother) with the daughters or sisters, Lacan reads Freud as having uncovered an even more profound taboo. This one is placed as an interdiction of "psychic" Oneness between infant and mother, a taboo against foreclosing the third term of "no" or Otherness by which exchange is born in the substitutions necessary to the "fall of the object (*a*)," lest the infant become psychotic. Thus, loss of the (*a*) gives birth to society, rather than to psychosis. Lacan's hypothesis ascribes a meaning to the incest taboo that concerns a survival of the species at a psychic level, rather than a reproductive or genetic one (cf. *Essays on the Pleasures of Death*, ch. 5).

Lacan's interpretation of male group bonding in *Totem and Taboo*, hypothesizes that Freud put forth a logic of male subjectivity and sexuation, but could only explain his own mythical theory of the beginnings of society in male bonding as a form of oedipal guilt caused by having killed the greedy Ur-father. Freud, therefore, could not ascertain the true logic of male sexuation.[22] Lacan defined male identification with the group of males, rather, as an identification with the symbolic phallus, the positivized phallic signifier that represents difference from the Ur-father as "castration"; that is, as a psychic reality, not a biological one. But given that oedipal competition also tugs at the lawful social bonds, Lacan pursued the logic of "lawful" cooperation in the realms of history, myth, religions, and government, where identification with a leader who is "supposed" to know the "truth," functions as a guarantee of how to act for one's own good ("good" taken in Jeremy Bentham's sense that one's utilitarian good is also true).

Insofar as every cultural truth also "has the structure of fiction—that which maximizes one's good qua personal desire—"[23] Lacan argued against Immanuel Kant's voluntaristic categorical imperative in which the good of one is the good of all; the group. Rather, he claimed, the fiction of an omnipotent Ur-father is a social supposition (even a requisite) of the One exceptional being who stands outside and above the law in order to guarantee its validity. Thus, any Ur-father can be seen as another form representing the real father of enjoyment whose symbolic effect lies on the slope of superego interdiction to Oneness.

Lacan's theory that an identification with the abstract signifier for difference— that is, castration—is taken as the base of law and reality means that although Freud did not place *Totem and Taboo* in the lineage of his writings on the Oedipus complex, Lacan did. Freud never got beyond the visual and biological interpretations of "The Three Essays on Sexuality" (1905) where he first tried to describe the difference between the sexes thus: A male decides he is superior to females because of his narcissistic interest in his penis, which he see as superior because of its size and visibility in contrast with the female organ. He quickly resolves his own Oedipus complex by coming to identify with men at the level of the law, internalized as the superego.

Lacan retained only the *structure* of Freud's observations: The sexual difference *is* constituted asymmetrically. But where Freud falls prey to imaginary thought, Lacan proposed that the phallus is linked to the particularity of fantasy through a "propositional" (symbolic) function, rather than directly to the real organ, or the imaginary body. Indeed, an explanation of the "substance of jouissance"—masculine or feminine—necessitates a topological logic of three dimensions (real, symbolic, and imaginary), not a scrutiny of two sexes (Morel, p. 23).

On the one hand, the male error seems imaginary. Imaginarily, males may mistake their being marked as different from the mother as an attribute of *being* the phallus—the desired object. Thus, he confuses being with sexuality insofar as the privileges granted him seem to concern his body. Actually, male privilege is granted by the Other whose attributes are symbolically (empirically) countable. It is not an imaginary phallus he valorizes at the level of cause, then, but difference as a countable symbolic value, difference as interpretations not subsumed by imaginary consistencies and misrecognitions.

In *Le séminaire, livre IV* (1955–1956): *La relation d'objet,* Lacan described each sex's relation to the object (*a*) and to its lack in terms of the imaginary father; that is, any figure or signifier that represents fatherhood, be it Daddy, an uncle, a priest, a river god, or any other such paternal sign, is not the real father of jouissance who communicates interdiction, or the symbolic father whose function is to introduce castration (or lack) into being, but a sign Lacan defined here as a mixture of the imaginary and symbolic.

Rejecting Freud's incomprehension of female sexuality, Lacan puts forth a logic in which females confuse their entire body as *being* the phallus—the *beloved object* (*a*)—at the point where love and desire equate her sexuality with her bodily beauty. Put another way, Lacan shows that a male is a male only insofar as he is a signifier that represents a subject for another signifier. He represents himself as a male to another male via his subjective identification as *different* from the mother qua Woman. At the level of empirical "controls," a psychotic lacks this identification for difference. Schreber, for example, identified *with* his mother in a push toward incarnating The Woman-who-lacks-nothing, and settled into the delusion of being the wife of God (cf. *S. III*).

Such a "mental" refusal of separation—a refusal to lose objects from the Other (O)—indicates one resolution of "being" that Lacan called the limit of freedom; an identification with a suffering that is antithetical to any myth of joyful transsexuality. Thus, psychosis, as a refusal of the oedipal "no," fails to evolve the symbolic lack that builds the capacity for dialectical thought around a third-term effect, produced by the fall of the object (*a*). The psychotic is affixed, rather, in a lethal proliferation of mirror-stage narcissistic refractions in which all others are equivalent to his or her Other as full, not decompleted, and all beings are submitted to the (*a*) he or she cherishes.

But most males internalize the oedipal injunction to difference. In compensation for this castration—this alienation from being One with the first object(s) of love and desire, given by the mother—they identify their being and knowledge with the structures of patriarchy: reality, language, and law, playing by the rules of the game of any local "universal" encoding of symbolic requisites. Male identification is, thus, defined in terms of the social body, which he, in turn, defends to the letter and spirit of the law. If not, he is outside the law, on the side of the feminine (or the negative masculine)—a place of joyful identification for the perverse subject and of sheer unmitigated torture for the psychotic.

The female is defined asymmetrically as *not all* within the order of the symbolic, *not all* under the phallic law. Insofar as she remains identified with the mother whose primordial being is corporal and real, the female is closer than the male to an identifica-tion with the real of the drives. This leaves open a question regarding females who identify primarily with their fathers. But, nonetheless, both sexes are identified with the real cuts out of which the void is first created by the losses of the (maternal) object's comings and goings. That these objects give enjoyment as a status quo of simulated wholeness means that the mother enters into the category of Woman, not only as sexual, or feminine, but also as holding out the hope of constancy as a deferral of the impossible real.

"Very different is the effect of the castration complex on the girl," Freud says. She acknowledges her castration, admits the sexual superiority of the male and her own inferiority, with three possible outcomes: (1) She turns her back on sexuality altogether, giving up her pre-adolescent (i.e., active/sexual) proclivities as well; (2) She clings to her threatened masculinity and develops a "masculinity complex." The third response a woman can adopt to what Freud calls castration is (3) the "normal feminine attitude" in which she takes her father as a love object, thereby arriving, *via castration*, at the feminine Oedipus complex. That is, by accepting that she is not a man, she becomes a woman, a sexual partner to a man who is not her father, thereby accepting "definitive femininity" (Freud, "Female Sexuality," p. 232).

Since Lacan viewed castration as a lack-in-being that characterizes both sexes, he saw both as required to fill that lack. While woman is drawn to the male's jouissance phallus via his social power, as well as by his *savoir* and his fantasy image of her, his attraction for her passes through the defiles of her imaginary lures that represent the partial phallic object as sublimated sexuality. Male sexuality is denoted by Lacan as Φ and (a), while female sexuality depends on words and identifications that fill the void of loss $(\varnothing)$ and suture the lack-in-being $(\cancel{S})$. But insofar as sexual pleasure itself is concerned, Lacan adds supplemental capabilities to the woman that emanate not only from her *not* identifying sexually with only one organ but also from a potentially limitless corporal enjoyment insofar as (s)he is not *all* identified with an abstract principle for law, language, and reality. Such a principle subordinates most men to the singularities of the positivized symbolic phallus and its mate, the superego. Feminine sexuation acts on both sides of the sexuation graph, bringing together sexuality, ontol-ogy, and epistemology.

Thus, Lacan's theory of sexuation puts forth a radically different image of the realities and causes of "female sexuality" than does Freud's. Most biological females are mentally castrated within a contradictory and paradoxical logic of double negation, he argues, because they are identified with the desiring and evanescent object $(a,)$ the negativized phallic signifier $(-\phi \rightarrow \cancel{S})$, and are proximate to the real of lost objects $(a) \rightarrow [\Phi])$. While the male sexuation symbols are Φ and a, the female ones are $\cancel{S}$ and $\varnothing$. And these verities obtain whether the man is heterosexual or homosexual, and likewise for the woman. Thus, Lacan does not divide the sexes as homosexual or heterosexual, but in terms of epistemological places built up as masculine or feminine responses to lack and loss.

Castration is not a fantasy, Lacan says, but is the real operation introduced by the incidence of the signifier in the rapport of (the) sexes. Loss must logically precede identification with the signifier. While man conflates desire and love with his fetishized penis and its fantasy objects (*a*), the Woman desires to be loved from the place where she represents the decompleted or incomplete Other (∅) for others, and thus she seeks reflexively to know who she is in their eyes. Quite different requisites are put on the male for obtaining jouissance. To "enjoy" a woman, the man's father must be (mythically) dead in the real—which Lacan defines as the impossible place of contradictory elements—of the impasses that reappear in the symbolic. The Oedipus myth is, thus, a structural operator of the real father (*S. XVII*, p. 144): The boy desires his mother, but cannot have her. If he gets her, he has overthrown the basic law of exchange by which sociey subsists. Freud erred in equating jouissance with the dead (Ur) father, Lacan says, thereby missing the point of what myth is. In enunciating the impossible ideal, myth moves to the "logical structure" that requires the father's murder as the condition of the son's jouissance; this is the antithesis of Nietzsche's foreclosure that would have God dead (*S. XVII*, pp. 138–39 and 143–45).

In "Identification," Joël Dor refers to Lacan's abundant work in rethinking Freud's three modes of identification. In 1962, Lacan said: "The affect of anxiety is, indeed, connoted by a fault in the object, but not by a fault in reality. If I no longer know anything about myself as the possible object of the desire of the Other," as Dor continues, anxiety arises as a small step from an identification that has been shaken.[24] With these theories, advanced in the 1960s and 1970s, Lacan stressed the sexuated choice of identification as masculine or feminine, a choice not determined by primary or secondary biological sexual characteristics but by the "identity" given a child by others and the Other: $\Phi/\text{\$}$. Up to 1974, Lacan had spoken of "sexuation $\text{\$}$ formulas" or "sexual identifications."

But in 1974, he advanced a new term—"options of sexuated identification," arising by the signifier as predominantly masculine or feminine. That is, language creates one's imaginary body and defines one as a signifier that represents a subject for another signifier in a chain of articulations:

The unconscious, structured like a language, cuts into or across the imaginary consistency of the biological body, bringing into language the effects—the *dits* or *sinthomes*—that create affects; not biology. This is the sense in which psychoanalysis can use the symbolic of one's *dires* and *sinthomes* to enable an analysand to reconfigure (reinterpret) the real of the *dits* that "speak" his or her desire from the radically absent place of the unconscious Other.

Such a view of (sexual) desire is far from Freud who maintained in 1931 that the pre-oedipal relation explains many puzzles of feminine sexual life. In married life, the wife treats her husband as she treated her mother, "regressing" to conflicts she had with her mother. Here Freud asserts another way in which the feminine Oedipus complex differs from the masculine one. Girls do not rival with their mothers (or each other) out of competition for their fathers, but on the basis of conflict with their mothers for the father's attention—conflict Freud attributes, again, to the magical power of the visible, to the daughters' seeing their mothers as castrated.

In her course, on *"La différence des sexes,"* Geneviève Morel points out that in his sexuation graph, Lacan describes a function on the feminine side that cannot be written in the real of the unconscious—$\overline{\exists x}\,\overline{\Phi x}$—where there is no exception to not being castrated. Women "see" the realities of a double castration on the male side,

$$\frac{\text{Man}}{\frac{\$}{\Phi}}$$

insofar as the symbolic names the male (Φ) as different from woman, yet he still depends on her to fill his lack ($\$$) in myriad ways.

But women do not consider themselves castrated insofar as the male organ is perceived imaginarily by both sexes as a separable partial object. Beyond these points, Lacan's focus is, rather, on the point of exception in the feminine universal (Morel, pp. 102–103):

$$\frac{\overline{\exists x}\,\overline{\Phi x}}{\forall x\,\Phi x}$$

Where there is no generic or universal Woman, no Ur-woman exception to the rule of all being alike insofar as none is a man, women are mythologized as retaining exceptional feminine traits or knowledge, or as possessing supramasculine powers. But they do not become abstract signifiers or principles that guarantee symbolic-order law, as does the Ur-father on the masculine side.

In the feminine logic, the double negative on the top line creates a double noninscribable function—that is, the real. One cannot inscribe the point of exception necessary to support a universal on the feminine side since the father (or his substitutes) are on the other side of sexuation.

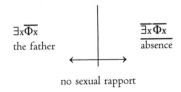

$\exists x\overline{\Phi x}$ $\overline{\exists x}\,\overline{\Phi x}$

the father   absence

no sexual rapport

Thus, one ends up in points of impasse. The formula for the real, "that which does *not* stop *not* writing itself," can only produce a positive number (the real squared) (Morel, p. 103): $\overline{\exists x \, \overline{\Phi x}}$. Since the consistency of the "whole," or *all*, resides on the male side—the universal of men $\forall x \Phi x$ is based on the father $(\exists x \overline{\Phi x})$—(Morel, p. 104).

Schema of the Man

Morel points out that Women remain concerned to supplement the masculine sexual formula written as $\exists x \overline{\Phi x}$. One reading of this formula is that the father cannot supplement his daughter's lack. Taken as an exception, he alone assures a universal consistency of the *all* to a social symbolic, that is, a limit; Creon versus Antigone. Lacan reproached Freud for his theory of a universal Oedipus, just as he critiqued the Aristotelian universal. Even though Lacan had a theory of the universal of men, it is based on a logic of contradiction: No man can be an exception to the law in addition to being its originator. This contradiction partially resolves the Oedipus complex by giving man a way out of his being *all* enclosed within the symbolic. Insofar as he is phallically castrated, he has a *possible* motive for reaching out to the other, to a partner, through his lack: $\$ \lozenge a$. But the phallus serves him contradictorily, also, negating the possibility of a universal male sexuality. The phallus is an obstacle to the other (the partner) for he desires the Other (sex), already constructed as his fantasy (Morel, p. 105).

On the feminine side of sexuation, Lacan adapts a model Aristotle rejected. What happens if one negates the universal quantificator $\overline{\forall x}$? One ends up with no universal of the feminine, even no logical limit to its contingencies. Lacan proposed that insofar as woman doubles herself, constituting a nonidentitarian logic of sameness—there is none who is not the same; that is, without the phallus—there is no "every woman" as a generic universal phallic class. Such a class has, at least, the male identificatory mark of difference as a "psychic" basis for attributing specifically "masculine" properties to difference. On the other hand, there is not one woman who is *not not all* $(\overline{\forall x \Phi x})$ under the local universal *all* of being somewhat outside the phallic exigencies of the symbolic. This new kind of logic led Lacan to postulate identificatory sexuation as that which necessitated modern logic and the mathematical theory of ensembles (Morel, p. 104). Looking to the French grammarians Damourette and Pichon, Lacan picked up on their use of a double negative that is not forclusive (Morel, p. 106). He described the feminine negation of the universal as discordential.[25]

Even though there is a universal of the masculine symbolic function—$\forall x \Phi x$—("one can say of any x . . . ,"), the possibility of this lies beyond itself in a logical exception. Having rejected the old-fashioned logic that derived negation binarily by simply negating the copula, the verb *to be*, Lacan did not leap immediately to the conclusions of modern logic that all statements are relative to a possible exception. Rather, he combined Aristotle's negation-by-separation with Freud's universality of the

Oedipus complex—that is, castration or separation of the infant and mother leads to a nonrapport of the sexes—that creates the obstacle that the phallic signifier puts under an early interdiction (Morel, p. 105). The feminine of this universal possibility lies beyond itself in a negation of the universal: $\overline{\forall}x\Phi x$.

In speaking of a universal masculine function, Lacan says psychotic men are not located within it while the feminine introduces a vacillation between what is phallic (symbolic) and what is not. Yet, the biggest obstacle to the sexual rapport comes from the male side, making of the feminine *not all* an ambiguous negation that marks itself as an inconsistency. Moreover, the silence of the Other (feminine) jouissance ($\varnothing$), when added to the fantasy and the word of love, make up what Lacan called the feminine *pastoute* ($\overline{\forall}x$), which passes through the phallic word, not through the real body (Morel, pp. 107–108).[26] Morel argues that the word of love supplements the woman's disappointment—not in the mother, but—in the father (p. 123). Thus, while jouissance equals love for a man, a woman needs the words of love. That is, for Lacan, "existence" has to demonstrate itself for either sex. It cannot be a simple enunciation of discourse.[27] Existence demands a material proof, an inscription. Lacan's sexuation graph is written thus (Morel, p. 111):

Man		Woman	
$(\exists x\overline{\Phi x})$ Necessary		Real	$(\overline{\exists x\,\Phi x})$
$(\forall x\Phi x)$ Possible		Contingent	$(\overline{\forall}x\Phi x)$

That is, the double negative of Woman's nonexistence ($(\overline{\exists x\,\Phi x})$—they are all alike— cannot be inscribed in the real. While the number 0 can be inscribed as a lack of something ($\emptyset$) and 1 can be inscribed as an S_I, a unary trait of identification, the mirror-stage number 2 cannot be made out of two persons whose refractions are lost in confused illusions of Oneness.

It is precisely the confusion between the numbers two and one that constitutes psychosis. Lacan started his career as a medical doctor, a psychiatrist who worked with psychotic patients for more than thirty years. In this period he made a long series of discoveries regarding the cause of psychosis that might be described as the identification of two as one, or the indifferentiation between a child and the other, or the foreclosure of a signifier for difference that creates lack whose inverse is desire for most people. That is, if a child identifies with the other as a totality—a superego posture— later he or she will not have the dialectical base of intersubjectivity from which to address others as (ego) ideals, similar to but different from him or herself. Insofar as there is no pregiven, innate inscription for (sexual) difference, but a oneness of seeming rapport between two separate individuals, the psychotic subject's refusal of the Father signifier creates an unstable third term in this subject for whom an imaginary prosthetic element functions as an ideal and the Other is taken as already complete. The Other is decompleted only when it offers a threat. The prosthetic imagined Other, then, falls apart in a psychotic break.

Having refused the signifier for difference, the psychotic lives in a profound identification with the primordial mother. Thus, the psychotic forecloses imaginary castration ($-\phi$) between the symbolic and imaginary that comes from dropping the object (a). The dropping of primordial objects ordinarily creates "identity" boundaries as a space of freeplay between imaginary being and symbolic thinking. Psychotic foreclosure refuses this loss, thus creating a surplus jouissance around the organs and objects implicated in desire. Foreclosing the real father's desire for the mother—that is, symbolic castration—means that the psychotic must identify with prosthetic imaginary fathers who serve as supplemental figures of the law. But the only source of law in which the psychotic truly believes is the mother's voice, her superego dicta: She (or her substitutes) serves as The Woman Who Exists and provides the missing signifier of law as an all-pervasive superego voice (or gaze).

While the idea of a logic of the same on the slope of the feminine may clarify some things connected with psychotic structure, Lacan does not actually speak of a "logic of the same," or a foreclosure of the phallus, for the feminine. Rather, he advanced the notion of a discordential logic of the "no" between the enunciation (the subject as desiring) and the enunciated (the subject as spoken). One could describe the logic as a feminine discord opposing masculine rules: the masculine $\forall x \Phi x$ versus the feminine $\overline{\forall x} \Phi x$ (Morel, p. 107). In her proximity to the thing in itself—the maternal "Good" one might describe as the real object—that Lacan locates on the feminine side of sexuation, not only is the mother confused with giving symbolic "gifts" that will stop the infant's imaginary frustration via a real organ, such as the breast, males, later, unconsciously solve the oedipal demands of difference by splitting women between prostitutes and virgin (mother)s. While Freud thought girls flee identification with the mother because of disgust with a literal castration, Lacan credits Freud with having discovered, rather, the lineaments of the dialectic surrounding the object a where the inside and outside concern proximity or distance from the real of sexual excitement, not different properties belonging to the object:

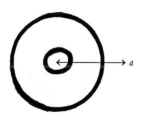

Insofar as extimacy and intimacy place perception and perspective within proximate realms, distance from the pure real of the object does not bear on incest as a morality or a genetic malady, but as the limits of mental and psychic confusion and collusion where the extreme merger with the object may result in psychosis, where two are (mis)taken as one. This is why the sexual difference needs to be created by the real father's giving of the symbolic law as a "no" to "psychic" Oneness. The phallic effect places males and females at a distance from the mother's embodiment of "essential" (libidinal) objects. Later, any dyad or couple will abound with nonrapports, although the "supposed" Oneness of two brings the myth of a grounding in unity as well as the death zone of the contradictions and impossibilities that usher the real into the life of a couple.

Although Freud conflated the "object" with a person, and the cause of feminine conflict with the mother's capacity to elicit disgust regarding her "supposed" castration, Lacan's description of the object (*a*) as the excess or surplus value in jouissance, can be applied to the same passage where Freud erred in attributing psychic cause to organ reality. Lacan suggests that the girl's disgust with her mother, noted by Freud, has much more to do with the young female's thrust toward individuation, toward difference or Otherness, than with biological organs per se. The object (*a*) satisfies in the particular, supplementing jouissance requirements derived from the structuration of desire in the earliest interpretations of the phallus and castration. But why would conflict or hostility be aimed by a daughter at her mother, Freud asked? On the one hand, childhood love knows no bounds, demands exclusive possession, and wants the intimate and extimate to be the same. But, Freud noted, the conflict between mother and daughter has no real aim. The principal reason it is doomed to end in disappointment is that it is incapable of providing satisfaction. That is, oneness of two is an illusion.

One can see in Freud's description of the child's goal of attaining all the mother's love for (him or) herself, and its vicissitudes in later life, a hazy sketch of Lacan's object (*a*)—an object representing a lost object—an object sought with the goal of reexperiencing a totalizing satisfaction. The primary object can never be (re-)found in its original form, for it was only ever illusory. One is, thus, cast back and forth in life between the fantasy, the drives, and the incomplete Other:

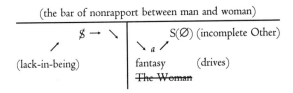

Lacan stressed that although the object (*a*) sought in satisfaction is never the actual thing one hopes for, this in no way attenuates the ardent and active human activity by which individuals pursue persons and objects with the manifest goal of being satisfied.

Little girls also turn away from their mothers, Freud suggested in his 1931 essay, because the mother prohibits the pleasurable activity of masturbation (p. 239). He concluded in his 1932 essay that little girls stop masturbating because the sight of the male genital organ makes them think they have an organ deficiency. They give up their own pleasure and decide to wait for the substitute replacements of husband = organ, followed by baby = organ. Morel gives logical sense to Freud's imaginary reductions of visible phenomena to "the thing" of fulfillment. The little girl's deception by her father gives rise to the common analytic and literary fantasies some women have of being a singular parent to a child, Morel writes. In fantasy, these women believe their mothering can compensate for any taint of "castration contamination." They wish to "mother" from the place of the ideal father. As such, they become exceptions to the rule of castration: $\exists x \overline{\Phi x}$—on the masculine side of sexuation. Such fantasies not only satisfy this mother's desire to be on the masculine side, they concomitantly have the effect of denying the feminine trauma in the real, based as it is on a double negation: $\overline{\exists x} \, \overline{\Phi x}$.

Freud's essays on the anatomical difference between the sexes have been dismissed both because they are incorrect, and because he uses those differences to establish a theory of how mind is formed. Only when one accepts that Freud was trying to understand the mental meaning of the conflicts and asymmetries that clearly mark the development of mind and being or, that when he speaks of women he is trying to understand why individuals with no deficiency feel oppressed by men all the same, can one grasp how he arrived at the biological and behaviorial reductionist conclusions, such as those advanced in his 1931 essay: "If we survey the whole range of motives brought to light by analysis for turning away from the mother: That she neglected to provide the little girl with the only proper genital organ, that she did not feed her enough, compelled her to share her mother's love with others, never fulfilled all the expectations of the child's love and, finally, that she first excited and then forbade her daughter's own sexual activity—all these seem adequate as a justification of the hostility finally felt" (p. 234).

Although Lacan does not directly answer Freud's comments, he deduces a fundamental lack-in-being (with the exception of the psychotic), posited at the site of the mother's unconscious desire toward each child as correlated with her own experience of castration. His sexuation tables, moreover, imply that the girl is burdened by an impossible—that is, identitarian—logic of the real which, having the negative (number-line) properties of real numbers (fractions), are inscribed as a weightiness of loss(es). Both sexes equate woman, alternately, with the mother of the drives and as a sexual "object" within the drives. Insofar as the drives are qualities, not (empirically countable) quantities, Woman is quickly mythologized. Lacan taught that myths begin precisely at the point where something is hard to quantify or qualify precisely because it is known only in terms of the jouissance properties that emanate from the real object (a), from the void ($\varnothing$), or from the negativized phallus ($-\phi$) (S. XVII; cf. ch. 8). We remember that Lacan equated the Borromean knot with structure and placed the a at its center, with the void located between the imaginary and real ($\varnothing$) and the split between image and word—first located between absence and presence of body parts—between the imaginary and symbolic ($-\phi$) (S. XX, p. 9):[28]

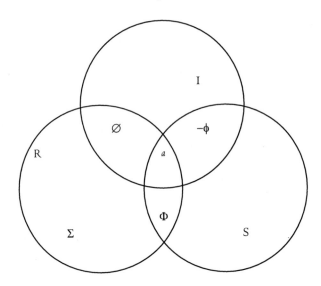

One values what one can count clearly and see easily. Yet, the unconscious "count" begins with valorizing the 0 that grounds being in the holes created or hollowed out in the real by the unary traits of identification. These "signifieds" are then esteemed as the I or (S_I) of difference in the symbolic. The 2 that merges the mother and infant into an imaginary, illusory "one" cannot be counted in the unconscious. That is, imaginary numbers are nonsensical and unthinkable. Lacan refers to unconscious counting as that which begins in the particular jouissance meaning of the drives, created by the "real" remnants left over from the loss of objects that first *caused* desire. Unconscious counting is an affair between 0 and I. The positivizable residue of the lost objects—the unary traits—bind themselves to holes and to the body. They consist of four that have different topological properties: The feces, for example, seem more substantial than the solipsism of the oral drive, first marked by the milk that flows silently between the mother's nipple and the baby's mouth. Because the feces are visibly solid and have dimension, they lie at the base of a later link between the visible and the jouissance surrounding a *counting* that is scopically libidinal. One counts money, cars, friends, orgasms. The feces are also on the border of the quantifiable symbolic in an imaginary equation of feces = phallus = "having."

Insofar as the mother is the first conveyor of the drives, Lacan's conflation of mother with Woman and jouissance gives a logic to Freud's picture of woman in "Female Sexuality." Although Freud found no universal law of ambivalence—love/hate—except as a characteristic typical of obsessional males, he argued in 1931 that the strength of the early female attachment to the mother gives rise to the daughter's subsequent ambivalence. Why, he wonders, do boys retain their attachment to their mothers without becoming hostile to them as girls do? Still, this may not be the case for boys, he suggested, since there is more work to do on the pre-oedipal in boys and on processes "we have only just come to know of" (p. 235). Still Freud never directly theorized the subsequent split between a supposedly asexual pure mother and the impurity of sexual women that marks male confusion toward the mother. Not only does the requisite of sexual difference cause this split, Lacan maintains, it is further widened in the distance imposed by the incest taboo. Indeed, rather than describe the male infant's phallus as an object of the mother's desire, Miller says it is closer to "an almost natural barrier" to jouissance.[29]

Although these oedipal issues concern identification, Lacan was at pains to provide a logic of how identification(s) are constructed, while still attending to the conditions of meaning via distinctions Aristotle had made between the logic of classes and attributes. Thus, he ended up linking mentality to sexuality—as sexuation—via that which appears between a subject (who is empty [$\cancel{S}$]) and jouissance (which is positive [a]). Lacan wrote the subject's enjoyment as a functional proposition of the Φ: (Morel, p. 66). But there is one relation to this signifier for men—$\Phi x \rightarrow \forall x \overline{\Phi x}$—all are castrated—and a different one for women—$\overline{\forall x} \Phi x$—not all are all castrated. The consequent access the woman has to the phallus is contingent: $a \rightarrow \Phi \rightarrow S(\emptyset)$ (Morel, p. 173).

Lacan presents a far different picture from Freud's phenomenological, observational, and positivist view of what a little girl asks of her mother regarding the nature of her sexual aims during the pre-oedipal period. The answer Freud garnered from clinical material was that the aims are both active and passive. The child wants to do what has been done to her (or him). Based on this observation, Freud stated paradoxically that the early mother-infant relation is an a-"sexual" relationship, even though much of the activity in it includes the real of corporal care and touching. Lacan objects that this view of development leaves out the concrete real of sexuality, while abutting in an erroneous conclusion: The mirror-stage dyad of mother and infant is romanticized as the paradigm of an ideal adult sexual coupling (Freud's genital maturity) based on a belief in the harmony of the One.

Freud wrote in his 1931 essay: "The first sexual or sexually tinged experiences of a child in its relation to the mother are naturally passive in character. It is she who suckles, feeds, cleans and dresses it, and instructs it in the performance of all its physical functions. Part of the child's libido goes on clinging to these experiences and enjoys the various gratifications associated with them, while another part strives to convert them into activity" (Freud, "Female Sexuality," p. 236). Given his discovery of infantile sexuality, Freud did not have to make a great mental leap to propose that libidinal energy is constructed in the earliest maternal care.

Lacan argues that Freud, nonetheless, confused the unique, particular elaborations of the partial drives around the objects-cause-of-desire—the oral, anal, scopic, and invocatory drives (whose fates vary with the structure of desire that marks one's oedipal fantasies as primarily normative, neurotic, psychotic, or perverse) with the adult genital relation. Lacan's sexual nonrapport means, among other things, that there is no genital drive: That is, there is no signifier for a direct rapport between organs—nor between man and woman, or infant and mother—that would give rise to a genital drive whose clear reciprocities would function automatically and cyclically as it does in the animal kingdom. Each person's partner is actually a relation to the Other (sex) of his or her earliest unconscious fantasies and to the repressed object(s) (*a*)—representative of the drive—that constitute the particular conditions of jouissance in his or her fantasies.

In trying to puzzle out the mysteries of feminine sexuality up to 1931, Freud sought to understand the sexual difference via a contradiction in passive and active behavior, these being the characteristics he assigned respectively to feminine and masculine sexuality. But, in 1931, Freud saw that all children want to convert passive behavior into active behavior: Do to the other what was done to them. Why, he asked in "Female Sexuality," do little girls *not* want to wash and dress their mothers as they do their dolls? Why seek a substitute figure, while directing an "oral, sadistic and finally even phallic" impulse toward their mothers? The answer he gave to this question was later developed by Melanie Klein: Infants fear being devoured by the mother, so they want to devour her in turn (p. 237).

Seen through a Lacanian grid, the identification with dolls is not gender specific, but an imaginary identification with images and with the symbolic effects of language that constitute a child's unconscious Other, which later seems as if it were detached from the mother's unconscious desire. Relating to enigmatic objects of desire, a child places its libido in language through metonymies whose referents may be the breast, a button shaped just so, and finally the amorphous desire to be held. This is quite a different theory from Freud's concept where two people relate harmoniously as whole bodies—boy and girl, or infant and mother—mirroring each other in a totalizing way through corporal completions where two whole selves create an ideal merger into one.

Lacan gives us, rather, a mathematically complex relation of parts of two beings dependent on one another. But the excluded middle of intuitionist logic is not valorized, as Kirsten Hyldegaard argues.[30] Rather, Lacan's bars, schemas, graphs, and use of the picture, all work toward giving a logic of the negative functions of lack, loss, castration, and cuts that intervene in all seeming totalities, such that even a triad cannot be formed without a fourth link (the knot) that unifies the orders by bisecting the triad into three realms, the knot itself making the fourth category of the symptom/*sinthome*.

Lacan questioned all theories that reduce perception to consciousness, or to the visible imaginary, or to intersubjectivity, or self/other relations. In such theories, no negative functions intervene at all except as simple seeming totalities. In the absence of a logic of negative functions, such as intuitionist logic, there is always an equation of perception with systems of consciousness, and the visible with the imaginary. When no unconscious splits intervene in being, body, or knowledge—as they do in Lacan's formalization of three jouissances—there is no way for libido to attach itself to meaning. In conscious life as depicted by Lacan, three forms of castration introduce alienation into language (a positivized castration $[\Phi]$); an encounter with the void in being and knowing experienced in moments of loss $(\varnothing)$; and the *dits* of the unconscious which language tries to translate in the *dires* of sense, or in the meaning of jokes, dreams, and so on, of the negativized (potentially separable) phallus $[-\phi]$.

In stressing the incompleteness of the Other as a set $(\emptyset)$ in *Seminar IX* on *Identification*, Lacan also emphasized the Other's impotence to respond, which comes from the limits of its knowledge. In bringing together Freud's conscious and unconscious with Aristotle's universals and particulars via the contradictory logic that topology makes truth functional, Lacan proposed three jouissance functions that enter language alternately as cuts, knots, or gaps in seemingly imaginary consistencies. The real actually cuts into an imagined "whole," uncovering hole(s) in symbolic narratives and in corporal homeostases. These attest to an ek-sistence of the real in conscious life (cf. "*La troisième jouissance*").

Giving a very different theory to the cause of mentality—to cover over the real and to negotiate desire—than Freud did, Lacan, nonetheless, maintains the sexual difference and the (oedipal) paternal metaphor as the basis of *how* meaning is woven together in the particular identifictory structures that constitute *sinthomes*. Indeed, the orders begin to intersect and weave themselves together as units of memory/mind long before two years of age when the infant advances to the mirror-stage identification by assuming a minimal image of a whole body gestalt, based on identifying with other(s). Later, he or she translates such primordial material through transformations that refer to the initial objects that cause(d) desire—the Ur-lining of the subject—once an incipient base of a grammar is acquired. In Lacan's teaching, any totalizing, holistic identification is a misperception, a fact he denoted by postulating the subject as an empty place($\cancel{S}$) filled by imaginary identifications of alienation and jouissance ($\sqrt{-1}+1$, etc.), where $\sqrt{-1} = i$, or imaginary numbers, equal an ideal image. The first signifiers to represent the subject through identifications are master signifiers $(+1)$ or S_1s.

Thus, Lacan writes: $\sqrt{-1}+1$, $\sqrt{-1}+1$ etc. (Holland, p. 64; Lacan *S. IX: L'identification*, Jan. 1962). When he added together the results of this formulation, he gave his first form of the paternal metaphor—Name-of-the-Father (Other/Phallus)—as well as the definition of a signifier as representing a subject for another signifier (Holland, p. 65; Lacan, *L'identification*). Herein, infant perception is first *created* in reference to the concrete realities of the experiences of loss ("0") and alienation (-1) that interpret the mother's unconscious desire vis-à-vis the Father signifier, the phallus, and castration. Later, the powerful effects of language as a body of knowledge (S_2) assign a place of "identity" to a child within the social field. From Lacan's viewpoint, during the early period Freud is describing, the desiring responses of an infant have already begun to be "written" in the Other in imaginary, real, and symbolic topological units, each of which encircles the object (a) in the center. When object satisfaction is lost, an infant seeks to retrieve some trace of the *object's* real metonymic properties $(+1$ or $S_1)$, or unary traits. Metaphorical substitutions of one thing for another are much more sophisticated functions which occur later as oedipal requisites: $i + \frac{1}{2}$.

The first losses of the object are registered as a tearing and splitting, as a breach between a "supposed" preexisting surface of smooth *material* thought to compose a whole body surface, and a sense of nothingness. Jeanne Lafont points out that "the hole is first before the surface itself."[31] This tearing away between the surface of the body and the object of desire is where imaginary *perception* begins to constitute the virtual real as a play between the rim and hole that constitute primordial perception on the side of jouissance from the start of life, rather than as a passive biological registering of sense data. The topological hole is created in the symbolic as a point zero of jouissance density, around which the libidinalization of language and fantasy begins to loop itself. These first splits are holes whose everyday existence *masks* their great topological sophistication (Lafont, p. 17).

In *La Topologie ordinaire de Jacques Lacan*, Lafont refers to Lacan's *Seminar IX* on "Identification" where he presents the four objects (a)—voice, gaze, breast, and feces—as having no specular image. The lack of a specular image in the Ur-lining of the subject enabled Lacan to distinguish between a false imaginary, which leads to mirror illusions, and a true imaginary that points to the holes in libido and knowledge where fantasy, desire, and anxiety seep into language via the body. Thus, the unconscious formation of the Ideal ego $I(a)$ is opposed to (a).[32] The topological referent by which the hole is known concretely is the surface or rim of an organ—the mouth, the anus, the aperature of the ear—which have been erogenized in the process of losing and refinding the object that first structures desire as the desire for an "object's" return. Lacan's "new writing," which includes unary strokes as well as topological forms, stresses that the desire(d) object was first composed of identificatory single strokes that, in turn, link desire to images and words. Although these inscriptions constitute the knowledge out of which the infant seeks to repeat or maintain a consistency in jouissance by fusing with other persons, this is not the true meaning of what Freud called an *incorporation*, Lacan maintained.

Although Freud explained incorporation in *Totem and Taboo* (1913) as the cannibalistic consumption of the Ur-father by the sons whose hope was to acquire his power and women—his jouissance—Lacan thought, rather, that incorporation (*Einforleibung*) was related to either foreclosing (*Verwerfung*) or affirming (*Bejahung*) the Father's Name. The first mode of Freud's identification with an interdicting father corresponds to identifying with the father in the real, an operation Lacan explains by the three algebraic axes of the torus as a central void filled (or not) by the (a):[33]

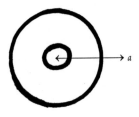

Lacan pointed out that the impossibility (the number 2) of imaginary fusions leads, later, to identification with a belief referred to a Father's Name signifier, taken as a guarantee or knot (Σ) of the three orders of knowledge. Such differences are between imaginary introjection (projection) of unary traits ($\sqrt{-1}$) and incorporation of the particular *sinthomes,* master signifiers, or *dits* ($+1$), that bespeak the real father. Lacan sees Freud's myth as an imaginary narrative that tries to explain the elusive real whose terrain Lacan maps.

Another feature of the pre-oedipal phase, Freud suggests in "Female Sexuality," is that because little girls are sexually stimulated by their mothers—albeit unawares—they often fantasize that their mothers have tried to seduce them (p. 238). Jacques-Alain Miller's clarification of Freud here broadens this to the near "universal" experience of the effects of castration. All representations compensate for the trauma of separation from pre-oedipal jouissance. Miller interprets Lacan's reading of Freud on the pre-oedipal phase to mean that since there is no signifier for jouissance, no *social* permission to enjoy, language and images will always cover and veil the libido. Thus, little girls do not automatically fantasize a mother who seduces them. They fantasize, rather, a replacement for lost jouissance that is inseparable from the mother's proximity to the real of the sexual drives. On the father's side, Lacan writes (Morel, p. 111):

$$\begin{array}{c} \underline{\text{Man's side}} \\ \exists \\ \text{Men } \rightarrow \text{ the father} \\ \forall \end{array}$$

On the mother's side, he writes:

$$\dfrac{\text{Woman's side}}{\text{one by one } \leftarrow \forall \leftarrow \exists}$$

Later efforts—of either sex—to recuperate primary jouissance will be linked to (substitute) mothers (or a mythic ideal Woman who is thought to exist as *the* feminine essence); or, in Lacan's terms, jouissance brings together pleasure and pain, *Eros* and *Thanatos,* because of its closeness with the feminine real and *its* proximity to loss $(J)/\varnothing$, a proximity based on the presence of the void. Although the infinite makes itself felt as such, on the side of real numbers that exist precisely to infer the subtraction of an incomplete ensemble, subtraction posits an end—a closed set—to a seemingly infinite flow of feminine desire, caught as it is in the regress of lack and loss. At such junctures, no woman thinks about limits or the finite end points of real numbers. Rather, desire seeks an object (a) to fill the lack within the logic of the *not all* which redoubles feminine jouissance by linking the void in the Other $(\varnothing)$ to the nonexistence of The Woman: $\exists x \overline{\Phi(x)}$. There is no essential Woman and no whole, self-sufficient mother.

Even though *desire* will always bear on the symbolic phallus (Φ), when raised to the level of secondary jouissance (or identification with the Ideal ego symbolic construct) it is also inseparable from the signifier for a Father's Name—$(\Sigma)/\Phi$—around which belief systems build up and elaborate the various structures of desire. Lacan called such belief the sublimation of the *sinthome*—Σ/S_1—which he placed in the real. One must always keep in mind that in Lacan's rewriting of Freud, two reals are at stake:

the biological "natural" one that enables reproduction, and the real of psychoanalysis where sex runs into the impasses caused by the fact that it can only be approached on the bias of language (Morel, p. 128). Thus, jouissance can only be apprehended when approached via desire/lack.

In this sense, desire has the familiar triangularity of Freud's oedipal structure,

as well as a triangularity that Lacan captures in rewriting the Aristotelian universal. Lacan points out that Aristotle's fallacy in his syllogism (A) with its attributes (I_1, I_2)—A: Every man is good; I_1: Some animals are men; I_2 Thus: Some animals are good—lies, not in the substitution of an attribute for a subject, but in the fallacy of the first enunciation (A) insofar as it depends on the limitation (I) which leads to a false conclusion. This syllogism, says Lacan, is a master discourse (Morel, p. 69). No universal should be based on an existence that is simply denied—that is, that some men are evil—Lacan argued in "L'étourdit" (1972–1973). For example, sexuation (masculine and feminine) depends on the particular truth-functional logic of contradiction where the universal contradicts the existential. Unlike Aristotle, Lacan placed the existential element (or *quantificator*) in the position of "Mistress" (Morel, p. 79).

We remember that the term *quantificator* was invented by Apulée, the author of a treatise on Plato, to designate the small words that characterized universals and particulars for Aristotle: *any, no, some—prosdiorismes*. Lacan called his own quantificators "quantors" because he did not want to allude to a "quantity" of attributes. For him the definition of *quantor* is "what links a variable in a propositional function." Before being linked, the variable is free, standing only by its own proper name (Morel, p. 74). In other words, having accepted the proposition that men and women define themselves "as such" in reference to a third thing—the sexual difference—and are thereby linked by that variable, Lacan proceeds to the Aristotelian universal statement that all men are castrated, which he then negates by a true (not false and thus not contradictory) existential proposition: One man is not castrated ($\overline{\Phi}$) because he stands (in myth) above the laws of men ($\exists x$). On the woman's side, he departs from Aristotle altogether and proposes a universal negative ($\overline{\forall x \Phi x}$): all are not all castrated. He follows this by a particular affirmative ($\overline{\exists x}\,\overline{\Phi x}$): There does not exist even one who is not castrated. On the man's side, something of the universal remains, while on the woman's side, an existential contradiction takes over a seeming "universalization" and, thus, is closer to modern logic (Morel, p. 77).

In Lacan's words, it is not on the universal qualification that the negative is brought to bear (*Le séminaire, livre IX: L'identification*, Jan. 17, 1962). Freud questioned the little girl's desire toward her mother. Lacan focused on desire's substituting someone or something else for the mother: S(ubject) → $\cancel{S}$ (subject division) → *a* or "things" that will fill the lack created by the separating: 1/2. The losonge symbolizes being alienated by language and separated from primary jouissance ($\cancel{\Phi}$ $\cancel{\partial}$ → <>), placing the structure of a split at the base of thought—$\cancel{S}$ <> *a*—for both sexes. In 1931, Freud described "the turning-away from her mother [as] an extremely important step in the little girl's development. It is more than a mere change of object" (p. 239). The further impact of such a change, based on clinical material he had observed, indicated a "marked lowering of the active sexual impulses and a rise of the passive ones" (p. 239). The negative consequences of this are profound, not only as a turning away from clitoral masturbation (which Freud called a repression of masculinity), but because dependence on the opposite sex, the father-object, increases the girl's passivity. Paradoxically, Freud recommended the development of femininity, at the same time that he outlined its injurious effects on the young girl's sexuality and behavior.

Perhaps the most important aspect of Lacan's having returned to Freud here lies in Lacan's insistence that Freud had found a structural logic that was separate from the content-specific conclusions he had drawn. Indeed, Freud's many impasses and quandaries led Lacan to posit a new logic of sexuation whose base is epistemological. We have said that the cause of conflict or mental anguish is not only "repressed" sexuality, or subject division, but also that the structures of desire from which sexuation arises are four interpretations or attributes of the propositions regarding the phallus and castration. These yield "normative" desire, based on a strong belief in a Father's Name and *repression* of the unconscious; or the neuroses that *deny* the sexual difference that founds the unconscious; or perversion that *repudiates* the difference; or psychosis that *forecloses* it.

In constructing the analytic real of the unconscious, the first "logical time" is that of the "natural," biological difference. The second "logical moment" occurs when sexual discourse transforms the "natural" organ into a signifying instrument regarding enjoyment: J/Φ. The third "logical time" is that of having assumed sexuation in reference to one of two different modes of (genital) phallic jouissance: the masculine or the feminine (Morel, pp. 128–29):

Although both males and females have equal access to genital (or phallic) sexual pleasure, females have a supplemental sexual pleasure that males do not (usually) have. Lacan called it the Other jouissance and located the enigma of the feminine elsewhere than in this supplemental sexuality. The feminine mystique, if you will, concerns, rather, the structural effects of woman's proximity to the real and to the object *a*, which place her in a special relationship to the cut that governs the drives.

Insofar as there is no essential whole Woman existing to fill up the real hole in the Other, or give an answer to the male lack that continually questions her, Woman's existential being is constantly jeopardized by the real. In *Seminar XX*, Lacan says he likes topology because it is interested in spaces and places and works with symbols and letters, but without any concern for how they represent themselves in space, even though his entire teaching always brings these back to individuals. In chapter I, he calls the "space" of sexual enjoyment for both sexes "compacity," or, a common space having the same structural impasse: A unique relation to the "absolute Other." This means that each man "relates" to Woman first as an absolute alterity, and only later as an other per se.

In "The Hypothesis of Compacity" in chapter I of *Encore: Seminar XX* (1972–1973)," Geneviève Morel tells us that a compact is defined in a space by the notion of closed and bounded aspects of metric spaces, such space being (*uni-* to *quatri-*) dimensional: from a real line, to a plane, to space, up to time. While Lacan defines male compacity in terms of closed space and female compacity on the basis of open (nonbounded) sets, jouissance, for either sex, is compact or bounded.[34] The man confronts the woman's sexuated body, which he must approach by the object (*a,*) the fantasy particular to him. As he takes women "one by one," he always seeks a repetition of the trait that causes his enjoyment. In this sense, man must seek his pleasure contingently, from the

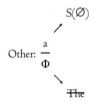

This is, for him, an equivalent of the feminine "*pas tout,*" which opposes his dependence on the fantasy *a* she embodies and the One of phallic jouissance on which his pleasure depends (Morel, *"La différence,"* p. 75). The Woman, by contrast, approaches her jouissance as a supplemental doubling due to her *not being all* under the phallic sway:

$$\frac{\text{The} \quad \Phi}{\forall \quad \diagdown} \diagup$$
$$S(\varnothing)$$

She is *not all* [*pas tout*] ($\varnothing$) on the slope of the barred Other who escapes the superego injunction imposed on the man who is under the phallic boundedness of the *all* (Φ) of the closed sets. Woman is, rather, under the phallic function which interprets the phallus as a signified; the one minus ($\Phi(x) \longrightarrow -$), the difference between the sexes (Morel, *"La différence . . . ,"* p. 96).

The mystery for Freud in "Female Sexuality" was centered on the study of Victorian woman subjected to male superego requisites of cultural requisites of the phallic *all,* referred only to the positivity in jouissance ($\Phi(x) \longrightarrow +$). "Why do libidinal forces suddenly go in a different direction for women than for men?" Freud asked. He answered: "Biological factors subsequently deflect those libidinal forces [in the little girl's case] from their original aims and conduct even active and in every sense masculine strivings into feminine channels" (p. 240). This gives one to think that biochemistry will one day find a male chemical substance and a female one, he suggested, immediately countering this statement with the observation that biology has not, for all that, isolated the causes of neuroses under the microscope: "Psycho-analysis teaches us to manage with a single libido, which, it is true, has both active and passive aims" (p. 240): $\Phi(x)(s<^+_-)$. This is the single libido Lacan translates in *Seminar* XX into *jouissance*, agreeing with Freud that there is only one (phallic) libido. And it is male *pas tout* in the sense of being a strictly genital jouissance, referring to the singular experience of orgasm for either sex.

By this Lacan does not strictly mean the penis, but the phallus as a sexual signifier of difference or castration, as well as jouissance. It is in the name of this duality that a division of the sexes is pronounced that puts men in one desiring posture and women in another. Although the phallus (as signifier of "no" to incest, the signified) is related to the penis as a real organ and is an image of it in the imaginary, its principle status is symbolic insofar as it signifies both jouissance and castration. When Lacan says the libido is masculine, he does not equate it with the biological male or female, then, but with masculine or feminine jouissance and castration—active or passive postures adopted in sexuality—which he calls identification as lover or beloved. In this sense, the *difference* between the sexes is situated by language at a signifying level where oedipal identifications create sexed positions in terms of unconscious desire.

Lacan argues that this *symbolic* status of the phallus is well exemplified in Freud's "On Transformations of Instinct as Exemplified in Anal Eroticism" (1917)[35] where Freud established a series of symbolic equivalences between the boy and his penis—excrement, money, and other metonymic substitutions, all referring to the symbol *phallus* defined as a positive element (+) that paradoxically opposes itself to lack (−). By connecting the penis to the feces in male perception, while connecting the phallus to the castration complex, one sees further evidence of Freud's efforts to solve certain "biological" enigma by postulating equivalence relationships in the visible imaginary. When Lacan argued in 1958 in "The Signification of the Phallus" that a boy can pass from *being* (identified as) his mother's object of desire to *having* the phallus (that is, being able to desire something else), he put forth a new psychoanalytic axiom that goes beyond Freud: The primacy of the phallus is correlated to the outcome of the castration complex.

Developing Lacan's four negations in the sexuation formulas, Geneviève Morel portrays the first as the sexual nonrapport marked by bars over the phallic, the universal, and the existential quant(ificat)ors: $\overline{\Phi}, \overline{\forall}, \overline{\exists}$. However, Morel says, Lacan's bar of negation does not work like it does in modern logic, where negation is placed before the proposition one denies. Not only is sexuation not true mathematics, neither does Lacan link the negating bar to the object under it (as did Aristotle). Rather, at the point of an impossible rapport on the feminine side, one finds the phallic function marked by this principle negation: "It is not that": $\overline{\exists x}\,\overline{\Phi x}/\overline{\forall x}\Phi x$. This means that the woman's jouissance is only figured in reference to the phallus taken as the key signifier which marks a gap or hole between the sexes: (Φ . . .) (Morel, *"La différence des sexes,"* pp. 94–96). The second negation, then, is castration—both possible and contingent—which means accepting to inscribe oneself as an "x," as a variable that represents one as sexuated within the phallic function of difference and lack (p. 96). The third negation is that of the negativized phallus or the postivized one: $\Phi/-;+$. What Lacan means by this is that "at least one" man says no to castration in the symbolic, thereby gaining the status of leader. This is not the foreclosure in the real that marks psychosis, but a structural paradigm of the grounding of law and logic in power, status, and submission: $\forall x \Phi x$. On the feminine side, Lacan eliminated the universal negative by a double contradiction, marking, rather, the absence of a point of exception that would support a (local) universal: $\overline{\exists x} \overline{\Phi x}$. This formula goes with his "There is no ~~The Woman~~," exception to the law (of the father), who instigates law on the basis of a true/false paradigm where the "false" is actually *"falsus"*—as in the semblance of an Ur-father—not false by empirical proof (Morel, *"La différence des sexes,"* pp. 96–103).

Thus, the fourth negation that Lacan calls the feminine *not all*—$\overline{\forall x} \Phi x$—is logically discordential, calling up Peirce's empty set as an equivalent of the unconscious, rather than Irigaray's idea that Lacan's $\forall x \Phi x$—universal of men—places madness and foreclosure on the feminine side (Morel, p. 104). In the field where the economy of negations means something, only the negations related to castration produce signifying feedback which, retroactively, resignifies earlier losses that were constituted by the *cut* that first produced the logic of separation. It is not severance or weanings Lacan means by separation, however, but that these experiences leave traces that can be re-remembered or repeated as countable unary traits that were initially inscribed at the moment of the infant's losing the objects mobilized when desire was first constructed as a limit to memory. Based on Lacan's psychoanalytic logic, the phallus-castration oppositions will be mapped onto all other (earlier or later) oppositions: masculine/feminine; active/passive; lover/beloved.

Lacan argued that Freud, without realizing it, posited the result of an interplay between the Oedipus complex and the castration complex, between different kinds of negations and lacks. But Freud did not realize that these negations were not biological. In his seminar on *The Transference,*[36] Lacan offered a new interpretation of Plato's *Symposium* in the first eight chapters, first arguing there that *active* and *passive* sexual postures concern whether or not one is in the position of the lover or the beloved. Such a theory takes away any gendered notion of "sexual" behavior, thus contradicting Freud's conclusion that the entire problem of female sexuality is contained in the existence of the passive aims of the feminine libido. Lacan interprets Freud's stress on feminine passive aims and masculine active ones as another way of saying that women depend on love at the point where men confuse love with sex.

Freud concludes in "Female Sexuality" that girls oscillate between choosing the abandoned mother-attachment and the father-object. His view typifies male sexuality rather than depicting its paradoxical logic: Dependent on the superego injunction to enjoy, while prohibited by the incest taboo, Lacan's greater focus was on the fact that no universal (master enunciation) determines a sexual logic. Rather, the exception confirms the rule of difference by denying the universal, showing the universal as empty and merely possible, not necessary (Morel, *"La différence des sexes,"* p. 71).

By fusing the "quantors" of modern logic—the (exception) and the (universal)—Lacan does not, however, give them a symmetrical status. Moreover, he keeps some affinity with Aristotle's "every" and "some," although he modifies them by giving priority to the "some." Most men (those who are not psychotic) are *all*, under the requirement of castration (Φx), because they have deferred to the real father's desire to have all the women—at least the little boy's own mother. Here, then, the exception ($\exists x$) gives the rule. Later, in sexual relations, the male experiences this symbolic no as a limit on the infinite push to enjoy the other via the fragile conditions imposed by tailoring his own fantasy to the Other's desire.

Lacan, like Freud, placed a more complicated sexuation structure on the feminine side, insofar as it does not obey Aristotelian logic (Morel, *"La différence . . . ,"* p. 76). Unlike masculine sexuality, the feminine one is an open ensemble that is not limited by an existential "quantificator" ($\overline{\forall x \Phi x}$). Although Aristotle retained the principle of contradiction in his logic, he considered it undemonstrable. Lacan asserted the principle of contradiction as basic to science, even arguing that sexuation sets forth the logic: Inconsistency is permanent from the moment "a" does not equal "a" (Morel, pp. 78–79). Thus, feminine sexuality, in containing a double negative—there is none who is not castrated—($\overline{\exists x \, \overline{\Phi x}}$)—opens onto the contradictory logic of the impossible real ("what does not stop not writing itself"): Aristotle's universal negative, without value, and C. S. Peirce's empty ensemble, lacking a negating principle.

Lacan's conclusion passes outside such blockages, beyond such contradictory abutments, specifying the feminine as also proximate to infinite sexuality, insofar as $\overline{\forall x} \Phi x$ means that *not all* of them are all castrated. This adheres to a contingent logic, derived from an open compact space that counts lovers (or orgasms) one by one, on a continuum of successions. Such a logic of the particular—one by one—negates the universal ($\forall$). Following the French grammarians Damourette and Pichon, Lacan, as we have said, named this logic discordential. This does not mean discordant, however, but a nuance between a probability and a desire that something might be so (Morel, *"La différence des sexes,"* p. 106). Put another way, Lacan arrives at an understanding of the feminine as dwelling on the side of the question, in the domain of the uniqueness of unary details, itself introducing into the closed bounded sets of masculine epistemology and sexuality the unbounded open sets that make room for the place(s) of equivocation, the *logic* of inconsistency, and an ungraspable vacillation that Lacan lovingly named the *not all.*

In Morel's terms, a feminine inconsistent logic (a logic such as Bertrand Russell tried to construct in mathematics) contains the coexistence of two contradictory positions: Being in the phallic function and not being in it. These are two inconsistent positions that cannot be joined into one (p. 108). One can only conclude that a feminine epistemology is of a piece with the supplemental feminine jouissance Lacan placed "beyond the phallus" in his chapter "God and Woman's Jouissance" (*Séminar XX*, p. 74).

Lacan had developed Freud's postulation of three modes of identification in *Le séminaire, livre XXI* (1973–1974): *Les non dupes errent*, and earlier, in . . . *Ou pire* (*livre XIX* [1971–1972]), where he had stated that subjects reject their natural sexual identifications based on anatomy: "They only recognize themselves as speaking beings, in order to reject this [anatomical] distinction by identifications" (Morel, p. 52). Before arriving at his "formulas of sexuation" that connected sexuality to ways of knowing, Lacan, as we have said, used the terms of *sexual identifications* or *options of sexed identifications*. By this, he meant that one chooses a masculine or feminine sexuation by the intermediary of the phallic signifier. While a "normatively" (castrated) person (male or female) will choose (on the masculine side)—will identify with what the Other desires in classifying a "real" man or woman—a perverse subject will identify with jouissance itself insofar as it fills the Other's lack. The Lacanian hysteric and obsessional are closer to Freud's term of *bisexual*, except that by bisexual, Lacan does not mean identification with anatomical traits or organs. He refers, rather to the family and culture-specific masculine and feminine traits that marked the mother and father and environment (Morel, p. 53).

By going back to Freud's three types of identification from "Group Psychology and the Analysis of the Ego" (1921), Lacan increasingly stressed the rapport between sexuation and the first and basic human identification with the lack in the Other: $\emptyset$. Having characterized this as the hysteric's identification with her father, he adheres to Freud in depicting this as the basic identification of any subject (except the psychotic) with initial cuts between the object of satisfaction and the infant's body. Insisting on the particularity of the signifier in composing the Ideal ego that defends against the void in the Other, Lacan stressed the desiring subject's identification with a unary trait. Indeed, the hysteric, sometimes, has identified with only one such trait. Lacan emphasized the *sinthome* Dora chose in identifying herself as sexually uninvolved—similar to her father's impotence—as well as her identification with her father's cough, a sign of malady. Rather than identify as "sexuated"—a bric-a-brac of multiple identifications not marked in this case—Dora's flight, her identification with a castrated father, *are* marked (Morel, p. 54). It is the primordial Freudian identification Lacan stresses in sexuation, then, not the other two levels of identification that concern group identity: ego to ego in a collectivity, or identification with a leader bearing a prestigious Father's Name, and, thus, worthy of representing an Ideal (Σ/Φ) for a cohesive symbolic order group.

"The signification of the phallus," Lacan writes in 1958, lies in its being the "privileged signifier of that mark in which the role of the logos is joined with the advent of desire" (*Ecrits: A Selection*, p. 287). What is veiled—Φ/Other—is its relation to the Other's desire. The phallus plays its role veiled, while paradoxically manifesting the Other's desire as that which must be recognized (p. 288). "Here," Lacan says, "is signed the conjunction of desire in that the phallic signifier is its mark, with the threat of nostalgia of lacking it" (p. 289). In this sense, its meaning turns around the personal demand for love and the social demands for particular conditions of *being* that elicit love. If one *"has"* the required "phallic" attributes—that is, those valued by the Other—one is "given" being in the social gaze; one is blessed; one is desired. In this sense, the demands for love are subjected to the function of the mask, to one's accepting the identifications and semblances the Other requires in the power dynamics of desire and love (p. 291).

Not only do desire $(a/-\phi)$ and love diverge, desire comes from being the "phallus" for the Other, first for the mother, while the phallic function refers to the mother's unconscious desire $(\Phi/?)$ vis-à-vis the masculine subject, her unconscious fantasy (Morel, p. 48). By approaching the sexual difference on the bias of jouissance and language, and not in terms of development, Lacan argued that sexuation comes from a logic that occurs in three logical times: (1) the natural difference between the sexes; (2) the sexual difference itself; and (3) the time of the choice of sex—masculine or feminine—by the subject. His construction must, however, be approached by the opposition of two reals: that of biological science and that of the psychoanalytic discourse (Morel, *"La différence des sexes,"* p. 127).

As early as the 1960s in his "Remark on the report of Daniel Lagache," Lacan wrote the formula for male desire as Man$/\Phi$ (a); and for female desire as Woman$/$ $\varnothing(-\phi)$.[37] The masculine here is negative, bearing the mark of castration rather than the positive mark of jouissance, insofar as it signifies a renunciation of masturbation in favor of choosing a partner. The other, the partner, will predominate over the male's narcissistic investment in his own body. The woman desires, instead, from an incomplete place, which constructs an excess of supplemental jouissance in her response to the totalized desire of male jouissance. While the man is troubled by desire—that is, by (non)performance anxiety—the woman is burdened, rather, by a demand for love, lest she touch on the empty place of the void in the Other (Morel, pp. 49–50). In this sense, Lacan depicts the boy as leaving the oedipal nexus by joining the group and submitting to its social conventions, while the girl enters the Oedipus by the problematic of castration she must solve, not only in terms of her mother's unconscious desire vis-à-vis her *own* veiled castration, but also in how she valorizes the Father's Name as a paradoxical signifier. The Father's Name signifier represents not only an imaginarily castrated man, then, but a symbolic function and an organ "fetishized" in the real.

In the real, the phallus signifies positivized jouissance, which impacts variously on males, in excessive valuation or elevation of the orgasm, double castration, seduction, and so on, (Morel, *"La différence des sexes,"* p. 47). In the symbolic, the phallus compensates for a lack, thus representing the cure for its own flaw by commanding the prevailing local universal symbolic view of reality: $\Phi \cong S_1, S_2, a$. At this level, Lacan equated the phallus with (secondary-process) language and called it the signifier of the language paradigm equated with the law, language, or reality taken as the Other's truth. On the masculine side of the sexuation graph, identification with the phallus is not however, static, but moves with the *Fort! Da!* rhythm around the presence or absence of the object *a* that lets desire and fantasy enter language. This is one meaning of castration. First the (imaginary) phallus is there and, then, it is lacking in reference to the sex who does not have it, and, moreover, is susceptible of being lost by the sex who thinks he or she has it. This drama of the real, whose effects create a representational trauma, enables us to understand the link between male aggressivity and its base in ego fragility as one response to the double castration that marks the male.

When, in 1971, Lacan began to develop a logic of femininity that dropped any Freudian equation of the feminine with a castration opposed to a masculine virility, he hypothesized the feminine as formed, not only as a way to work with the phallic *pas tout* of a contradictory universal symbolic—$\overline{\forall}x\Phi x$—that is determined as universal by a negation, not all under the phallic identification of a given symbolic-order convention of reality. And, furthermore, this identification outside the law culminates in a sexual jouissance supplemental to male phallic enjoyment. This is a feminine enjoyment of the *pas tout* located within the realm of infinitude.[38]

Femininity is neither to be found in appearance nor in the traits inherited from the Other. Rather, the woman's rapport with the imaginary remains crucial (Morel, *"La jouissance . . . ,"* pp. 54–55). Imaginary identifications give women a way to think about themselves as loved, as well as offering a precise antidote to the symbolic/phallic/ "having" equation. This equation marks the masculine concern with work, prestige, and the immediacy of orgasm, as opposed to the feminine preoccupation with supplementing her narcissism by various means of attenuating the lack that *is* being. Lacan might be read as arguing in *"La troisième"* (1975) that the third jouissance between the imaginary and symbolic ($-\phi$) is unconscious fantasy, a kind of meaning playing at the edges of clear signification. Such "meaning" is libidinal in contrast with the closed master discourses that mark symbolic-order uses of language as phallic alienations from the real.

Insofar as man relates to the phallic signifier and the object (a), not to Woman per se, except insofar as she grounds him in a myth of the mother that unconsciously guarantees an essence of the whole, masculine knowledge and being are protected from any encounter with the void. Lacan situates jouissance outside the body, in the fantasy and in the drives. And the drives come from outside the body, making a split between aim and goal in response to the phallic signifier that anchors and orients them as normative, neurotic, perverse, or psychotic (*"La différence . . . ,"* Morel, p. 56). Neither fantasy, drives, nor phallic signifier are in the body. These principles of jouissance are outside the body, which Lacan call a desert of jouissance that takes on a semblance of consistency from language. Bodily homeostasis is closely linked to the "law" of a particular phallic signifier that orients by organizing one's relation to lack. In conclusion, let us remember Morel's stress on the degree to which the drives' being outside the body calms the real and gives one a position in the symbolic order of the group.

3

Feminine Sexuality, or Why the Sexual Difference Makes All the Difference
Lacan's "For a Congress on Feminine Sexuality" (1958)

Lacan commented in his "Congress on Feminine Sexuality" (1958) that nothing had been heard about feminine sexuality since the 1920s and 1930s when Sigmund Freud, Karl Abraham, Ernest Jones, Karen Horney, Helena Deutsch, and many others talked and wrote prolifically about "the true nature of woman."[1] While this was true in 1958, it seems strange to refer to "nothing heard," given that since the 1960s reams have been written about female sexuality in terms of psychological profile, physiological analysis, and feminist rights. Everyone is familiar with Masters and Johnson on clitoral orgasms, Judith Butler on gender trouble and bodies that matter, Irigaray on the two lips, and myriad others on the inability of men to satisfy women sexually, the greater sexual pleasure in lesbian life, and so on.

In addressing the topic of *feminine* sexuality by considering the ways in which the debates of the 1930s were taken up again and carried forward by Lacan's return to Freud, we will continue to focus in this chapter on: (1) what Lacan means by sexuality; (2) what he notes as particular to feminine sexuality (as opposed to masculine sexuality); and (3) what some of the consequences of his theory are in regard to current feminist debates. We remember that Lacan coined the term *sexuation* to describe a subject's choice of sex as masculine or feminine in assuming an active or passive position vis-à-vis his or her object of desire. One's psychic sexuation does not conform to anatomy or gender, but to the structure of the paternal metaphor—Lacan's rewriting of the Oedipus—complex out of which his or her desire arises as an interpretation of the mother's unconscious desire vis-à-vis her own castration.

Lacan establishes a *logic* of feminine sexuality wherein a certain precise relation of identification, desire, and jouissance constitutes not only a uniquely feminine organization of sexuality, but an epistemological position as well. And until Lacan returned to Freud's efforts to articulate the logic of feminine sexuality as different from masculine sexuality, this "dark continent" had, indeed, lain dormant. Moreover, Lacan's statements about feminine sexuality have not yet been fully explored, nor have his work on hysteria or his theory of a feminine supplemental jouissance. Far from being a phal-

locrat who would annul feminine sexuality, as some have thought, Lacan opined in
Scilicet that feminine sexuality was fundamentally perverse;[2] that feminine jouissance was
first genital and secondly a supplemental bodily enjoyment that can go on infinitely,
even after genital enjoyment.[3] Lacking a universalizing signifier—"The" Woman—
that would point to some essence of Woman, human beings who do not identify with
having a penis, identify, rather, with the real which inserts a lack in the symbolic ($\varnothing$).
The real itself delimits the void—$\varnothing$—whose differential opposite—Φ—on the
graph of sexuation attributes signifiers of having to being. These symbolize masculinity
as a countable identity—that is, that which has value—in the symbolic sphere of
public worth.

In this sense, feminine sexuality is not "equal to" masculine sexuality. It is
different from masculine sexuality. It is asymmetrical to it, even though both are
constituted *dialectically* within a *combinatory*. Put another way, dialectical meaning is
establishable only on the basis of oppositional terms; thus, there is no learned representation of the feminine or the masculine, except in terms of one another. Surprisingly,
this means that the masculine and feminine are not simple binaries, interchangeable
collections of words and letters that constitute a *logos*, as Derrida has argued. Rather, the
secondary feminine is constituted by a logic of that which differs from the symbolic—
$\forall x \Phi x$—is even radically Other to it, while the masculine is defined, paradoxically, by
its differences from the primordial feminine—$\forall x \Phi x$—the masculine being an abstraction, a representative of whatever a particular society defines as the social norm of
masculinity.

One will understand that not only are the masculine and the feminine redefined;
sexuality is redefined as well. Freud's surprising find at the beginning of the twentieth
century was that sexuality is not in and of itself natural, nor does it coincide with its
reproductive ends or, necessarily, with pleasure. In other words, sexuality is *constructed*,
but not by a desiring self in some Foucauldian recasting of a "free will" of desire into a
sexual "self-fashioning." It is laid down piece by piece from the beginning of infancy,
from the particular master signifiers Lacan calls identificatory traits (S_1) that come to
constitute any person's libido in terms of absolute unary traits that Lacan called both
S_1s and the object *a* part. Jean-Paul Gilson characterizes Lacanian sexuality as "an
eroticism submitted to the law of the signifier by the fact of the *parole pulsionelle* (drive
signifier)." This means that the erogenous zones are actually constructed as primordially repressed traces of the *lettre*—Lacan's word for the join of language to body
(vocal *lettre* joined to *l'être* [being]). Freud supposed a pregiven causal substance—the
libido—at work in the vicissitudes of the goals, ways, and means of the drives. Yet,
both Freud and Lacan stressed that on their path toward sexual pleasure, the drives are
marked by tension and conflict. Lacan argued that this is because sexuality is more often
in the order of missed or traumatic encounters, than those of satisfaction (Trobas, p.
125).

In "Beyond the Pleasure Principle" (1921), Freud implied that fixations to
unpleasant and repetitive ways of thinking and being, and rather than developmental

stages, govern sexuality in a logical time, not a biological one.[4] Lacan described the constant ebb and flow of sexual excitations as the ups and downs of jouissance in the field of the partial drives—Freud's positive libido—which continually places the real of repressed bodily tension (i.e., the desire to fill lack by aiming the drives toward libidinal goals one just misses) in language and thought. Freud's polymorphous perverse infant is, in Lacan's teaching, a myth, a signifier by which Freud sought to represent the real of constantly intrusive jouissance that touches adults and children alike. Yet, one cannot equate sexuality with jouissance. And this is the surprise. Sexuality describes a consistency of meaning between body and thought that quickly bears on the death drive; that is, the *fixions* in archaic memory that keep people attached to static fantasies that block them from realizing Eros in the newness of desire. Sexuality appears in the excitements that make one attempt to recapture the jouissance lost in the myriad cuts of the signifier ($\Phi;-\phi$) and the constant losses of objects ($\varnothing$) that caused desire in the first place.

It was through his work on the logic of psychosis in his doctoral thesis and later in *Seminars* III and XXIII that Lacan gradually came to an understanding of how human sexuality is linked to jouissance as masculine or feminine, regardless of the gender— that is, the biological sex—of a person.[5] Sexuation, in other words, derives from the way a subject is split by language (or not) in the oedipal experience of identifying as primarily masculine or feminine and with preference for a particular libidinal mode:

a	of psychosis (the object as real);
$-\varnothing(\rightarrow \$)$	of perversion (game, fantasy, fetish);
$J(a); \Phi; S_2$	of obsession (the symbolic as imaginary);
$\varnothing; \$$	of the hysteric (the imaginary as the real)

By the 1950s Lacan had figured out that the structure of psychosis lies in an indifferentiation in identification between a mother and child. The object *a* never falls, but continues to be hallucinated as the fullness of no lack. The psychotic subject does not undergo the alienation or castration (that Lacan symbolized by $\$$) of losing the illusion of being One with his or her mother. This is one response to the oedipal call for identification. The signifier for the Father's Name—that is, the signifier for difference itself, the phallic third term taken as the difference between the masculine and feminine—can be *foreclosed (Verwerft)*.[6] Russell Grigg writes: "Using the four discourses, it is now possible to say that in psychosis the master signifier, S_1, is missing from its place; and this has the consequence that the S_1s do not locate the subject within (social) discourse, but outside it" ("Lacan's Four Discourses," p. 35).

One might say of hysteria that the S_1 is also missing from the place of master signifier as the agent of speech or thought. What locates the hysteric *within* social discourse is her attachment to one key phallic signifier, an S_1 put in the place of the other, not a body of knowledge per se (S_2), as is the case for the obsessional. Lacan responded to Roman Jakobson's communication theory of discourse with his own psychoanalytic definition of *discourse,* based on the idea that "discourse makes a social link" and love is a *sign* that one has *changed* discourse: "A change of discourse—things budge, things traverse you, things traverse us, things are traversed . . . , and no one notices the change. . . . I can say until I'm blue in the face that this notion of discourse can be taken as a social link . . . , founded on language, and thus seems not unrelated to what is specified in grammar, and yet nothing seems to change."[7]

Arguing that although psychosis is outside discourse, it nonetheless has a logic, a rationality, Lacan was able to go on from there to formulate the differential logic(s) of neurosis, perversion, and the "normative" masquerade. As we remember, these are four identificatory (oedipal) responses by which a subject inscribes him or herself for the sexual difference in reference to the symbolic phallus (Φ), imaginary castration ($-\phi$), and the loss of the object a ($\mathcal{S};\varnothing$). Here sexuality constitues mind as libido in that it is constructed in reference to separation from the primordial objects that cause desire for their return precisely because they were lost. Thus a central loss, the loss of the ongoing search for jouissance, places a "no" in the center of language for everyone but the psychotic. The concomitant lack-of-being that Lacan named castration determines that no one "be" all masculine or all feminine in the unconscious, except the psychotic who has the illusion of Being all one sex, one with the primordial mother (and, in this sense, has no unconscious, no repression). Sexuation is never separate from being, then, insofar as castration—an interpretation of the phallic signifier—determines the parameters of "sexuation" by way of the responses to it that create oedipal identifications in the wake of traumatic experiences of the loss of primordial objects, as well as the loss of being all One sex.[8]

The Unconscious

In the third phase of his teaching, from 1974 to 1981, Lacan equated sexuality with the unconscious—repressed memories—arguing that an *unconscious* part of the mind governs conscious life, as Freud first thought. But at the site where Freud located biological instincts, Lacan found the language bank of each subject's memories (the treasury of the signifiers in the Other) and the drive fixations (jouissance constructed for meaning) by which language and sexuality are linked to each other, although they ultimately compose two different meaning systems: the representational system of language one might call secondary process and the jouissance system of fantasy and desire one could characterize as primary process. The human "animal" uses language to symbolize (and hide) the real of jouissance. That is, the "object" of thinking, speaking, writing, and reading is to acquire, reproduce, and maintain jouissance, which Lacan defined as a logical (or imaginary) consistency in the symbolic. In this context, one cannot possibly separate *sexual* being from conscious or unconscious thought because their base desiring substratum is the symptom (or *sinthome*), which is a Borromean signifying chain of endless associations of words, images, and traumas that continually realign themselves so as to produce jouissance. One loses jouissance in cuts and castration(s), which, in turn, motivate one to use language at all. Moreoever, conscious use of language is subjectivized in being linked to the imaginary body that produces thought as jouissance (*S. XX*, p. 131).

Jacques-Alain Miller returns to Lacan's *che vuoi?* graph ("You say that, but what do you [really] want?") of 1960 to argue that the demand or drive is itself an object of jouissance where the interior signifying chain (s[O]) of the graph concerns the effect of meaning and the superior chain(S[Ø]) concerns jouissance. In other words, jouissance is not natural or instinctual. It depends, in Miller's felicitous phrasing, on a "*sens-jouis*" [a sense of a meaning enjoyed] where the word *sens* implies both meaning and the "sense" of the "five senses."[9]

But although no one doubts the *existence* of the demand for jouissance, be it for the jouissance of food, love, or sex, the unconscious is another matter entirely. How does one *prove* the existence of the unconscious? It is by definition, Lacan stresses, the *Unbewusste*, the unknown, the dark-sided face of God. Nonetheless, Lacan taught, the unconscious is *there*, not only where Freud found it (i.e., in dreams, wit, parapraxes, and the *Fehleistungen*), but also always residing *in language* in unary traits which are the unbroken lines of master signifiers of identification from the real. The unconscious reveals itself when the speaker stumbles upon an impasse (of the real) that produces an enigma, a question, or a doubt that conscious memory cannot adequately represent at the level of language. Because Freud never figured out how the unconscious comes to think, he gradually dropped the idea that an unconscious (structured like a language) part of the mind governs conscious thought. Lacan maintained that Freud's early "find" was correct; Not only does the unconscious think, it thinks in language, in words, whose *structure* works by (secondary) metaphorical substitutions for the (primary) metonymical displacements that record traces of evaporating lost object(s) of desire.

Freud had also intuited that concerns of memory and language bear on sexuality. But what is Lacan's proof that the unconscious thinks, moreover, in the language of "sexual reality"? Lacan maintained that Freud's never having backed down on his theory that sexuality confers its realistic character on the unconscious, despite the disagreements of analysts such as Karl Adler, Gustav Jung, and others, meant that the *cause* motivating conscious "behavior" was something hidden. For Freud this was first the interdiction of sexual enjoyment with one's mother, whom Lacan describes in *Seminar VII: The Ethics of Psychoanalysis* as the primary good, indeed, the only Good.[10] Does this mean, then, that the unconscious fantasy of incest constitutes the foundation of sexuality for both sexes? It would seem so, at least at the level of the demand, where the demand for love (i.e., recognition) was first structured as the aim of (re-)*capturing* the mother's gaze, voice, even incorporating simulacra of her breast (a thumb, a pacifier, etc.), as a way to maintain a consistency of oneness in jouissance. Having removed Freud's explanation of causality from the field of biology and literal sex acts to the field of language, Lacan demonstrated in the third and fourth periods of his teaching, how language is linked to the drives via jouissance.

In "To Interpret the Cause," Miller postulated that the Freudian Oedipus—inscribed by Lacan as the paternal metaphor—translates itself from an unknown jouissance to the "phallusization" of jouissance; that is, to a "significantization" of jouissance. And this is something a bit different from what we have seen before:

$$\frac{F}{M} - \frac{\Phi}{X} \rightarrow \frac{O(\text{ther})}{J(\text{ouissance})}$$

Here we are at a level where something that is *not* a signifier is substituted for by something that *is* a signifier. Indeed, the secret of the Oedipus is that it enables jouissance to be inscribed in the symbolic order. And that is why at the moment Lacan found the phallus as the signifier of jouissance, placed there where the residue between the libido and language is an *excess* or surplus of jouissance—(the *[a]*)—he could say that something that is *not* a signifier is substituted for by something that *is* a signifier: The signifier for sexual difference. And this move—the oedipal move—causes jouissance to be given meaning.[11] One can infer, then, that jouissance substitutes for what one has repressed about the primordial mother of the drives and the oedipal mother of unconscious desire.

Maintaining that Lacan's return to Freud gave a unified field theory of psychoanalysis in his elaboration of precise laws of cause and effect, Miller says that in sexuation, for example, biological sex is "significantized" for psychical sex insofar as the infant is the mother's phallus—that is, a third term between the mother and Father, as signifier, who is interpellated at the level of sexual jouissance. Lacan puts together the series of The Woman, jouissance, baby as phallus, and the object (*a*) in answer to how biological sex takes its meaning as "psychic" sex. In *Seminar XX*, he proposed that there is paradoxically no signifier for Woman: no "The." Since there is no universal woman—although there are myths of great women and histories of unique figures—Woman as an essential being or category does not exist—not even as a mother (*S. XX*, pp. 72–73 and 80). She exists as a countable being insofar as she is in the symbolic order where the Other names her as a signifier: the daughter or the wife of; the partner of; the possessor of; the woman who has, does . . . , and so on. But there is no generic class of women who constitute themselves as such except in reference to the phallic signifier of the symbolic order; that is, as *not* [being] all within the symbolic order of the difference from Woman by which males define themselves as men.

This is where the (*a*) comes into play insofar as jouissance is inscribed via the pathway of the drives (oral, anal, invocatory, and scopic). In the third period of his teaching, Lacan argued that jouissance is constituted by the *effects* of language or representation (Φ) given by the Other (O) in reference to the object of desire. But he also means the primordial Other, as he argues in *Television* in 1975. The primordial *dite maternelle* or *la lalangue* (the earliest murmerings) create the particular conditions that will later produce *jouis-sens* for each subject in the gaps between the word and the image of a thing ($-\phi \rightarrow \not{S}$).[12]

At one level, one could say that jouissance is a case in the particular real of each infant's lost maternal murmerings that surround each object that causes desire. At another level, each drive field—oral, anal, invocatory, scopic—is constituted by the effects of an interplay of the S_I, (unary trait) identifications, with their co-respondent objects that first caused desire such that jouissance not only—replaces lost primordial objects or the enigma of the mother's unconscious desire, but does so in a logic of negations or castrations that Lacan formalized in his Borromean structure of inter-linked categories that compose the signifying associations of the Other as real, sym-bolic, and imaginary. The logical responses to primary and secondary castrations follow: Loss of the (a) yields confusion about who has/is the phallus, producing a cut in the Other. The lack of objects and the lack of being all one sex are the causes that produce the effects Lacan calls the phallic signifier's "no." The losses are filled by the substitutions for lack that are language and law.

Human sexuality is, perforce, constituted on the bias of language, which remains, de facto, an imaginary "body" which is "beyond" or Other to the jouissance of the real body qua physical organism. It follows that the interdiction of jouissance (that Freud calls the superego) will itself be an effect of language built upon a paradox: When someone says to you, "Do not enjoy. It's forbidden," the immediate response is a desire to enjoy the forbidden, to transgress the law. This, in turn, divides a subject between lived jouissance—the silence of the drives $J(\emptyset)$—and the language that determines one's alienated reality in the Other (Φ). We can see that Lacan made a dialectical turn or torsion here at the point where Freud ran into an abutment. By trying to define the reality of the unconscious in terms of organ reality, Freud ended up in the untenable position of having to deduce mind from organ function.

In *Le séminaire, livre XX* (1972–1973): *Encore*, when Lacan first began to elaborate the theory that characterizes his third period of teaching, he argued that the uncon-scious thinks by enjoying in language. Lacan gave multiple glosses on *how* the uncon-scious thinks in language. In 1964 he had conceptualized it as alienated, describing a concrete division or gap between the speaking subject and the unconscious memory bank of his or her words $(\emptyset)$.[13] The point is that the gap is itself a function in language. In other words, the subject is not composed of only language or writing, slipping from phoneme to phoneme, as post-structuralist theory has maintained. But the gap is not outside language, either. Indeed, the gap is an effect in language around which a person's cause was first organized in the paths of desire, via the loss of objects. Lacan called this the logic of alienation:

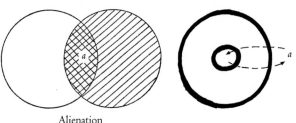

Alienation

The object (a) has the shape of a torus—tridimensional—indicating that it is both inside and outside the gap, its properties transformed by metaphorical substitutions that displace metonymical desire.

If unconscious thoughts are, moreover, as Freud maintained, *Vorstellungen*—things that stand *before* something else; that is, primary fantasies—then, preconscious *thought* is made up of *Sach* and *Wort Vorstellungen*. Preconscious language would be a second-level *Vorstellungen*, then, and *as such* has the double structure of metaphor where one thing can be substituted for another. In preconscious language, subjects "think" at one step removed from the unconscious real of metonymic displacements contained in the drive signifier that Lacan described as representing the already represented [an image of an image], but absent, unconscious idea. The *Vorstellungsrepräsentanzen* would seek to give form to the repressed "memories of experience" that Freud called elementary hallucinations and Lacan called primary fantasies. But what has been "introjected" is not the object itself, *à la* Melanie Klein, be it letter or image, but a signifier, which is not usually taken as a thing. It ordinarily (except in psychosis) functions dialectically to make meaning in reference to another signifier. The object-of-desire, either absent at the level of the *Niederschriften*, as in unconscious fantasy, or present, as in hallucination, is not a signifier. Nor is the master signifier of unary identificatory traits dialectical. It is absolute and, thus, links directly to desire and starts producing word pictures that speak to the sexual longings of fantasy ($\$ <> a$), fears of loss ($\varnothing$), reifications of "phallic" pride ($-\phi \searrow \Phi$), and so on.

Lacan argued that Freud had chosen a variety of words to represent different, but similar, phenomena. Freud tried to say that only in the articulation of the subject's *own words*—be it in analytic free association or the *recounting* of a dream—can he or she perceive something of his or her own *unconscious* language of *ideas (Vorstellungen)*. Although this language was laid down in an initial synchrony as *Niederschriften*, or traces, which are retrievable later in images and words because dream messages return via the laws of metaphor and metonymy—that is, distorted by condensation and displacement—they must be deciphered in the analysis of repeating fantasies and symptoms, both of whose guide is always a signifier.[14]

Miller has clarified Lacan and Freud further to show that even though the words one speaks (S_2), one's knowledge, *hide* unconscious traits (S_1), some part of these details can still be recuperated through attention to the *lettre* or drive signifier because they coalesce around what Lacan called the object-cause-of-desire. Indeed, the structure of fantasy ($\$ <> a$) denotes just this: The subject is pushed by (unconscious) desire to seek something lost as a substitute for the first object-*cause*-of-desire. Desire resides in the fantasy as lack because the object (a), denoting the radically lost object-of-desire, can only refind itself in the traces of jouissance in the signifier, in an image, or in affect.

Perhaps an example from the Dora case will clarify Lacan's reworking of Freud here. When Herr K. asked Dora for a kiss beside the lake, saying to her, "My wife gives me nothing," *nothing* describes the wife at the level of an object-cause-of-desire within the series of eight primordial objects-cause-of-desire Lacan listed in "Subversion of the

Subject and the Dialectic of Desire in the Freudian Unconscious."[15] That she gives nothing to him means that she is not the *cause* of his desire. She causes him to desire someone else. In this example, one sees language functioning metonymically—that is, Herr K.'s desire emanates from the Other qua unconscious, as repressed, thus placing some real part of his being-for-jouissance in the field of language where desire peeks out from behind the egoistic narcissism that usually hides one's desire.

Put another way, the pleasure principle's goal is fundamentally autoerotic. It seeks pure body pleasure of a primary homeostasis. But the reality principle—based on the secondary-process law or functioning of the interdiction of pure jouissance— thwarts the autoerotic aim, *its* goal being, rather, to maintain the ego goal of secondary homeostasis or imaginary consistency. Lacan pointed to this paradox: The reality principle keeps subjects imprisoned in identifying their words with their narcissistic ideals and prevents them from admitting the truth of the sexual unconscious. In conscious life one is usually lost in a forest of words, only ever close to the unconscious goal of realizing desire when the actual referent is a drive object $(S <> a)$, made so because a trait of the object retains some remnant of lost desire. Lacan will later speak of drive representatives as the language of the *lettre*, or divine details that join the signifier to the object *a*, in his "Hommage fait à Marguerite Duras."[16]

What Is Sexuality?

In chapter 15 of *Seminar XI: The Four Fundamental Concepts of Psychoanalysis*, "From Love to Libido," Lacan compares the unconscious to a pulsating bladder—rather than to the cellar or platonic cave of familiar comparison—which alternately reveals and conceals the subject of the unconscious.[17] The subject that is alternately revealed or concealed there appears in the light of the partial drives—oral, anal, scopic, invocatory—"which necessitate us in the sexual order" (pp. 188–89). That is, the push for jouissance makes a demand, issuing from the real, a demand to the Other to give satisfaction and, thus, fill up lack-in-being. But this is not easily accomplished, for love ordinarily bears the burden of negotiating between drives and desire.

In chapter 14, "The Partial Drive and Its Circuit," Lacan makes a major departure from Freud in arguing that all emotional investments, most particularly the transference relation in analysis, manifest real love, not a transference neurosis. And he asks the obvious question, given that psychoanalysis is a clinic of sexuality: "Does love represent the summit, the culminating point, the indisputable factor, that makes sexuality present for us in the here and now of the transference?" (p. 174). Lacan stresses that the central import of Freud's writings concerning the drives and their vicissitudes, rejects such a view in the clearest possible way: "Freud says quite specifically that love can in no way be regarded as the representative of what he puts in question in the term *die Ganze Sexualstrebung* . . . the tendency, the forms, the convergence of the striving of the sexual, insofar as it culminates in *Ganze*, in an apprehensible whole, that would sum up its essence and function" (p. 175).

Arguing that the drives are partial "with regard to the biological finality of sex"—that is, reproduction—Freud separated them from love, attributing them, rather, to an archaic and autonomous id. Lacan, argues, to the contrary, that the partial drives enter human relations (the analytic one included) as love, real love (pp. 176–77), "that the transference is what manifests in experience the enacting of the reality of the unconscious, insofar as that reality is sexuality" (p. 174). The purpose of love is not to be correlated with its biological result, Lacan insists, for there is no representation of (no signifier for) reproduction, no drive signifier that represents the totality of the sexual tendency in the psyche (p. 204). In other words, there is neither a reproductive instinct, nor a genital drive per se. But, if this is the case, where do the drives come from? Lacan argued that even though the *partial* drives dwell on the side of the real of the biological organism, they have the structure of the signifier. "Sexuality comes into play only in the form of the partial drives. The drive is precisely that *montage* by which sexuality participates in the psychical life, in a way that must conform to the gap-like structure that is the structure of the unconscious" (p. 176).

Let us go step by step in considering what Lacan means by saying the drives have the structure of the signifier, and the unconscious has the structure of the gap. Doubtless, statements like this have led certain critics to reduce Lacan's words to a topology of non-sense, to metaphorical forms of literal gaps, or to literal representations of letters and sounds. But this is not what Lacan meant. By jumping forward to chapter 16, "The Subject and the Other: Alienation," in *The Four Fundamental Concepts*, we can answer the two questions just asked with some precision. This will allow us to go forward a bit in understanding Lacan's rethinking of what sexuality is and how it bears most pressingly on the necessity of redefining knowledge in reference to the masculine and feminine that give it its contours.

In the opening sentence of chapter 16, Lacan says that "if psychoanalysis is to be constituted as the science of the unconscious, one must set out from the notion that the unconscious is structured like language. From this I have deduced a topology intended to account for the constitution of the subject" (p. 203). Let us go slowly. The unconscious is the reality of sexuality in function; the unconscious is structured. *Like* a language. In other words, sexuality is structured—that is, imposed from the outside. Lacan's point here seems compatible with sociological feminisms. One "learns" one's sexual identifications—one's sexuation—from the symbolic order, but as correlated with imaginary identifications, not biological anatomy. Yet, his is not a sociological theory of role behavior, for the "interpretation" of an infant's gender begins before an infant's birth into the economy of the Other's desire. The mother cannot help taking a position toward the child's possession of the imaginary phallus (or not). Lacan argued that since both the masculine and the feminine have the phallus as a referent, the phallic signifier becomes a symbolic-order interpretation one must perforce give the infant, taken as the phallus or third term between the mother and the father. The meaning given to the child's sex becomes the *phallic* signifier of his or her *la lalangue* by which language will try to *represent* the real of what the sexual difference actually means in a primordially repressed place that emits fragments of "sense" all the same.[18]

But how is sexuality imposed from outside the biological organism? Lacan takes Freud's radical discovery in the 1925 essay "On the Psychological Consequences of the Anatomical Distinction between the Sexes" as a point of departure.[19] Not only is the sexual difference not innate to anatomy for the male or female, as Freud had previously thought, the very notion of femininity as a universal category is incorrect. Lacan stated this as: "Woman can only be written with a bar through it. There's no such thing as Woman . . . indicating the universal . . . because in her essence . . . she is not-whole . . . "The" 'Woman' (*la*[the]) is a signifier. With it I symbolize the signifier whose place is indispensable to mark—that place cannot be left empty" (*S. XX*, pp. 72–73). The "nature of things" being the *nature* of words, "Woman" is a signifier constituted by language as an interpretation of the oedipal symptom one might describe as the fiction of a father.[20] One truth repeats itself over and over in analytic treatment: *Being* a woman or a man is not natural or normal. Each subject of analysis unveils in microcosm the norm of human suffering that fuels the social macrocosm. Each analysis repeats endless variations on but one theme: Each subject feels in some way that he or she is a *failed* man or a *failed* woman.

Freud realized this at a structural level. Describing an ultimate impossibility in psychoanalytic cure in 1937 insofar as the feminine position is rejected by men and women alike, he focused on masculine (castration) anxiety and feminine (penis) envy.[21] Lacan translated these terms into the positions of lover and beloved, masculine and feminine,[22] arguing that psychoanalysis must *begin* at this point of impasse, of the sexual nonrapport, there where biological men spend their lives trying to be "it"—that is, a real man—and women spend their lives trying to figure out what a "real" woman must do to attain pleasure in jouissance and status in the symbolic. Lacan says in *Seminar XI* that "the ways of what one must do as man or as woman are entirely abandoned to the drama, to the scenario, which is placed in the field of the Other—which strictly speaking, is the Oedipus complex. . . . The human being always has to learn from scratch from the other what he or she have to do, as man or as woman" (p. 204).

In 1974, Lacan said of the oedipal experience that "the family order translates only one thing: That the father is not the genitor and that the mother remains to contaminate the woman for the *petit d'homme;* the rest follows from that."[23] The mother's unconscious desire will bear on castration and the phallic signifier. In other words, the father's position in the family affair is at best unstable. The real part in the oedipal myth *says* this to the son: Your father is not your father—that is, not an interdiction to your desire for your mother. And in the order of the real, the order of the drives, this is true. The father is a fiction in the symbolic order. But, a necessary fiction lest psychosis ensue in the unimpeded Oneness of mother and child.[24] And that is the point where woman contaminates her child for the *petit d'homme;* that is, both the man's offspring and the phallic symbol of sexual difference mark the *cause* of man's desire, not the organ qua potent or impotent, but the beloved qua cause. How does the mother deal with the phallic function insofar as it marks her castration in a different way from the man's? *Not* [being] *all* in the symbolic, woman's jouissance goes beyond the phallus onto a supplemental plane that lets women possess the men and makes a joke of "putative frigidity" (*S. XX*, pp. 74–75).

Although each subject assumes his or her sexuality via concrete identifications with particular signifiers and with the palpability of the object-cause-of-desire, the central identification around which all others coalesce concerns the effort to align a sense of *being* as a man or as a woman with anatomy. Yet, one asks, why, if sexuality is not natural, should anyone be concerned about this difference? Poststructuralism has given us the answer of either/or, both/and. And certainly Freud had already asserted that everyone is always both one and the other in the unconscious: bisexual. Lacan wrote the logic of the "polymorphous perverse" signifier in *Seminar XI* by the vel of alienation (p. 211):

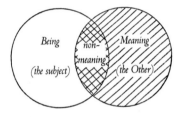

In other words, in constituting the being (of the subject) from the Other of meaning, a part overlaps. This part, lost from consciousness, is what Lacan describes as the non-sense or object (*a*) in the middle. This *a* part, the excess in jouissance, becomes the *cause* of the subject of the unconscious, the subject itself taken as an object, a response of the real.

Psychic malaise—a problem of being—which Freud described in "Symptom, Inhibition, and Anxiety" (1926), derives from a lack of alignment between a subject's sexuality, the (*a*) part, and his or her experience of the "law" of lack on which the social is based.[25] Freud called these misalignments pathologies. Lacan called them structures of desire. In either case, they are constituted as particular orientations in reference to the paternal metaphor whose coordinates are the mother's desire and the signifier for the Father's Name. Psychosis, for instance, is the condition of having no inscription for *being* either masculine or feminine, while neurosis is characterized by the refusal to *be* one or the other. Perversion repudiates the necessity of making a choice at the level of *being*, thus dramatizing a particular psychic relation to castration in fetishized scenes and rituals where the real of jouissance is transformed into social law.

Lacan departs from Freud's use of myth and story to give us the paternal metaphor as the structure of the oedipal myth: Freud, vindicated by Lacan. One cannot say, as did Jung, that the unconscious is a rich container of primordial material, made of sparkling images or poetically shimmering words. Rather, the unconscious *is* sexuality in function, all conscious life circulating around the central dilemma of an impossibility: How can one be a "real" man or a "real" woman when neither is signified in the unconscious? The masquerade of identifying as one or the other means precisely that: To play at *being* a man or woman in order to *be* in the social field of exchange and difference. Lacan's is quite a different concept from Judith Butler's notion of masquerading the masquerade, however. Her imaginary theory leaves out the real of loss and the cause of suffering from the lack-in-being that necessitate the masquerade as a sham in the first place. When Butler postulates the loss of an originary homosexuality as the cause of mourning, she assumes that all desiring structures function in terms of the same logic. For Lacan, "sexuality is established in the field of the subject [the autoerotic subject of experience (s)] by a way that is that of lack" (*S. XI*, p. 204). We can understand several things by Lacan's words here. Not only is sexual difference constituted on the basis of lack, lack is also equatable with the structure of a void place created by alienation, not lack of an originary homosexuality. One cannot equate homosexuality or heterosexuality with the void.

Whether one focuses on the drive as orienting a subject in the field of sexuality, or whether one looks at the drive as the psychical representative of the consequences of this orientation, Lacan's point remains the same. The sexuality of a subject is deduced from something other than sexuality itself. And that something else is constituted by the joining of two lacks where one kind of meaning overlaps with another. The signifier of meaning (the Cartesian "I think") obscures the subject qua sentient being (the Cartesian "I am"), alienating each part from direct awareness of the real of his or her lived experiences. Thus, alienation is occultation by the signifier; that is, castration of the real. The second vel Lacan writes in *Seminar XI*, the vel of separation, refers to an earlier lack; the real intersection that Lacan locates at the level of the living being who loses a part of himself by reproducing himself through sex—through the drives—which introduces the subject to the second death (beyond the biological death of the animal) in the dependence of the living being on another person for satisfaction (p. 205).

In love relations—be they heterosexual or homosexual—individuals seek their other half in their partner. The mystery of love seeks its resolution, not in a complementary partner, then, but in a sexual partner who has enough particular jouissance properties that he or she is thought to *be* the lost half of oneself. Put another way, loss occurs at the level of the real that Lacan placed on the side of the feminine in the sexuation graph (S[Ø]). But the loss that enters the partial drives, among them death drives, does not refer to a lethal feminine element, to a bad mother, to loss of a breast, or to any other attribute of woman qua Woman. Rather, loss—all loss—repeats the primordial loss of *das Ding* or the primary Good where the mother is sexualized around the object (*a*). Continually lost in bits and pieces (the breast, the gaze, the voice, etc.), not as a whole person, she will only ever be whole in the nostalgic memories that (mis)take the part for the whole, and jouissance for the essence of woman.

And, although these particular losses constitute the partial drives within the field
of the real around partisan objects, the larger issue is that a child must experience a
break in the continuity of jouissance provided by the mother in the imaginary and the
real in order to join society. In this context, one sees why Lacan placed jouissance on the
slope of the death drive. There is no universal Eros because of Thanatos. That is, two
do not make a harmonious one, as Freud thought. Rather, oneness reduces everything
to dust. The one (the psychotic) who believes in a universal Eros lives outside the
symbolic order, rigidified when confronted with the possibility of exchange or reciprocity. Although most people are not psychotic, the experience of loss obliges every
subject to confront the unbearable fact that the void is *in* one's own *sense* of being, not
outside it in heaven or hell as, for example, religions claim. Thus, subjects cling to
semblances of *das Ding*—the object (*a*)—in order to retain the illusion that the
mother's semblance at least, and various names-of-the-Father—God the Father, for
example—serve as guarantees against loss, as shelters from anxiety.

Masculine and Feminine Sexualities

The point is that sexuality is not where we think it is—that is, in sexual acts, be they
those of ordinary or extraordinary copulations, peep show exhibitions, or any other. *It
(ça)* is, rather, *in* the parade (*défilés*) of signifiers that makes up the subjective chain of any
person's knowledge (S_2) about jouissance. But let us stop for a moment to define the
word *parade*. In dictionary terms *défilé* means "a naturally enclosed corridor, so narrow
that one can only pass through there single file." Lacan chose this word to stress that no
subject has access to all language, only to the *défilé* of his or her own signifiers where
sexuality is fastened down by the jouissance that marks sexual fantasies with "perverse"
traits. But much more than sexual fantasies is at stake. Lacan taught that the key to any
person's life choices—mate, career, ideology, or whatever—lies in the way jouissance
inscribes itself in—even as—his or her thought. From this point of view, sexuality
cannot be dismissed or glossed over in any responsible establishment of a theory of
what knowledge is and how it functions.

A further clue to a subject's sexuality—hidden as it is in the secrecy of
fantasies—lies in the particular traits that mark what Jacques-Alain Miller calls "the
conditions of love." These are concrete details that sketch the ideals one seeks in terms
of physical appearance, social standing, ways of being, such as voice tone, and so on.
Such "divine details" establish a concreteness to the oedipal experience that determines
the kind of person with whom one will identify in love.[26] And all of a subject's chosen
relationships are marked by these traits, not only the one specific choice of a life
partner. Put another way, sublimation does not mean neutralization of the drives, but
the eroticization of human relations.

Freud concluded his 1925 essay "On the Psychical Consequences of the Anatomical Distinction between the Sexes" by saying that although masculinity and femi-

ninity are the two central axes on the basis of which male and female beings define themselves, "masculinity and femininity remain theoretical constructions of uncertain content" (p. 258). Lacan demonstrated how the content of each is shaped by a logic that gives a certain predictable structure to it. And since these structures are ahistorical at the level of the local universal, marking, rather, *jouissance knowledge positions* within language, not knowledge as content, it is crucial to any feminism to consider that no matter how the attributes that characterize the specifics of the masculine or feminine vary from historical moment to historical moment, the logic of their asymmetry will remain constant.

Feminine sexuality will be constituted by an imaginary identification with the real of a lack ($S[\varnothing]$), a castration that is interpreted in the symbolic order of the masculine as based on an imaginary identification with the symbol—the lowest common denominator of "visible language" attributed to the male—the phallus ($-\phi$) insofar as it marks difference via its properties as a potentially separable image belonging to neither sex. Since the sexual difference itself is an abstraction, a third term, the feminine real always escapes the rules of the symbolic, in part, while masculine identification with the symbolic order suffers from foreclosing the real. Lacan returned to Aristotle's categories of the universal and the particular into which he had integrated his discoveries regarding the masculine and the feminine, thus supplying the causal connection Aristotle could not make, thereby demonstrating how the masculine and the feminine *come to exist* as recognizable *places* that are concretely constructed in the three different orders of language (the symbolic), images (the imaginary), and the real of trauma as registered in anxiety, envy, or excitement.

The masculine defines itself in terms of *One* signifier, the S_1 of the master signifier that gives substance to the idea of a unified reality principle. The feminine defines itself in a double reference that refers both to the lack of a natural signifier for law in the symbolic, the ($S[\varnothing]$) representing encounters with the void in the Other, and to the positivized phallic signifier which anchors the feminine in the Name-of-a-Father (taken on as a reality principle). Although these *psychic* identifications do not adhere to anatomy, each one is, nonetheless, constituted in the precise terms of a sexuation logic whose pivot is the central lack of a signifier for Woman (The Woman—qua essential category—does not exist) and the inadequacy of the phallus to its task of representing man qua man in groups of symbolic ensembles.

There is no essence of Woman, no female nature, no "natural" woman, no eternal feminine, not even a guarantee at the level of Woman qua mother. The "the" (*La*) that makes of Woman a universal category is barred in Lacan's sexuation graph (L̶a). And the phallus is only a symbolic-order construct—a representation of the effects of difference—that denotes the effort to define man qua man in terms of his difference from Woman. "This little bit of reality" is elevated to the function of a signifier which, paradoxically, will give rise to the concept of Man as the norm, the standard. Put another way, the standard or norm means the symbolic order where the rules of the game are established on the basis of the local (universal) Law (of difference). When a woman enters this terrain, her rules become the boys' rules. The salient feature in the construction of sexuality around difference is this: Both male and female desire ($\not{S}$) find their cause(s)-for-being on the side of the *pas tout*, among the primordial partial objects (the breast, the feces, the gaze, the voice) that give rise to the (partial) drives (oral, anal, scopic, invocatory) that materialize language for jouissance around the void place cut in the beginning by their loss.

Jouissance is *caused* at the level of the (a), which determines how each subject will then treat the loss occasioned by the lack of a signifier for "The" Woman, or "The" Mother. The answer arises on several levels. Is one the lover ($\not{S}$) or the beloved (a) in sexual identification? What unary traits compose one's fantasy scenes and object(s)? From what drive field(s) will one choose semblances to fill the void: Will consumption go toward the anal (acquisitions and controlling) or toward ingesting (food, words), for instance? The (a) is constructed out of the particular experiences of each subject, the point being that whether a subject is biologically male or female, phallic (or genital) jouissance is always excited by the object (a) of one's own references. In a larger sense, the sexual difference makes all the difference in that the *feminine* calls to the *masculine* whose quest is not primarily for orgasm per se, but for the reparation of the feminine *pas toute* where desire was first structured for both sexes around the real of loss:

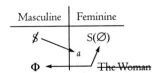

Contemporary feminist conflation of the masculine with the male voyeur and the feminine with the position of victim, not only misses the subtlety of distinguishing lover from beloved as positions taken on in the masquerade, it misses the more fundamental principle within sexuality itself: The desire to enjoy another, that Socrates observed in his students, does not have sexual pleasure per se as its goal, but capturing the "more than you in you" of the other's *agalma*. In the chapter "On the Baroque" in *Seminar XX*, Lacan says: "The unconscious is the fact that being by speaking, enjoys, and," I will add, "wants to know nothing more about it . . . know nothing about it at all" (p. 105). Lacan points to a paradox here. What we call idle talk is not idle at all. We "enjoy" as men or women in the precise words we choose. Miller has clarified Lacan here by his own return to Freud. Jouissance and language are incompatible, Miller argued in his course of 1987–1988, "Cause and Consent" ("To Interpret the Cause," *Newsletter of the Freudian Field*, vol. 3, p. 31). Subjects do not "come" in language all the time. Language is, rather, a supplement to desire that marks a *loss* of jouissance, rather than a surfeit of it. It even serves as a defense against that loss. Moreover, Freud signaled that jouissance can be ignored by the subject who can easily dwell on the repetitive side of Thanatos.[27]

What Lacan calls a jouissance of speaking or thought in *Seminar XX: Encore* is, rather, the partial drive dwelling in language, pushing language to satisfy its jouissance, such as the demands made for love (or at least a modicum of recognition), and so on: see me, hear me, feed me, take care of me. The unconscious function of sexuality is in language, then, but as the desire for love, not as a pregiven jouissance. We "enjoy" when we speak, Lacan says, and don't want to know anything about it. What we enjoy in language, I would suggest, is repeating the jouissance knowledge that already anchors our *fixions* (fixation/fiction) of being, our repressions of desire. In 1972 Lacan proposed that the repression of jouissance is not a property of the male or female, but of the metaphorical function wherein one meaning is substituted for another, the laws of rhetoric paralleling the way the drives are inscribed in language. We deny, repress, joke about, dismiss as nothing, the real of the (sexual) impasse that language touches on all the time.

In his course of 1993–1994—*Donc*—Miller continues his clarification of Lacan's later claims that jouissance is a meaning system.[28] But rather than refer to a diffuse sexuality, ever present in speech, Miller refers to the particular conditions that give rise to *desire*, touching via fantasy on the real of jouissance. While Lacan focused on the sexual difference as constitutive of an impasse between the sexes, Miller hones in on the precise organization of the details that give rise to the search for jouissance as the search for a set of concrete conditions, sometimes conscious, often radically unconscious. This is a different picture from Lacan's depiction of a global jouissance in language. The "I don't want to know anything about it" of unconscious desire resides on the masculine side of sexuation, within the field of language. Miller points out that no one wants to know anything about the *particular* sexuality behind his or her language, because language, by alienation and repression, already guarantees being by filling up the hole in the symbolic order (∅) from which anxiety emanates as real:

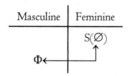

And the masculine side, the field of the reality principle of language, exists to deny this fact: The Other or second jouissance that Lacan places on the slope of the pleasure principle resides in the field of the feminine which opens onto the corporal real of Thanatos—structured by identification with the losses of objects—that lies beyond identification with the closure and Oneness of phallic jouissance. Yet, there is no *the* masculine or *the* feminine because both are, finally, inseparable insofar as each exists only in reference to the other. Lacan's arrows indicate this, as does the long and painful battle of the sexes, a battle not only between the genders, but between the masculine and feminine in relationships, the "longest revolution" of masculine versus feminine would-be harmonies with no ending in Oneness possible.

Lacan corrected the biological bias in Freud's postulation of a reality principle and a pleasure principle, pointing out that Freud could not solve many of the problems he kept raising because he believed the pleasure principle and reality principles to be oppositional. Freud did not understand that there can be no opposition except in terms of relationship, no thesis/antithesis without dialectic. Examining the relational aspect of these two principles, Lacan came to see that the fundamental structure of any person's being, as constituted in the experience of the paternal metaphor or the oedipal myth, is first a response to the enigma of the sexual difference within the field of the *visual*, or the world of forms where oppositions have the character of that which is potentially separable. That is, in the imaginary the little boy (and the father) have the penis and the mother does not, a reality that each child later translates as a castration trauma. Lacan calls *this* the impact of the primal oedipal scene on him or her. Veering away from Freud's anatomical reductionism, Lacan states in 1958 that the biological difference is translated by the child into a plus or minus of value that then functions mathematically. The plus or minus is confused with the primordial demand for love, however, taken as a demand for "more" which converges with the desire to *be* the phallus, that is, the one who "has" (all the mother's love).[29]

The distinction between having the phallus and being the phallus enabled Lacan to understand the masculine and feminine as a division more fundamental to being than that of biological male or female. Having or not having is *psychic* (*tychic*, of the real) in the determination of the subject of the unconscious. And the real is an impasse whose social effects go from the prostitute at the bottom rung of the social ladder to Medieval eschatology's splitting of being into the high function of mind/spirit and the base, animal function of the carnal/flesh. Lacan confronts us with a logical extension of the proposition he calls "an untenable truth": "The reality of the unconscious is sexual reality—an untenable truth" (*S XI*, p. 150).

But the language of the *tout* ($S_1 \rightarrow S_2$)—that is, the use of language to seek the closure of an answer in keeping with the masculine logical mode of the necessary—reveals the impasse in its own search. The quest for meaning turns on the demand for love, which aims toward the nonclosure of the *pas tout*, or the feminine contingent ($\overline{\forall}x\Phi x$)—$\$ \not{\diamond} a$—that one might describe as the implicit question posed by the masculine to the feminine. One sees in the one-way directionality of the arrow from left to right the impossibility of intersubjectivity that Miller describes as the impasse at the base of Lacan's efforts to design the mirror-stage in the Schema L.[30] Although he never worked out its precise causes, Lacan nonetheless took seriously the formula Freud defended—the untenable reality of sexuality. "Why is it an untenable reality?" he asks (*S. XI*, p. 150). Why does most everyone impute a low motive to sexual realities? Since Freud's day we have made a little progress in understanding sex, Lacan says, just a bit. It is now admitted that sexual division ensures the survival of the species, that if a species does not reproduce, does not copulate, it dies. So we can say that sex and death are fundamentally connected. We can even say to philosophers and theologians, Lacan continues, that *existence*, thanks to sexual division, rests upon copulation, accentuated in two poles that time-honoured tradition has tried to characterize as the male pole and the female pole, be it as anima and animus, or sun and moon, and so on.

Other things are grouped around this fundamental reality, such as the knowledge that the elementary structures of social functioning are inscribed in a *combinatory*—that is, oppositional—pair such as Yin and Yang. For example, it is matrimonial alliance, not natural generation, that links man to woman; the law of generation being the law of the signifier, the "You are my wife" conferring the meaning of "you may bear my children" (*S. XI*, p. 150). But the difficulty of linking the reality of the unconscious, insofar as sexuality is its reality, to an archaic junction in thought, is stupendous, Lacan says in 1964, immediately countering would-be objections to his proposition by pointing out that pansexual theories, such as Jung's, that neutralize libido, miss what Freud made present in its function: "The libido is the effective presence, as such, of desire . . . which is there at the level of the primary process" (*S. XI*, p. 153)—at the level of the primal fantasies by which an infant negotiates its first demands.

What seemed stupendous to Lacan in 1964 has since been radically developed and elaborated in the Freudian field around an ever-increasing knowledge of what constitutes the real and jouissance. Indeed, the theory of jouissance or libido, taken as a real substance that moves in the body and coalesces around vital organs, negatively (Thanatos) and positively (Eros), places psychoanalysis—the "talking cure"—in conflict with medical discourses that treat the symptom and not its cause. If, in fact, sexual energy is first and foremost *constituted* around the objects-cause-of-desire, as energy that courses in the biological body in a silent witness to blocked jouissance—whose referents are the particular constitution of each subject's primordial experiences of jouissance—one can say that jouissance inhabits language, but negatively, and positively.

In answer to the question What is sexuality? Lacan says "the nodal point by which the pulsation of the unconscious is linked to sexual reality . . . is called desire . . . the function of desire [being] a last residuum of the effect of the signifier in the subject (*S. XI*, p. 154). The operational word here is the *effect* of the signifier in the subject. The *residue* left over by the effects of the signifier is the (*a*), the kernel of one's being, one's cause as hidden in the fundamental fantasy, a cause that makes of the subject an object resonating in his or her own discourse as a metonymy of being ("a little shit"—a *rien*, "a nurturing maternity"—a good breast, etc.). And not only is desire first constituted by the effects of speech that create being and subsequently depend on the demand in drive, that is, on asking the Other for what one wants—which one does not necessarily consciously know—moreover, the (masculine) reality principle of language and law is, by definition, a resistance to the (feminine) pleasure principle on which reality depends as an escape from the strictures of the symbolic. When one desires objects, saying "I want this or that," it is not (usually) physiological need that speaks, but the more than need in need, the desire to be as in "being wanted." Thus, the function of desire sexualizes objects—that is, makes a libidinal investment in—forbidden objects (*S. XI*, p. 155). One wants what the Other forbids. The law of "no" begets desire. And so, paradoxically, as Jacques-Alain Miller argues in "Duty and the Drives," one desires the most where there is prohibition. Here, law and desire are one.[31]

Freud opposed the pleasure principle to the reality principle because he could only think of reality as desexualized. Lacan teaches that no libidinal investment can be desexualized even though the sexual element may be repressed through denial, repudiation, or foreclosure. The jouissance investment in the phallic signifier (Φ) is precisely a desiring identification with some ideal of the Father's Name, desire lying between sublimated sexual reality and jouissance as an imaginary mode of consistency. In this context, any investment of (cathexsis of) jouissance one makes in others (and in causes) is sexualized. Sublimated means eroticized, not neutralized; moreover, it is sublimated around the signifier for the Father's Name—away from the mother in the signifying "name" of the father. Thus, group phenomena, beliefs, ideologies, political platforms, are sublimations. Yet the symbolic Other defends its existence as Other to itself, defends the "purity" of its laws or rules, by denying any sexual element in group identification (although this has not always been true in History. Lacan gives the examples of Socratic philosophy and courtly love). At a fundamental level, however, in any era, law is the law against sexuality, the forbidding of jouissance that comes to guarantee the *solidity and unity* of a social body organized in opposition to and denial of the real of the drives.

Lacan adhered to Freud's view of the pleasure principle as sexual, but not because there is an innate or instinctual id pushing individuals to attain satisfaction. Rather, the pleasure principle is the quest to recapture the jouissance lost in the primordial experience of the cut. There is, however, the Catch-22 already mentioned: First pleasures are quickly *fixed* as experiences one wants to repeat, even as anticipated consistencies. And repetition works against change, against desire, thereby placing death right in the center of life. In seeking to "find satisfaction" (fill up the hole in the Other—the *place* of an "interior" emptiness), any subject will continually bump into the effects of loss. Lacan locates the experience of the real of the body on the side of the feminine, insofar as women identify with a logic of the *not all*, but he does not mean a lack of sexual organs by this. He means that woman is defined as *not all* within the symbolic order. This is not a pregiven or an innate reality, as we know, but a "knowledge" that arises out of the symbolic's and imaginary's structuring the real for meaning. The point is that the real is not biology or Marxist materiality or some kind of spirituality. It is a radically repressed category of meaning.

Geneviève Morel writes that feminine symbols only take on a sense in the imaginary and are, thus, subjected to other symbols in the unconscious. Moreover, Freud sensed this or he would never have attached such a surrealistic idea as the castration of the woman—that is, femininity—to a "complex" of castration, or to a mythically castrated mother. Yet, Lacan's thesis is this: An infant's early experience of the mother is of continual losses of the object(s) of desire. And even the invisible object(s) (*a*)—the voice or the gaze—become appended to images of the infant's *environs*. The symbols and images of woman cannot be isolated from those same images and, moreover, many feminine images, both visible and invisible, will be registered in the unconscious on the side of a lack. The image seems stable—full and whole. But it disappears. This is why Lacan writes it as a $\sqrt{-1}$: It has a negative function that inscribes both loss and opacity. The mirror-stage drama surrounding the *Fort! Da!* of the Freudian bobbin-reel story is repeated myriad times. Every time the mother takes away the object (*a*) grounding the infant in an illusion of its being whole within the scopic field, the void of *absence* is opened up ($-\phi \rightarrow a$). Only the mastery of language—substituting words for evaporating things—allows the "mirror-stage" infant a way to substitute the world of words for the evanescent semblance of the world of things. Words come to seem more reliable (more "real") than the images whose meanings are more proximate to the world of silence and the arbitrariness of the content, or the names(s) given them.

Lacan introduced us to a *structural reality of the unconscious* insofar as the phallus, the One signifier for the male, is immediately conflated with the concept of gain due to its comparative visibility, but most particularly by its signification of a difference left to be interpreted for the infant from the mother's *la lalangue*.[32] If one considers Lacan's theory in Freudian terms, "the same as the mother" means lacking the organ that differentiates her from the father. While the breast is real, primordial, and inseparable from need and the frustration concomitant with getting food, the phallus is that around which other objects are organized in the abstraction of *mentality*. The problem Lacan solved that Freud did not concerns the particular way in which this knowledge about who has the phallus is inscribed for meaning, a knowledge which, although repressed, determines the outcome of each subject's sexuality as a way of relating to the Other—as knowledge of the "normative" masquerade, neurotic denial, perverse repudiation, or psychotic fore-closure, all positions taken toward the object (*a*) one seeks—in persons, activities, intellectual pursuits, work endeavors, and so on. In other words, repression, denial, repudiation, and foreclosure are four attitudes vis-à-vis the phallus, "habits of mind" one might equate with Lacan's modal logics: Foreclosure is concomitant with the impossible (no one has the phallus); repudiation, with the possible (none does not *not* have the phallus, thus, all *may* have it); repression is concomitant with necessity (someone has to have it—i.e., the law, the power); while neurosis leans toward the contingent (either you have it or I do; the difference makes no difference).

Feminine Sexuality

At the level where one becomes a woman by identification, Lacan points to a logical contradiction within the sphere of the feminine. There is no woman who is not under the law—that is, who has not been castrated (except in psychosis). That is, there is only one symbolic, only one register of language and the signifier, not different symbolisms for everyone. It is in this sense that Fenichel could make the equation girl = phallus.

Lacan follows Fenichel here to show that the woman's body becomes her equivalent of not having the phallus, thus becoming the focus of adornment, her body being the phallus. So why would the little girl inscribe a lack in her unconscious? Morel explains that insofar as the first and real privations for any infant derive from frustrated (i.e., imaginary) demands for the breast, for example, any subject—male or female—(who is not psychotic) installs himself or herself as having a lack-in-being, but the little girl (unlike the little boy) registers the particular lack of the phallus, a symbolic object attributed to boys, as a privation.[32]

And there is no exception to this within the spheres of normativity or neurosis. By definition, a woman is one for whom there is no exception to the law of being under the law. Insofar as a woman is a woman in *differential* opposition to the masculine signifier for difference, the signifier Woman dwells under the law of castration (Freud), difference (Lacan)—$[\overline{\exists x \Phi x}]$). This double negative creates a strange effect at the level of universal meaning, the effect being that no woman is *all* under the law $(\overline{\forall x \Phi x})$. In other words, a law that does not base itself on an exception to itself cannot find a basis in the universal except as a logical impossibility. Thus, women dwell closer to the real of the drives because they are not defined as being wholly *in* the symbolic order of the group. In having one foot outside the symbolic, women have the other foot in the real, the place of loss from which the most radical of jouissance effects emanate.

In "*De la femme aimée à la femme désirante*" ("From the Beloved Woman to the Desiring Woman"), Carmen Gallano describes Lacan's contribution to the enigma of Woman as having situated her sexual being within the logic of the *pas tout* of castration.[33] But he does not mean what Freud did by this. Having deduced that castration is a response to the lack of a penis, Freud thought the oedipal father was the cause of *Penisneid* (penis envy). The oedipal father is not the *cause*, Lacan said. Castration is caused, rather, by the *loss* of jouissance from the body because the signifier for limits (the "no") cuts into the child's libidinal pleasure of oneness, installing lack alongside the deferrals of desire. One is *not all* (*pas tout*), one does not have everything, one cannot be just anything. There are limits, lacks, losses, for everyone, except in psychotic delusion where metaphor fails to work substitutively because this child was sacrificed to his or her mother's jouissance.

There is no ratio for a rapport of harmony or Oneness between the two sexes, Lacan said, arguing that, indeed, the two sexes are structured as different races. At the level of structural logic, Lacan further contributed to understanding feminine sexuality: The Other jouissance, the feminine one, is a correlate to the phallic jouissance of the symbolic. Lacan does not say Woman is the same as or "equal to" man, or potentially his equal, or vice versa. He says that the logic of feminine sexuality is a correlate to that of masculine sexuality, albeit asymmetrical, indeed supplemental. The difference is constituted in and by the symbolic order, although it is today incorrectly interpreted by biological or sociological reductionisms that are, then, treated within the imaginary order of totalizing judgments, where black and white moralizing platitudes (such as better than/worse than) hold sway. Totalizing reeducation programs win out over truth. Moreover, the means the sexes have of reaching one another have already been blocked by all the cuts into jouissance, all the taboos forbidding oneness. Repression is, if nothing else, a testimonial to the fact that jouissance does not automatically facilitate a *psychic* rapport between the sexes, or in sex.

Implications of Lacan's Theory for Feminist Debates:
The Logic of the *Pas Tout*

At this juncture, it may be well to emphasize something not immediately obvious when one speaks of Lacan's return to Freud: Lacan found the only hope for radical change (i.e., cure) within the logic of feminine *sexuation* that he named the *pas toute* of radical castration. If one goes no further than Lacan's saying that women suffer from phallic lack and men from the threat of castration, it will seem that Lacan has not advanced one step beyond Freud's biological reductionisms. But Lacan always takes the literalism of Freud's terms to the level of structure before he threads them back into the sexual drama of organ functions. Indeed, this move allowed Lacan to see the epistemological positions constituted by the different ways of being sexual of the masculine and feminine.

When referring to the phallocentrism of the unconscious, Lacan means quite simply that genital sexuality per se is not the referent, but the phallus taken as a *symbol* of difference—that is, the visible sign of desire rendered imaginable. Such an inscription has many vicissitudes: The hysteric retains the phallus unconsciously, denying that she *lacks* anything, while her "normative" sister seeks the phallus in her partner and then "envies" it, "envy" meaning both "desire for" and jealousy of. The obsessional male is not sure whether he has the phallus or not, while psychotic males experience the male organ as alive, as real (i.e., not symbolized in the unconscious). The foreclosure of this symbol sends psychotic women in quest of a Oneness with The Man for whom she is The Woman. Perverse subjects use the organ to teach others that the law of life is the law of jouissance.

Whereas Freud first thought little girls constituted their sexuality around the love of the father for whom their subsequent loves were substitutes, Lacan took these fixations of love to be the basis of female suffering. Carmen Gallano describes the Freudian "normative" woman thus: She does not love her mother since her castration anxiety makes her choose her father. But since her husband has married her as a substitute mother for himself, his highest Good being the harmonious oedipal rapport between a son and his mother, his value to her lies in his being the father of her children. The Freudian woman is above all a mother, then, one whose children compensate her for the phallus she lacks. And her husband is just one more child. This is quite different from the Lacanian woman for whom jouissance is not compensatory, but *supplemental*, and for whom *volupté* is not guilt, but a *desideratum* (Gallano, p. 92).

One must know, Carmen Gallano writes, that "the Freudian woman does not love men, but that she is nothing without the love of men and that when she loves, she loves as a mother" (p. 93). Gallano's conclusion here holds stunning implications: Freud's woman is on the masculine side of the sexuation graph, identified with the phallic signifier (Φ). Any woman who loves a man in the masquerade, by making herself the object he lacks, by trying to *be* what she thinks he wants, has given up on her desire. And loving as the passive object she supposes will correspond to her lover's fantasy of Woman, she partakes of the logic of narcissism. In Lacan's teaching, narcissism will always open onto the death place of fixated jouissance. Freud's woman does not love as a desiring woman, then, but as a *pastiche* or *semblant* in the sexual masquerade, wherein the masquerade is always designed to *compensate* for the confusion that reigns regarding having the penis, being the phallus, or acting on one's own desire.

In trying to deduce the "true nature of woman" from the oedipal model of the little girl desiring her father, Freud found something hidden behind this: The mother. And in looking for the true nature of woman within the mother, he found, instead, maternal lack. Lacan symbolizes this reality by the question mark regarding the mother's desire: If she wants something, then, what does she lack? The implication of this formula is that neither the husband nor the children are sufficient to fulfill a woman at the level of desire. The *being* of the woman is not correspondent with her desire. Nor is desire reducible to sexuality. In Lacan's teaching desire is a structure as well as a content.

It is this second point that suggests a new orientation for contemporary feminist debates. Lacan solved a problem Freud never could. Not only is the nature of feminine desire different from that of masculine desire, its structure lies on the side of psychoanalytic cure. Freud's "cured" woman would be one who loves *like* a man. By identifying with a masculine ideal ($\Phi \rightarrow \Sigma$), she *finds* the "self" outside herself, sacrificing her desire to being-for-another. Such totalizing love—trying to be the phallus the partner lacks—can only stifle the particularity of desire and keep a woman from loving from the place of feminine sexuality.[34] One runs into this paradox: "Selfless" imposes a love limit and, as such, is masculine. I would add to Carmen Gallano's thesis that the Freudian woman loves from the position of the male who loves a woman qua Woman, since "The Woman" does not exist *as such* at the level of the essence imputed to her: The male or female who seeks "her" will suffer from trying to make *a* woman into The Woman, sacrificing the truth of his or her particularity to a narcissistic universal. The lie between such partners can only produce conflict, the domestic quarrel.

But how can "normative" feminine (passive, selfless) love be masculine? In "The Dream of Being the Most Beautiful," Sylvia Tendlarz argues that the *particular* conditions that cause a woman to love a man require that he have a fantasy of her as unique.[35] From this angle one can say that a woman loves the picture a man gives her of herself, not him qua man in the singular. Such love can only be imaginary, then, based, as it is, on an idealized "fantasy" picture of the one she hopes he thinks she is, aiming at closure—Cinderella bedecked!—not desire. And this poses problems for feminine sexuality. Insofar as a woman already does not love a man qua man, qua father, nor qua possessor of the penis, but loves in him, rather, the fantasy he gives her of herself, what about *her* desire?

Lacan found this to be a pressing question concerning feminine sexuality. Because love *as such* is empty, is poetry, or a *meaning* whose words function as a filler to lack—as an object (*a*)—love quickly brings a woman face to face with the void in being, which bears on the object of the nothing. Love defines woman outside sex (*horsexe*), functioning as a supplement to the inexistence of the sexual rapport. Unlike Freud, Lacan did not think that women need a man as a husband or as a father, foremost; but, he argued, women *need* to love because only the *semblant* of a beloved partner can fill the empty place where the woman's being is inadequately covered by the veil of the phallic signifier; that is, there where the confusion between having and being is at stake.

Moreover, because "life, the vital feeling, is signified by the phallus as the signifier of desire, love which does not converge with desire sends the subject to the meaning of his emptiness as equivalent to death" (Gallano, p. 95). Desire divorced from love opens onto the emptiness of the void ($\varnothing$) where pure angst and desolation reside as the inverse face of the real. A lot is at stake in Lacan's ethics of psychoanalysis, argued on the side of the truth of desire. Instead of masquerading as the narcissistically beloved object—pretending she is the phallus lacking to men—the Lacanian woman is a desiring woman, taking her strength from the relationship she has to something like a sense of infinity that comes from having accepted castration. And here "desire must be taken literally."[36] In refusing imaginary, sacrificial love, the woman in analysis may pass from a masculine way of loving (a/Φ) to a feminine way, where an identification with the Other jouissance ($S[\varnothing]$) "beyond the phallus" infuses her body with desire. In this "pass" to a supplemental jouissance she loses the phallus (the hysteric), or her desire for it (the feminine masquerade), and gains access to the real of a lost jouissance which a woman can only (re-)find by dropping her phallic semblance.

More precisely, I would say, that which woman can experience but man cannot is an acceptance of a knowledge that already circumscribes her body. The question is whether she will inscribe this energy within the economy of Thanatos or that of Eros. In this context, what is generally called "affect" is only a series of relations to the real and jouissance whose referent is the object (*a*) and the hole in the Other ($S[\varnothing]$) from which the real emanates, marked by the shadings of inhibition, symptom, and anxiety in sexual desire. And this real may travel in woman's body as the *globus hystericus* of the imaginary loss of an imaginary phallus, or its substitute in the guise of a person.

The Lacanian woman does not have the penis. She does not want to be the phallus. She acts from her desire, for herself, not for any Other. And, as such, she incarnates desire up to the crescendo of a jouissance of being that is itself subversive of the ordering of the symbolic. But this jouissance of the *not all* is not circumscribed only by the limits of the supplemental jouissance, for sexual experience is inseparable from one's position in knowledge insofar as one works from a master discourse of the *all*, or from a feminine discourse of the *not all*. Lacan discovered that psychoanalysis can cure masculine and feminine beings of their suffering insofar as they realize their castration/lack and inscribe themselves in the not-all of the group. Totalizations throughout history, such as monotheism, monogamy, or motherhood, are not solutions to desire. When taken as such, blind suffering ensues.

4

A Rereading of Freud's 1925 Essay
"Some Psychical Consequences of the Anatomical Distinction between the Sexes" through Lacan's Theory of Sexuation

Lacan pointed out, as we have said, that the furor surrounding Freud in the 1930s (Karen Horney, Ernest Jones, and others) focused particularly on the question of woman's nature.[1] In this period, debates raged around Freud's theories of the castration complex, the Oedipus complex, and the meaning of the phallus.[2] Those who disagreed with Freud argued in various ways that the sexual development of males was equal and symmetrical to that of females. Freud never let go of the idea that there is only one libido—the phallic or masculine one, which might be treated as "genital" and active— for both men and women. He also knew that castration fears played a role in male acceptance of a subjective masculine sexual position. Although Freud considered the penis as causative of sexual anxiety in males because of castration threats and anxieties regarding who did or did not have one, or concerning its size, or its potential loss (cf. Little Hans), Lacan's focus was not on biological gender. He depicted castration as the mental effect on being of perceiving a gap of difference between the sexes.

Lacan gave to psychoanalysis what Freud could not: an understanding of how masculinity and femininity constitute sexuation as an unconscious knowledge about desire. Sexuation is the outcome of a subject's interpretation of sexual difference by imaginary identifications with symbolic-order others who have or do not have ("phallic") power there. Freud's "Little Hans" case is paradigmatic of the theory. Hans's obsession with whether or not his mother possessed a penis and, if so, how large it must be led Freud to think the organ was the thing itself.[3] Lacan argues, rather, that the presence or absence of the penis makes the first level of castration a logical operation that links being to body by negation of an image; that is a visible representation of something is perceived as potentially there or not there by both sexes. Lacan denotes this by the matheme for the negativized phallus: $-\phi$. An imaginary interpretation of the susceptibility of loss of a body part ("partial object") becomes a symbolic order reality written by the matheme for the positivized phallus: Φ.

By working with the psychic difference Lacan ascribed to the sexes, we shall see how Lacan got out of the impasse where Freud left off, writing at the end of his life in

"Analysis Terminable and Interminable" (1936) that even the best analysis was de-feated on the "rock of the castration complex" in men and "penis envy" in women (vol. 23).[4] This offers an entrée into an understanding of Lacan's theory of "sexuation" wherein sexuality is a matter of how jouissance conditions are logically written in the unconscious as positivized interpretations of the lost phallus. These interpretations create a lack around the sexual divide that Lacan called castration.

The Phallus and Castration Reconsidered

As we know, three of Freud's essays were crucial to Lacan's rereading of the meaning of sexual difference: "Some Psychical Consequences of the Anatomical Differences be-tween the Sexes" (1925) (*SE*, 19: 243–58)[5] lays the groundwork for his reconsider-ation of Freud's two famous essays on feminine sexuality: "Female Sexuality" (1931) and "Femininity" (1932). Where Freud evolved myths of women derived from imagin-ary male reductionisms to anatomical organs (*SE*, 22: 112–35),[6] Lacan deduced a logic of the unconscious based on loss and lack.

Unlike other post-Freudian analysts who started their study of Freud at the point where his theories on feminine sexuality ended in a series of impasses, Lacan argued, that the sexes are not fundamentally equal and symmetrical. Nor can they be made so by clinical treatment, or reeducation. Nor can one truly claim that the difference does not matter, whether it is said to be created by words and language games or by genes and biology.

Lacan advanced a logic that explained Freud's conclusion that the sexual differ-ence is constituted as an asymmetry between the sexes. In other words, the phallus and castration are symbolic-order myths that link organ differences to being and having in terms of having, not having, or potentially losing the representations of a separable "part object." Insofar as identification as masculine or feminine grounds "gender identity" (or sexuation) in four potential postures of unconscious desire that con-cern how one identifies with lack and/or with the object (*a*) that fills the lack-in-being ($\emptyset \; \maltese \; a$), radically repressed sex and imaginary narcissism lie at the base of all thought. To develop such a logic, Lacan turned, not to Freud, however, but to Aristotle's efforts to delineate the universal from the particular by modal or qualitative logic. Whereas Aristotle was concerned to explain the cause of an *act* as necessary, efficient, material, or instrumental (that is, as representable or quantitative), Lacan's interest lay, rather, in uncovering the causes of different libidinal (thus, qualitative) modes of response to the sexual difference.[7]

Arguing that the static prime mover of desire is no substance, but loss itself, Lacan says loss first catalyzes desire as the movement that becomes an act, its inverse face being *lack* or "want." He thereby postulated a reason for progressing beyond the Aristotelian unmoved mover as a theory of cause to a theory of lack and losses as themselves causative of *acts* of speech, being, and body, acts for which Aristotle could deduce no motive. Having posited desire as the cause and jouissance as its goal, Lacan isolated the jouissance modalities he then attributed the masculine and the feminine. He depicts the feminine as divided between the *contingent* and the *impossible*. The masculine adheres to the *possible* and the *necessary*. Divided by the third-term effect of difference—itself an abstraction—Lacan placed a bar down the center of the sexuation graph that functions as the phallic signifier which denotes difference as the lack of being whole, or as the loss of one's other half. The phallic signifier functions both imaginarily in the cut that separates one from a desired object and symbolically through the power of the name to simultaneously create a reality and to alienate one behind that "reality." Sexuation is never a binary in Lacan's teaching. Starting with the visible perception of a (potential) loss and the naming of that effect whose cause evaporates into lost memory, Lacan's closed-set masculine ensembles and open-set feminine ones both rely on a concept of the infinite. But this is postulated in reference to a point of finitude—as is repetition for Freud in *Beyond the Pleasure Principle*—which disqualifies them from being deconstructed as opposing binaries.[8]

Lacan's theory here concerns the logic of limits placed on any infinity of intervals between [0,1]. We remember that unlike whole numbers, the real numbers are rational numbers (fractions) whose limit is 1.114, the numerical limit of a set or series. Indeed, any real irrational number functions as a stopper on a series, or on the rationals (the Cauchy series). We pointed out in chapter 1 that in Lacan's theory, infinity—in math and in life—is based on Zeno's paradox: Neither Achilles or the tortoise can arrive at the limit. "It is on that basis that a number . . . can be defined, if it is real. A number has a limit and it is to that extent that it is infinite. . . . Achilles can only pass the tortoise—he cannot catch . . .up with it [except] at infinity" (*S. XX*, p. 8; Morel, p. 71). That is, the tortoise and Achilles will always be in different places vis-à-vis one another, as will the two sexes.

Moreover, Lacan's sexuation graph is not susceptible of deconstructive opposition because neither the masculine nor the feminine is whole. Thus neither identification acts in accordance with an ideal, or a totalized masculine or feminine self.[9] The bottom part of the sexuation graph seeks to demonstrate that insofar as the lack-in-being is contingent, characterized by a logic of the possible that "ceases to write itself," it is on the masculine side of potential fulfillment of sexuation. When the castrated subject reaches across the sexual divide by an arrow joining it to the object (a) it reaches the feminine, across a chasm of alienation and separation. The void in the Other on the feminine side (S[Ø]) is connected to the positivized masculine phallus (Φ) and simultaneously to the lack of an essential woman (~~The Woman~~). This lack of an inmate feminine essence makes the void a place of potential angst and paradoxically, requires women to have one foot in the symbolic. Thus, the subject of lack is not only *not* an essence, it is also a fading evaporating presence.[10] The subject is, thus, suffering and pathetic when anxiety reveals internalized loss in a temporary separation of the absent primordial object—the breast, the feces, the gaze, the voice—from it's substitute object (a) in reality. Then the real overtakes the symbolic.[11]

Lacan's modal logic writes the particular conditions of jouissance he had elaborated to explain, in part, the impasse between man and woman. This impasse gives rise to three subjective identifications in jouissance, identifications often at odds with biological realities. One identifies with the reality of power (Φ), or with the gap between the image and the word (−φ), while a third is with the hole in the Other (∅) that unveils the empty center of any set, an encounter with pure angst. These positionings vis-à-vis the sexual difference mark it by placing limits on the sexual asymmetry at the interfaces of the real, symbolic, and imaginary. Lacan described these as symbolic castration, imaginary frustration and real privation. Between the imaginary and the real, the Other jouissance is encountered: ∅. Between the imaginary and symbolic the local (universal) social reality appears: Φ. Between the imaginary and symbolic one finds the separability of image and word—of the "word" that the "thing" has already created as unconscious meaning. Lacan postulated three solutions to filling the gap. It can be filled with the Other, the phallus, or the *jouis-sens* of meaning. Each of these temporarily sutures lack or loss:

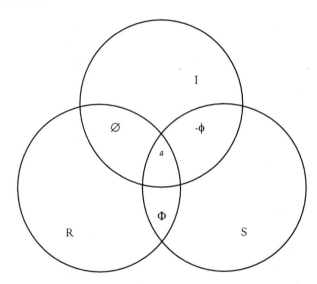

The "early" Lacan spoke of the lack of an innate object of satisfaction in the 1960s. A decade later, his descriptions of the lack or loss of the object took on topological affinities with different subject positions in the drives. But prior to this he had correlated lack and loss with demand, desire, and need. Lacan added his modal logic of the 1970s to his 1960s theories of the signifier, and the logic of the cut. One remembers that the cut begins with infancy when the baby tries to annul anxiety by recuperating an identificatory trait of an Ur-object's loss; loss, that is, of a semblance of fullness or presence. When an object of fulfillment is extracted from one's symbolic universe by certain demands or desires made by the Other, a void and a unary trait are left over. If the Other fails to answer one's demand, the void is encountered. Lacan's topology oscillates between the void in the Other and the object (a). For example, an oral object is demanded from the Other, while an anal object is taken as a demand made by the Other. A scopic object is experienced as the Other imposing its desire, while an invocatory object is "felt" as a desire for the Other.

In all phases of his teaching, Lacan insisted on the centrality of the phallus in the symbolic taken inversely as the male's susceptibility to being castrated. This is of a piece with his theory that the unconscious is structured like a language. That is, the unconscious is marked by lacks between differential references of one term to another. Thus, even though a little girl will represent her body by many images in the unconscious—made up of the traces, memories, and identifying signifiers of her world—she will not represent herself as having the penis, except in reference to its lack. The real knowledge a girl has of her body, such as infantile explorations of her vagina, cannot be symbolized in the unconscious because no *image* opposes the vagina in the imaginary world of symbols and images.[12] Thus, in 1958 and 1959 Lacan accepted Fenichel's formula of "girl = phallus," still thinking imaginarily in terms of a girl's "being the phallus" in sexuation and in modal logic, or a boy's "having" it (Morel, *"La différence des sexes,"* p. 27).

Sexuation and Modal Logic

To truly grasp Lacan's move in the 1970s to interpret the sexual difference via a modification of Aristotle's modal logic, one must look to Aristotle's *Rhetoric II,* 25, 1402a and *Topics VIII,* 2 157 ab and *II,* 115b (*S. XX,* p. 70).

But first, let us remember Lacan's thesis that a subject's psychic sexuation is constructed as a dialectic between the real of repressed fantasy,—which, by definition, resists interpretation—and a void place in one's own being, body, and knowledge ($\emptyset$). This dialectic occurs between the primordial objects-cause-of-desire and the unconscious (Other) signifiers of one's own subjectivity. Lacan argued that at the very least we must confront the question of what or who the agent of psychic reality is if it is no longer exterior versus interior monologue, or a dialogue of bodily complaints, or history, or a malfunction of the father as function-of-the-law, the Lacanian father being, finally, a legal fiction. The answer Lacan gave had multiple components, such as his notion of the "subject" which runs counter to a presence of identity, self, or ego. It is defined rather, as the inheritor of an initial foreclosure of a hole or gap that marks the return of repressed—unconscious—signifiers whose only traces are composed of the circuit determined by symbolic "words" that mark imaginary symbols.[13]

In *Seminar III,* Lacan wrote:

There is a subjective topology here that rests entirely on this which is given us by analysis, that there can be an unconscious signifier [whose effects can be measured by the unbridgeable difference between the signifier and signified]. Here we must conceive of space talking as such."[14]

He offered two modes of the feminine—the *contingent* and the *impossible*—and two modes of the masculine—the *necessary* and the *possible*—as epistemological ways of interpreting desire. And desire's limit lies in masculine phallic jouissance—the necessary and the possible—or in feminine supplemental jouissance. Insofar as jouissance forms each person's limits in thought, one encounters the limit of one's knowledge in sexuation in the writing of one's own Other. Here writing is defined "as what language leaves by way of a trace" (*S. 20*, p. 123). Elsewhere, Lacan calls this *la lalangue* (language as its own object). The traces may seem unrelated to one's conscious thought, Lacan says, more like a "cloud of language" linked to something beyond the effect of rain (*S. 20*, p. 120). But they are "presumed in certain words . . . and 'substance' [libido]." "Being" as form is not—but is the basis of—the "subject" that speaks without knowing one's being as body makes an "I," or the subject of a verb (*S. XX*, pp. 118–19).

In "Aristotle and Freud: The Other Satisfaction," Lacan says things do not succeed harmoniously between the sexes because the object (*a*) fails to translate the jouissance that would be necessary to create a civilization of "contents." And it "fails" in four different modes of logical negation (*S. XX*, p. 59). Aristotle's logic of the *necessary* becomes, for Lacan, "that which does not stop being written" (*ce qui ne cesse pas de s'écrire*). But, instead of being linked to the *contingent* (except in love), as it is for Aristotle, Lacan joins it to a logic of the *impossible*: "That which does not stop not being written" (*ce qui ne cesse pas de ne pas s'écrire*) (*S. XX*, p. 59). On the top left corner of the sexuation graph, Lacan places the *necessary* as the logical whole or *all*: $\exists x \overline{\Phi x}$. To perceive things as whole, even universal, is a required condition for a society to exist, then subsist. It is *necessary*, then, that most people believe in a superior being or principle—a symbolic-order Father's Name signifier—that transcends the law, in order to establish the law as a basis from which to "write itself" in reference to something. This creates a masculine or master discourse logic of the "at least one" who says no to castration—the Ur-father—and provides the model of an exception to the rule that gives rise to the concept of a social convention or "norm" of reality. It does not matter to those who believe in such a supreme being that his or her existence is *impossible*. Thus, the *impossible* is made out of the necessity of the impossible, taken as the basis of belief in the One-who-knows.

The mode of the *possible* is situated under the logic of the necessary, which Lacan writes as: $\forall x \Phi$. The *possible* is that which ceases writing itself (*ce qui cesse de s'écrire*). It depends on Lacan's view of the universal as that which contains itself by an existence that denies it, or repression.[15] In *Le Sinthome* (*S. XXIII*),[16] Lacan makes explicit the link of the *possible* to castration, as he does also in *D'un discours qui ne serait pas du semblant* (*S. XVIII*).[17] Here he proposes that any discourse is a discourse of the *semblant*. In *"Joyce le symptôme II,"* he refers to *Le sinthome* as giving the "only definition of the possible," that "it cannot take place."[18] In sexuation, for example, it cannot happen that all the brothers defer to the father for "at least one" will try to best him. Joining this category of the possible with *Seminar XX*, Lacan says no "possible" jouissance can cancel the unconscious by arriving at a point of infinity, an impossible universal doxa, which would hopefully close the surface of a fantasmatic sphere (cf. ch. 1)

In *Seminar XVIII* (*D'un discours qui ne serait pas du semblant* [1970–1971]) and *Seminar XIX* (. . .*ou pire* [1971–1972]),[19] Lacan argues that the *possible* is the "accepted" near universal reality of castration and that only in psychosis, where no law has been introjected, does the *possible* not write itself. Indeed, in masculine logic, the "possible" need not even be explained. What keeps writing itself are the conditions of law that make language, exchange, identity, and so on, possible. Thus, $\forall x \Phi x$ exists only in reference to the postulation of a law in the first place—$\exists x \overline{\Phi x}$—whose terms place a barrier between the mother and infant Oneness and eventually build the possibility of a society. In *Le Sinthome* (1975–1976) Lacan equated the *possible* with death and castration, veering toward the feminine logic of *not [being] all* under the sway of phallic interdictions. In Jack Stone's words: "Castration is the death that marks all that can be legitimately called progress, and may be the only true universal recognized in Lacan's teaching. Paradoxically, it is a universal that renders any truth claiming to universality 'not all'." [20]

The *impossible* logic says there does not exist one, as subject, who says no to castration. Placing this on the feminine side of sexuation—$\overline{\exists x \Phi x}$—Lacan says all women negate (imaginary) castration because not one of them is susceptible to it (some men negate it as well). In "Knowledge and Truth," Lacan elaborates these four modes as a limit point of libido or jouissance that responds to the potential meanings of desire (normative, hysteric, obsessional, perverse, and psychotic) in interpreting the phallic signifier. In other words, desire joins thought to jouissance. Adding the feminine *contingent* to the *impossible,* and the masculine *possible* to the *necessary,* he says the *contingent* "*stops* not being written" (*ce qui cesse de ne pas s'écrire*) (*S. XX*, p. 94; cf also Gilson, p. 68): $\forall x \Phi x$. The *possible* "may" stop being written (*ce qui cesse de s'écrire*—the all-men-are-right of "patriarchal" thought—making it a closed place in knowledge. Lacan's point is that the *necessary* and *possible* masculine logics depend on an illusion of the whole (or *all*) as the beginning and end of knowledge, while the *impossible* and *contingent* are *not all* based on the fear of castration, a fear that elicits closure. At the least, the feminine logics allow for an undecidable: The *impossible* pushes a subject to flee the unbearable, while the *contingent* lets in enough love to allow deadly repetitions to be rewritten. Thus, Lacan places psychoanalytic and cultural hopes for change in feminine logic.

Lacan read Freud's *Totem and Taboo* (1913) as having isolated "structural" realities of unconscious logic that Freud himself did not understand. Extrapolating his sexuation logic from Freud's 1913 text, as well as from Aristotle's *Rhetoric* and *Topics,* Lacan recast Freudian psychoanalysis, giving new explanations for seemingly disparate theories, such as Freud's principles of reality (the *all*) and pleasure (the *not all*). Arguing that interpretations of sexual difference cause the unconscious to desire particular traits of jouissance, he portrayed oedipal structure as a paternal metaphor: FN/MD · MD/? → FN (Other/phallus). The phallic signifier that first delineates difference serves as a symbolic-order referent for the limit of law or the reality principle

(Φ) of the Father's Name. One adheres to a group in reference to what a particular Father's Name signifies. And it substitutes for the mother's unconscious desire vis-à-vis the phallus. Standing in conjunction with the maternal real $S(\emptyset)$ of the pleasure principle—as Eros or Thanatos—the mother's desire determines whether the infant's void is filled by desirable objects or poisonous ones.

The Father's Name signifier can be understood here as symbolic-order language that tries to negotiate the enigmatic real of (the mother's) desire, which structures the drives via jouissance conditions. Another signifier for the Father's Name is the symbolic order itself. It functions to defer or cover over the real void of the partial sexual body created by cuts and losses of the object (a)'s comings and goings. In this sense, the Father's Name denotes the commensurability of the "law" of language with the particular equation of "reality" adhered to by a local universal set of ideas and beliefs while the sexual body uses the language of the symbolic to fill the gaps at its surface. Moreover, Lacan showed how language can substitute for a direct rapport with the "objects" of the outside world by the dialectical dependence of metaphorical substitution on metonymy's transformations of primordial desire into cultural meanings. Thus, Lacan (re)defined metonymy as the fading displacements of the real (lost) objects that mark other objects by the particularity of *contingent* desire. This dynamic brings into language nostalgia, or strange, and "uncanny" effects, all experienced within a flight of apparent sense: $2/1$ or S_I/S (metaphor) $/ S \dots S_I$ (metonymy). Indeed, elsewhere, Lacan defines the object (a) as the metaphor of the subject of jouissance (Gilson, p. 101).

In "Analysis Terminable and Interminable" (1936), Freud wrote sorrowfully of his failure to find a balance between the pleasure and reality principles, pleasure losing out. Lacan argued that Freud could not understand either the tension or connection between the pleasure and reality principles because he had not grasped that the "unconscious" can think only by an interplay of metaphor and desire (metonymy), that links language to objects, and the absolute to the dialectical. Neither could Freud decipher the enigma of conscious energetics: What causes (or drives) humans to act. It is not an accordance with an innate internal strife between the sexual id and social superego. Indeed, language aims to recuperate the loss of objects.

Lacan recast the Freudian cause of human *behavior and motivation* away from anatomy and biology to the subjective sexual identifications he called differential structures of desire. Each structure of desire establishes a pattern connecting it to jouissance depending on the way lack ($\$$) is filled in reference to the Father's Name (Φ) and the object (a) that marks the primordial subject as real. This real Ur-lining is subsequently reflected in the imaginary lure objects that attract a subject, or as a semblance of being, located between the symbolic and the real. Thus, one thinks/ desires as a neurotic who denies the lack-in-being; as a psychotic who forecloses the lack; as a perverse subject who repudiates it; or as a normative subject who represses and masquerades around it.

These four possible interpretations of the sexual difference arise as categories of logical negation, thereby bringing negation (or lack) into sexuation as the enmeshing of these parts. Each makes a precise linkage of the reality principle (Φ) to the pleasure principle (S[$\varnothing$]) We know that Lacan's pleasure principle is not Freud's. And Lacan redefined the reality principle as the symbolic phallic signifier (Φ) that constitutes a social form of law by a concrete identification with the rules and conventions of a given symbolic. The first referent of the symbolic is the abstraction of the effect of the sexual difference in sexuation, phallic reality joining the S($\varnothing$) or barred Other:

$$\Phi \mid S(\varnothing)$$
$$\underset{\text{The Woman}}{\underline{\hspace{3cm}}}$$

The pleasure principle seeks real jouissance as a Freudian homeostasis, then, by filling its own lack(s) with incorporated objects and object traits that resemble one's already constituted Ideal ego formation.

Insofar as the mother's unconscious desire is inseparable from her being in the Other, her primordial *la lalangue* and her body catalyze the partial drives (oral, anal, invocatory, and scopic) to which an infant first responds. The mother is the first Other. She carries the objects that cause desire, and the demand to satisfy desire is directed toward her. Lacan portrayed the breast and feces as a first version of the subject's identification with the object (*a*), and the voice and gaze as a second one (Gilson, p. 137), even though the voice and gaze are primordial. These objects are organized in reference to the symbolic phallus, which is a complement of the real Other in sexuation. Thus, the phallic signifier, or the Father's Name that represents it, function to differentiate the outside world of language away from pure bodily jouissance of objects. In this sense, the phallic signifier will always refer to *that* in experience which is both oppositional to *and* related to the mother qua Woman.

In Lacan's logic, it is impossible for there to be an opposition not based on a prior relation. Morever, the traces of identificatory bonds remain as mental associations, however vague or opaque they may be. Indeed, that the Father's Name becomes the phallic or signifying equivalent of each subject's reality principle occurs only insofar as the "law" of the social prevails over the maternal real. Since the pleasure principle is concomitant with a primary feminine experience of the drives for both sexes, it later manifests itself in a subject's (contingent) *efforts* to attain pleasure through recuperating aspects of primary maternal jouissance: $\mid a \rightarrow S(\varnothing)$.

Not only is the "reality" (pleasure) relation attached to the lacks in a particular mother's signifying chain of unconscious *desire* (vis-à-vis her own experience of the phallus and castration), any infant's sexual or libidinal enjoyment is also delimited by the myriad "no"s that language itself imposes on the incestuous oneness of mother and child, alienating an infant from the "silence of the drives." The blockages between reality and pleasure also come from repetitions, as Freud discovered in *Beyond the Pleasure Principle* (1921). The *pathos* for humans unveils their paradoxical efforts to attain pleasure via repetitions that yield archaic, fixed signifiers, not the livingness of jouissance born ever anew. This is how Lacan explains Freud's theory that Eros turns around the Thanatos of knotted signifiers that unveil the unconscious significations from which subjects unaware take their conscious knowledge of how to lead their lives. Borromean signifying units are ossified at the crux of the symbolic and imaginary axes, where they form the Ideal ego construct that gives the grounding from which one lives as *if* his or her being were whole and reliable.[21]

Returning to Freud

In rereading "Some Psychical Consequences of the Anatomical Differences between the Sexes," Lacan linked language and the drives to Freud's view of psychoanalysis as "a clinical approach to sexuality in human beings as subjects of the unconscious" (Brousse, *NFF*, p. 119). More particularly, he aligned sexuality with a category of his own invention; the real. Indeed, a study of Lacan's and Freud's writings about sexuality culminates in Lacan's declaration in *Seminar XI* that the unconscious *is* sexuality and the real is the sexual—whose logic is that of psychoanalysis. Freud's ground-breaking essay of 1925 returned to some of the problems he had addressed in "Three Essays on the Theory of Sexuality" (1905) where he first wrote that the sexual life of men "alone has become accessible to research. That of women . . . is still veiled in an impenetrable obscurity" (*SE*, 7, p. 151).[22] He added in his pamphlet on lay analysis that the sexual life of adult women is a "dark continent" (*SE*, 20, p. 212).[23] Yet, his work on the Oedipus complex is more germane to contemporary gender studies than these essays insofar as his theories of identification gave Lacan a basis for rethinking not only analytic structures, but also how they are constructed.

Early on in *The Interpretation of Dreams* (1900) Freud gave his first full account of the Oedipus complex.[24] Assuming a heterosexual norm, Freud presented both sexes as later becoming libidinally attracted to the opposite-sex through first having loved the opposite sex parent: the girl her father and the boy, his mother (*SE*, 4, p. 257). This theme is repeated in his study of Dora (*Fragment of an Analysis of a Case of Hysteria*), where he sought to demonstrate that the problems of hysteria, feminine sexuality, and female psychology are different, although interlinked. Yet, he did not publish any decisive statement on women until fifteen years after he published the Dora study in 1905, a study he continually emended in added footnotes (*SE*, 7: 3–122).[25] Nonetheless, in 1916–1917 during the period of his first topic, he wrote in the *Introductory Lectures:* "As you see, I have only described the relation of a boy to his father and mother. Things happen in just the same way with little girls, with the necessary changes: An affectionate attachment to her father, a need to get rid of her mother as super-fluous" (*SE*, 16, p. 333).[26] He has thereby made an obsessional male of the little girl.

In his "Three Essays on Sexuality" (1905) Freud had tried to explain the development of infantile sexuality—a revolutionary concept at the time—by arguing a theory Melanie Klein later developed to its highest point in object-relations analysis: That the first sexual object of any child is the mother's breast, which serves as the prototype of every later love relation (*SE*, 7, p. 222). In this essay, Freud stated clearly for the first time that a little girl could not arrive at a "normal" resolution of the Oedipus complex—that is, to love a man—without changing her interest in her leading sexual organ (the clitoris) and her principal sexual object (the mother). He proposed nothing less than a reformulation of biology and ego.

Arguing that a twofold change had to occur for little girls to become psychically mature, little boys, on the other hand, did not have to change their interest in their principal sexual organ or in the principal sexual object. Thus, the boy's sexual resolution of the oedipal conflict would, at least, be easier than the little girl's. We know that Lacan does not follow Freud's view of male sexuality, anymore than he does Freud's work on feminine sexuality. Still, Freud's essay written in 1925 opened the way for his later development of what he described as the "pre-oedipal phase": This emphasized the mother as basic to the development of both sexes.

Although Lacan dispensed with the pre-oedipal phase in all of his teaching, given his stress on the shaping power of language, one could argue that he rethinks it in his various theories of the object and the object (*a*), and later in his topological theories. Not only does the infant experience the primordial mother's real body through imaginary frustrations occasioned by the Other's incursions that disrupt the pleasure of imaginary unity, the real organs themselves—the breast, the voice, the gaze, the feces— are first received as gifts of the symbolic order, according to Lacan in *Le séminaire IV* (1956–1957). Lacan developed his triadic interpretation of the mother as symbolic *agent* in relation to the real *object* and its imaginary *lack* as early as 1956.[27] Yet, it is the real father who introduces the signifier ("no") of symbolic castration that divides the child's dependence on the mother's desire and jouissance between the symbolic (Φ) and the real part of the (*a*). The infant experiences his or her mother as a semblant, dwelling between the symbolic and the real (*S. XX*, p. 90). However, in *Seminar IV*, Lacan presents the symbolic and the real mother as obscured by the omnipresence of imaginary confusions, illusions, and frustrations.

In *Seminar V*, Lacan is still far from developing the topological science of the real that marks *Seminar XX*. He speaks of elementary signifiers that make the word tremble before an encounter with lack in the drives (*S. V*, 1958 p. 478). Nor is this the Lacan of *Le séminaire, XXII R.S.I.* (1974–1975) who presents the Borromean knot as supporting both body and mind as the real sinthome which is poked full of holes by the symbolic which, in turn, incorporates the real part in the signifier that one must finally define as a hole in a word, or that which makes a hole (April 15, 1975).[28] The latter theory goes along with Lacan's idea that to name is an act: The *dire* (the saying)—not the *dit* (the said)—is an act that makes its own frame out of words and gaps punched in to seeming imaginary consistencies. The real is just beyond the imaginary/symbolic. It ex-sists by wedging individual Borromean knots,

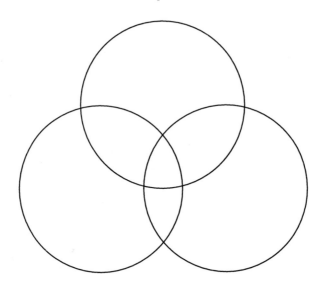

into corners of the three orders (March 18, 1975).

In "Some Psychical Consequences . . . ," prior to his proposal of a pre-oedipal phase, Freud too was preoccupied with asymmetries and even fragmentations, although they were not triadic or quattrocentric as are Lacan's. They are the familiar binary ones of simple oppositions. In his detailed development of the different relations of boys and girls to the castration and oedipal complexes, he proposed a further difference in the construction of their superegos. Revisiting Freud's major ideas, including Freud's view that males are more subject to superego guilt than females, Lacan gave a different explanation. Lacan's obsessional male for example, is preponderantly guilty because his mother preferred him to his father.

Even though Freud referred to feminine sexuality off and on after 1905, he was always dissatisfied with what he could say about this topic in the studies he published between 1915 and 1925, including the study of a female paranoiac in 1915, a female homosexual in 1920, and theories on feminine masochism and the infantile sexual development of girls that he advanced in his work on the fantasies of "a child is being beaten" in 1919 (*SE*, 17).[29]

Freud's increasing distinctions between the psychic development of the sexes appear first in "A Child Is Being Beaten" where he declared himself dissatisfied with his earlier precise analogy between the sexes, stating that "the expectation of there being a complete parallel was mistaken" (*SE*, 17, p. 196). Yet in a paper published in 1923 on the "phallic phase" of infantile genital organization, he still felt that "unfortunately we can describe this state of things only as it affects the male child; the corresponding processes in the little girl are not known to us" (*SE*, 19, p. 142).[30] Since Freud had begun to correct his view of how infantile genital organization is constructed in 1915, he redescribed a theory he put forth in 1935 as initially based erroneously on the paradigm of male children (*SE*, 20, p. 36).[31] He simultaneously began to advance new ideas on feminine sexuality in "The Ego and the Super-Ego (Ego Ideal)" (1923), in "The Dissolution of the Oedipus Complex" (1924) (*SE*, 19).[32] In "The Ego and the Super-Ego (Ego Ideal)," he compared the outcome of the little boy's Oedipus complex with that of the little girl's, making them symmetrical: "In a precisely analogous way, the outcome of the oedipal attitude in a little girl may be an intensification of her identification with her mother (or the setting up of such an identification for the first time)—a result which will fix the child's 'feminine character'" (p. 32). By 1925, he had abandoned this idea.

In "The Dissolution of the Oedipus Complex" (1924), Freud argued that the female child does not discover her genital organ when boys do, a theory Lacan and others before him have long since proved false. What does interest Lacan is Freud's theory that a female does not perceive herself as physically castrated, but assumes simply that she, like her mother and other females, has already lost an organ of equal size to the boy's at some earlier date. But not until the 1925 essay ("Some Psychical Consequences . . .") does Freud state clearly and for the first time what he later develops in his 1931 essay ("Female Sexuality"), in lecture 33 of *The New Introductory Lectures* (1932), and in his posthumous *Outline of Psycho-Analysis* [1938/1940]:[33] Not only are male and female sexual development asymmetrical, the Oedipus complex raises one more problem for girls than for boys (*SE*, 23, 141–207). Indeed, this 1938 essay contains a complete reevaluation of all Freud's previous views on the psychological development of women.

But the theories of infant sexuality Freud advanced here in 1938 as a paradigm for adult sexuality still did not offer a clue as to how women became women, sexually and psychically different from men. In 1915, Freud had added "the libido theory" to his 1905 "Three Essays on the Theory of Sexuality," where he had first suggested that because the principle female sexual organ is the clitoris, "the sexuality of little girls is of a wholly masculine character" and "a wave of repression at puberty" is required before the clitoris can give way to the vagina, thus ushering the little girl away from a sexual masculinity to the femininity of womanhood (*SE*, 7, 219–21). One might suggest that Freud's imaginary interpretations of feminine sexuality are equations of the vagina with the uterus, both romanticized in a masculine, essentialist logic of the whole or *all*. Here Woman is "birth"-giving and "life"-giving.

Lacan attributed such male myths regarding The Woman to a confusion between female sexuality and some presupposed innate essence of motherhood. But why would males mystify motherhood, or confuse the mother with an Essential Woman who is alternately goddess, savior, mother earth, or, in turn, whore, harridan, and a curse? Lacan's theory of a mirror-stage illusion of Oneness would suggest that the symbiotic paradigm of the mother/child dyad is the structural grounding of such myths. Moreover, this theory can be verified at the level of lived experience in terms of Lacan's later topological theories wherein a demand made to the Other for an oral object is a demand made to a "supposedly" essential mother capable of making her child or her partner whole and safe by love, advice, sex, and so on. We might turn this around and say that any demand made for love is an oral demand, asking for the jouissance of immediate gratification, rather than accepting the deferrals of desire.

Indeed, Lacan's topological "science of the real" proposes that the *dits*—the sense of *jouis-sens* as meaning ($-\phi$) beyond the *dire*—is the link to his four "modal places" in the discourse structures: The S_I (or master signifier) emanates from the real traits of identification that "ek-sist" as somewhat open and consistent (Stone, p. 52; Gilson, p. 214). These traits inhabit language and insert unary strokes from the real into assumed consistencies of the imaginary body and into symbolic narratives. Lacan's porous scaffolding of the psychic gestalt can only lead him to dispute Freud's myths of an Essential Woman. His axiom "The Woman does not exist" means that woman cannot be equated with an *essence* of wholeness, oneness, goodness, and so on. Man's belief that she does is his symptom (*S. XX*, pp. 80–81). In his "Seminar of 21 January 1975,"[34] Lacan argued that not only is woman man's symptom, she is his (fetishized) sexual symptom, thereby enabling him to ward off a direct contact with his unconscious ($\not S <> a$).

In the relation of feminine sexuality to the foundations of logic and language in males, Lacan proposed that something strange is at stake: The male fantasy of woman Freud unveils is woman equals mother.[35] In 1915 Freud saw the passage from girl to woman as a matter of preparing to receive males by experiencing vaginal sexual pleasure, believing that organ complementarity equaled sexual complimentarity and the psychological preparedness of women to be *harmonious* companions to men.

One could suggest that sexual and psychic oneness describe, rather, the dyadic structure of the mirror-stage infant's illusion that two are one. (Even in mathematics two is a fuzzy, irrational number.) Indeed, Freud's theory of sexual oneness was not so much a proof of oneness, as the construction of a developmental theory of psychic and sexual maturity. In this evolutionary paradigm, genital maturity was equated with vaginal orgasm for women and reciprocity and generosity of character for both sexes—a "genital" stage beyond oral greed and anal acquisitiveness. But beyond his ever-changing ideas regarding women, Freud's outrageous claim that the libido was phallic fueled the quarrels of the 1930s. Not until Lacan took up this thesis was Freud's claim taken seriously as having a logic—albeit a nonbiological one—at the level of the unconscious.

If we read Freud's two well-known essays on feminine sexuality in terms of Lacan's qualitative logic of three kinds of jouissance established via negations, we have the basis for recasting Freud's theory of the phallus. It is reinterpretable as an effect whose cause is the difference between the sexes. The way is then opened for a theory of *identification*—not with an organ or a standard of behavior, but—with the signifier of ideals (S_I) that build into an Ideal ego at the base of Lacan's graph of desire ("Subversion . . . ," p. 315).

In Lacan's sexuation graph,

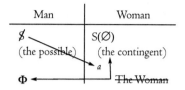

the phallic signifier (Φ) is concomitant with alienation (or castration) by language. (Earlier on, we linked this to the *possible* via the *necessary*). As one of two symbols or mathemes that joins the masculine, or symbolic side of the tables to the feminine side, it supports Lacan's logic(s) of the *possible* dream as masculine, and the *contingent* encounter in love as feminine. From the feminine side, an arrow points in two directions, to the positivized Φ and to the signifier for a radical incompleteness in the set of meanings that constitutes any ensemble of the Other (S[$\emptyset$]) (*S. XX, Encore*, p. 78). While, on the one hand, the Φ is the symbol for Freud's theory that there is only one libido for both sexes, a masculine one, Lacan clarifies the meaning of the masculine libido, beyond the male's genital orgasm. The phallus signifies the point of identification a person has with a place in the symbolic order; not only identification with the male sexual organ or male sexual pleasure. That it is *necessary* that at least one person—$\exists x \overline{\Phi x}$—not be castrated, that such a person exist, if only in myth, means simply that each subject may aspire to "order" in their lives by identification with others—over the chaos of the real created by the Ur-father—thereby gaining a place in the symbolic. The *necessary* element of castration gives rise to the social order via a masculine logic that leads to the *possible* insofar as it—$\forall x \Phi x$—requires turning away from the feminine as Other by accepting castration, that is, the rules of the group.

Lacan made the innovative point that *sexuation*—the subjective sexual identification a person takes on—is constructed not only in regards to sex, but first in reference to the signifier for sexual difference itself, taken as a signifier without a signified: Φ. Producing itself as a set of unary traits (S_1s [$S_2 S_3 S_4 S_5 S_6$]), a swarm of identifications with particular social Ideals—I (O)—the phallus takes on a symbolic "value" in the Ideal ego *unconscious* formation. It is equal to the knot or sinthome that sustains thought and body in three different psychic experiences of castration: The reality Φ, the structure of lack ($-\phi$), and the $\emptyset$, or the cut. And each castration produces a different relationship of the (Ideal) ego to meaning: (1) The phallic signifier (Φ) is *foreclosed* in psychosis, which subject requires that castration (or the experience of a lack-in-being) *not* cut into his or her Ideal ego; (2) The phallic signifier—index of sexual difference— is *fetishized* in the perversion typical of fantasy, wherein sexual jouissance sets the standard for social law; (3) The phallic difference is *denied* in neurosis, such that the neurotic tries to impose his or her Ideal (ego) narcissism on social law, thereby giving prevalence to the imaginary. The normative represses the difference and acts out whatever characterizes the sexual masquerade in his or her social order.

Lacan reads Freud's theory of castration, not as the fear of organ loss, but as a process of unconscious desire wherein identifications (S_1s $\rightarrow$ Ideal ego) construct any person's subjective sexual position as the outcome of his or her interpretation of sexual difference. In the feminine logic(s) of the *contingent* and the *impossible*, contingency accepts that the impossibilities of the sexual nonrapport may cease producing impasses long enough to allow for love. The *necessary* and *possible* masculine logics pretend that neither desire, fantasy, nor jouissance enter language and actions, except in some category of the already known that is codified in institutions (church, school, war) through polite formulae of agreed-upon knowledge and rituals of convention. Given that the phallus is a referent for each formula, repression, denial, repudiation, or foreclosure, of the modal logic(s)

$$\exists x\overline{\Phi x} \mid \overline{\exists x\Phi x}$$
$$\forall x\Phi x \mid \overline{\forall x\Phi x}$$

each of the various meanings is qualified by its relation to the existential quantifier ($\exists$) and the universal one ($\forall$). It follows that Lacan viewed the differential phallic signifier (Φ) as one of the base elements of human mentality. Along with it, he adds the subject of desire ($\$$); the master signifier made up of unary traits of identifications (S_1); the signifier for knowledge (S_2); and the excess of *jouissance* of the objects (a) that fill the concrete lack that is desire's inverse side:

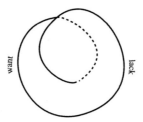

In bringing together desire and the phallic signifier as that which comes to the place where a signifier for self is lacking in the symbolic, Lacan shows the metaphorical properties of the phallus. It substitutes for the lure objects meant to satiate desire. It is, thus, in response to the "what do you want"—the *che vuoi*—that the lack of a signifier for the subject in the unconscious enters the symbolic order as the desire for a filler to lack: $\$ <> a$.[36]

One cannot say, then, as does James Mellard, that "desire" is just an early Lacanian concept, superseded by drive, jouissance, and the real (Mellard, p. 395).[37] The first eight objects that cause desire make it the desire of a desire for a return, desire being constituted only as a response to the loss of an object. What remains as a real nonspecular Ur-lining of the subject as desiring are the unary traits that glue themselves to each object-cause-of-desire: the breast, the feces, the voice, the gaze, the imaginary phallus, the urinary flow, the phoneme, and the nothing. Such traits return in the real, symbolic, and imaginary as reflections of the forms already given in the symbolic and imaginary orders. These forms appear as details, affect, enigmata, in the gap between the word and image, revealing castration or lack to be a foundational corner of the master discourse where the unconscious base lies in fantasy:

$$(S_1 \rightarrow S_2$$
$$\$ \leftarrow a)$$

The idea of the phallus, as a third symbolic effect caused by perceiving the sexual difference, makes sense of Freud's failures in "Some Psychical Consequences" to explain the asymmetrical psychological development of male and female sexuality by sexual organs. Freud wrote later in "Analysis Terminable and Interminable" that "at no point in one's analytic work does one suffer more from the oppressive feeling that all one's efforts have been in vain and from the suspicion that one is 'talking to the winds' than when one is trying to persuade a female patient to abandon her wish for a penis on the grounds of it being unrealizable, or to convince a male patient that a passive attitude towards another man does not always signify castration and that in many relations in life it is indispensable" (Freud, "Analysis Terminable and Interminable," 1937, p. 270).

Lacan's return to Freud via a complex logic of the phallus depicts female penis envy as the desire to be *identified* with an Ideal in the symbolic, while male castration anxiety concerns a double defense against the real of loss, anxiety, and trauma. Not only does the male stop up the void place at the center of being with the reality paradigms that represent a given phallic (symbolic) order, he also takes a partner (an object of desire) as a buffer against acknowledging unconscious lack. Male castration anxiety, is further denied by the closures into symbolic structures of masculine bonding one finds depicted in the upper left corner of the sexuation graph.

Although ideals are structured by the symbolic order of any given historical moment, they are realized in the imaginary others who appear as desirable figures because they embody certain ideal traits. Such "phallic" identifications—be they men or women—mean a positivization of phallic jouissance insofar as it is prescribed by the social Other's approving gaze. Within this context, male castration anxiety manifests two levels of identification: Identification with the primordial, real (maternal) Other as The Woman who *could* exist—within a *contingent* logic—to annihilate the void in the Other (S[Ø]), and identification with the secondary, symbolic (paternal) Other (Φ) who is "supposed to know." The male's fear of being a passive object at the mercy of other males reveals the symbolic as itself a defense, not only against his own agressivity, but also against a fear of separation from the mythical Woman who is assumed to protect males from encountering the void in the Other (Ø).

Freud emphasized the (sexual) competition he called oedipal rivalry, while Lacan stressed, rather, that male bonding in the symbolic is a structural necessity imposed on the little boy from having deferred to the person or signifier that represented the father for him as law/reality/"no." Adult men make the abstract leap to believing in a superior "father" who stands above and outside the law, thereby dictating its terms to them. Lacan's theory of sexuation brings together Freud's essays on the sexual difference and his enigmatic theories on male bonding from *Totem and Taboo* (1913),[38] along with Aristotle's efforts to define being.

Refuting the biological basis of Freud's idea of an active masculinity and a passive femininity, Lacan says not only did this idea not solve the problem of the sexual difference, it also failed to stress that neither tendency ever disappears from either sex. In other words, the "active" component in feminine sexuality that Freud associated with masculinity becomes, for Lacan, an imaginary feminine confusion among seeing, having, and being. Since Freud tried to solve the problem of sexual difference imaginarily, much as Immanuel Kant had tried to separate the beautiful from the sublime by arguments regarding visibility and magnitude, Freud portrayed the girl who lacks the penis as one who can be compensated by a baby—a bigger and better imaginary phallus. While Freud worked with geometry, quantifying by empirical, metrical measure, Lacan's realm of the visible is topological: The gaze of consciousness means seeing oneself being seen and, as such, equates dissimilar things in a link of metaphorical, metonymical substitutions; "having" a beautiful girl (car, etc.) is merged with one's desirability. The scopic drive aims to validate, even elevate, one's being via sublimation, by conflating the aim of the drive with its goal.

Although the problem Freud actually wanted to solve was what caused the sexual difference, his detours—such as seeing the wish for a baby as a substitute wish to compensate the girl for sexual or psychic passivity—led him to the impasse of making *feminine* sexuality equatable with motherhood. Urging his interlocutors to see passive and active tendencies as characteristic of both sexes, Lacan unveiled male castration anxiety as in and of itself an implicit admission that having the penis does not make one the desired object—the phallus—nor does it protect the male from the castrations implicit in his depending on the Other. Lacan portrayed the Freudian female as ending her analysis by wanting a positive ("active") identification in the symbolic, (S_1), while the male ends up defending against being separated from the maternal Other, and at the mercy of the paternal Other's desire (i.e., admitting his own "passive" lack [$\emptyset$]).

If, as Freud opined, female castration anxiety were to resolve itself in penis envy, one can only wonder why any other object would not serve as an adequate *substitute* for something supposedly lacking or lost. One could argue that *wanting* or *having* a baby may well be the signal for some women that they have attained a position in the symbolic order, for example through alliance with a Father's Name that gives the mother social status. The feminine drama concerns value (self-worth) and meaning, not organs, organ size, passive sexuality, or an innate maternal instinct.

Lacan arrived at his conclusions by carefully reading Freud in German. Strachey, Freud's major translator, indicates in an "Editor's Note" to the *Standard Edition* that Freud became strictly occupied with the issue of feminine sexuality, starting with his rethinking of the Oedipus complex in "The Ego and the Id" (1923) and "The Dissolution of the Oedipus Complex" (1924). Reading Freud in German (a language of expertise for Lacan), enabled him to stress how careful Freud had been in choosing his words. His 1925 essay begins: "In my own writings and in those of my followers more and more stress is laid on the necessity that the analyses of neurotics shall deal thoroughly with the remotest period of their childhood, the time of the early efflorescence of sexual life" (p. 248) ("*Die zeit der Früblüte des Sexuallebens*").

Although a *Früblüte* or "efflorescence" of a beginning moment cannot be recuperated as such in memory, having been transformed by condensation (metaphor) and displacement (metonymy)—and, thus, being unanalyzable as conscious memory—nontheless, a beginning moment gave rise to an endpoint which Freud named as analyzable—an analysand's sexual life. The route to understanding neurosis is to be found in these very earliest moments of sexual development. Lacan stressed that the language of the unconscious dwells in the marginality of the "language" and images of fantasy, desire, jouissance, and in the unary traits inscribed in the real. Thus, nothing can be known of primordial sexual experience except insofar as it is recounted in language, but not the conventional language of grammar or the familiarity of repeated narratives. Rather, the signifieds of *jouis-sens* run counter to the signifiers of narrative (cf. ch. I, S. V).

Lacan listened to the language of primordial murmurings (*la lalangue*), to the flights of meaning into wispy evaporations of "sense" surrounding the objects that cause desire, projecting traits of the real at the rims of holes poked into language. Although no person ever has words to describe those first experiences, one can subsequently reconnect individual threads of the drive to the desire emanating from non-specular objects that first created a dialectic between drive and desire, a dialectic out of which fantasy is built.

Freud left his readers in the impasses that have given rise to contemporary psychology and classical psychoanalysis which, in his wake, have focused increasingly on "behavior," whose causes are easily attributable to the biological organism as causative of its own effects. Yet, if one reads Freud in German, one immediately sees that Strachey's translation introduces distortions. He writes "the first manifestations of the patient's innate instinctual constitution," where Freud had written "the early efflorence of sexual life" (1925 essay, p. 248), "efflorence" meaning to bloom or to leave behind a "chemical" deposit from a process. Freud said one must look to this early *material* that has been remodeled and overlaid, leaving his followers with this contradiction: If neurosis is *caused* by early sexual experiences, how can these be "instinctually" innate? And insofar as associational memory is radically individual, how would one neurotic subject differ from any other? Moreover, if "innate instincts"—supposedly common to all—constitute the early "flowering" of a sexual life, why would feminine sexuality differ from masculine sexuality?

Long before Lacan gave *Seminar IX: L'identification* (1961–1962) where he began to develop the logic of the topological overlaps of forms that allowed him to elaborate a truth-functional category of paradoxes and impossibilities—the real—which registers certain effects of the "world" as contradictory, he had already begun to "translate" Freud's idea of complexes into primordial matrices of concrete images in *Family Complexes*.[39] And in the 1930s before he had conceptualized the object (*a*) in *Seminar VIII: Le Transfert* as a matheme representing an effect whose cause is invisible or absent, but whose effect is still present, Lacan had begun to reach for this conclusion. By arguing that "complexes" are not innate or biologically constituted, but are composed of images and words taken in from the outside world, he can say by *Seminar XX:* "I have never looked at a baby and had the sense that there was no outside world for him. It is plain to see that a baby looks at nothing else but that, that it excites him, and that is the case precisely to the extent that he does not yet speak. From the moment he begins to speak . . . I can understand that there is some repression. The process of the *Lust-Ich* [pleasure principle] which Lacan defines [as that which is satisfied by blah-blah] may be primary . . . but it is certainly not first" (p. 56). Alienation (behind language and images) is first, for without it pleasure cannot be imagined, conceptualized, or sought as a freedom from it.

Lacan explains where Freud took the wrong paths, the ones followed since by classical post-Freudians. But Lacan's post-Freudianism gives value to the structure of Freud's arguments by an inverse logic. Before the "pleasure principle" appears, for example, one encounters the "reality principle" of traumatic losses, which catalyzes the quest for pleasure via the search for repetitions of lost experiences. Lacan's theory is that the unconscious subject can *only* follow the predictable paths of its own structurations because they have already constituted a series of limits in finite ensembles of signifying material that surround the various objects (*a*) that cause desire. Given that the structure of limits is Borromean,

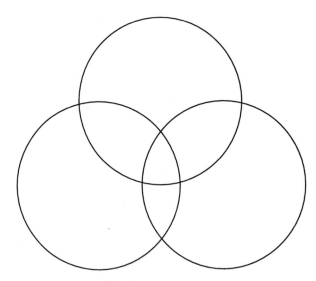

made up of intersecting parallels that give the topological dimensions of a surface, one sees Lacan moving from first symbolizing structure, then topologizing it.[40] Passing beyond imaginary schema that stratify the planes of the image, the surface prevailing there, he moves on to the graphs that inscribe symbolic space, and the picture that presents sites as real places.[41] One can see the difference between the "real" Lacan aims at with topology, and the imaginary nature, for example, of the Schema L.[42]

Lacan's point is that the content specific to the real, imaginary, and symbolic orders is secondary to the structures that are formative of a mind-body interlinking. Although Lacan adhered to Freud's idea that there are two orientations in neurosis— obsession and hysteria—he stressed that every neurosis is a case in the particular of a given set of associations of master signifiers that constitute the unconscious networks of language (S_I) and the jouissance(s)—(a)—that compose any person's fundamental fantasies around an ideal construct of "self." Thus, no theory of neurosis can be based on a universal model of biological or sociological development. Rather, the neuroses are constituted as modes of sexuation that *deny* that the sexual difference matters or produces an effect of trauma, while awaiting release from the impossible paradoxes denial creates. For Lacan, obsession, for example, is a male identification with knowledge that tries to diminish the power of the feminine in it by replacing the openness ($\forall x\Phi x$) in desire with closures of knowledge. Hysteria is a (generally) female identification with her father's lack-in-being that leads her to sacrifice her jouissance in an attempt to take on the burden of his castration, thus inverting her own Ideal ego with the ego ideals of others.

Strachey's translation of the "instinctual constitution" of the earliest experiences of a person's sexual life is Freud's use of *Triebkonstitution*. It is only by analyzing *what constitutes* the *Triebe*, or drives, that one can "accurately gauge the motive forces that have led to his neurosis," Freud writes. In *Freud and Man's Soul*, Bruno Bettleheim argued convincingly that Strachey's translation of *Trieb* as "instinct" has destroyed the meaning of a major concept in Freud's work: Freud rarely used the word *instinct*, and even then only in reference to animals, using the word *Instinkten* to mean "species-specific instinct."[43] When he used *Trieb*, on the other hand, there was always an implicit or explicit reference to a join between the human biological body and psychic forces. In other words, a native speaker of German will understand *Trieb* in a psychological sense.[44]

In Freud's German, the "motive forces" that lead to the neuroses—one of his concerns in this essay—are *Triebkräfte*. The English translation of *The Standard Edition* leaves out the word *Trieb* in "motive forces," which ought to mean the "motive force of drives." In both words—*Triebkonstitution* and *Triebkräfte*—Freud sought to explain the cause of neurosis in terms of some fate of the drive: Not as "innate instincts" or biological "motive forces" propelled on their own energy. Freud's German shows his attempts to understand the neuroses in relation to the earliest experiences of a person's sexual life as hinging on a question regarding the enigmatic nature of the drives. "This requirement," to examine the first manifestations and earliest experiences, "is not only of theoretical but also of practical importance," Freud stressed, *"for it distinguishes our efforts from the work of those physicians* whose interests are focused exclusively on therapeutic results." Having referred to the patient's "innate" drives (*mitgebrachten;* i.e., what one brings with one), Freud immediately, and paradoxically, sought to distance his work from that of physicians who look to behavioral changes as "therapeutic results" in proof of cure; not to causal factors ("Some Psychical Consequences of the Anatomical Distinction Between the Sexes," p. 248). Furthermore, even the word *mitgebrachten* does not mean biologically innate. The correct German word is, rather, *eingebornen*.

Apologizing for having had neither the time nor experience to give the proof of universal applicability, Freud says he still feels justified in publishing the findings he had evolved at this stage of his work in 1925. He recapitulates his ideas on the Oedipus complex in boys: In the first stage the little boy "cathects" the object of nursing—his mother—with his libido. Lacan will critique Freud's idea that a libido can *act* as an agent, while Bettleheim also criticizes this theory by questioning Strachey's translation of *besetzung*—which means to occupy a place, or to place something somewhere, or invest in something—as "cathect." The "investment" of jouissance creates the libido, Lacan argues, by the boy's attributing to his mother the identifying unary traits of jouissance Lacan called master signifiers of enjoyment (S_1). Freud names the agent that "cathects" (or invests in) the mother, the libido.

Once one uses *besetzung*, rather than "cathect," the problematic of how matter constitutes mind presents itself. Object-relations theorists have spoken of projection, introjection, and incorporation as operations or laws that wield an active unconscious fantasy system, sometimes supposing such a system to be innate or a priori, rather than constructed from the outside.

To counteract Freud's biological theory of instinct as causative of behavior, Lacan developed the imaginary order, derived from the premirror- and mirror-stage relations between mother and child, to explain how one becomes "informed" by the societal conventions of the symbolic order. Infants take in the data of the Other/other by incorporating traces of the first objects they desire, but come to know only in losing them. The hole punched into their perception by loss(es),

might be equated with the torus, of the null or empty set [ ] (*S. IX, Identification*, 1961–1962, March 14, 1962, unpublished seminar); "Torus is reason, since it is what allows for knots" Lacan says in *Seminar XX* (p. 123). That an infant desires—and acts—in order to replace a lost object answers the question of how the libido is linked to meaning by desire.

This is not disconnected from the problem posed by Freud in his 1925 essay on the anatomical distinction between the sexes: What constitutes the drives and what motivates them? The question he could not answer was how the libido can equal itself as both agent and object. His multiple answers were finally resolved in "The Ego and the Id" (1927),[45] where he depicted the erotic libido as transforming itself into ego by desexualizing the id and sublimating its libido in order to master sexual tensions (p. 46). But he still has not answered how the "derivatives of Eros" become the libido that Lacan parceled into three forms—$\Phi;-\phi;\varnothing$—all surrounding the object (a) that causes desire and that one, in turn, seeks to recuperate in all life's acts, rituals, and repetitions.

Lacan asked, what is the libido and what has it to do with the drives? In *Seminar XI* he described the libido as a *lamelle*—a thin flat scale or part as one of the thin plates composing the gills of a bivalve mollusk or of a mushroom—and the drive as a montage made of signifiers and partial objects in the three orders (p. 169). This is closer to the amalgam of identifications that allows one to "think" via "being . . . presumed in certain words . . . that constitute form [as] the knowledge of being" (*S. XX*, pp. 118–19), than to Freud's unified (genital) sex drive, taken as the momentary triumph of id over ego and superego. Freud's notion simply does not explain how drive becomes desublimated or unrepressed, despite his spurious references to love, survival of the species, inverted sex acts, and so on. And although Freud talks about refinding the object, it is as a substitute person, not an elaborated, albeit a refracted form, of the primordial Ur-lining of the subject, the lining first laid down as the infant's corporal/ mental relation to eight "essential" objects that link his or her body to forms in the world.

Because language covers over the real, it automatically defers the signifier of sexual difference away from presence into an alienation or distance from these primordial libidinal objects (a)—first linked to the mother—placing difference on the masculine side of the symbolic and proximity or distance to or from sexuality in the real of the feminine side. Thus, the autoeroticism of the sexual real would be found on the feminine side of sexuation, there where there is greater proximity to the primordial object (a), as well as to the open, void place of trauma, anxiety, and sexual excitement: ($\varnothing$). The void or null set comes into being along with alienation into language. We remember that it is created by the initial losses of the primordial object(s)-cause-of-desire in the moments of the cut, desire giving rise to the drive to reinstate the causal object. In the second period of his teaching, Lacan described the drive as a *montage*, equating it with a demand made in language ($\$ <> \text{Demand}$) to fulfill desire, thereby attenuating effects of the void—$\varnothing \rightarrow \$ <> a \rightarrow \$ <> D$—with the stabilizations offered by the symbolic order and the possibilities of fulfilling fantasy, sexual or otherwise.

Increasingly, between *Seminar XI* (1964) and those following, until *Seminar XX-VII* (1981), Lacan's gradual development of the topology of the three jouissance(s)— $\Phi; -\phi; \varnothing$—poses the question of whether or not libido is a drive. The drives produce sublimated libido, which is known as such only once it has been lost. But, it is not desexualized. Thus, libido is neither agent nor subject, but rather, an affective "substance," which is a veiled reminiscence of the effects of meaning one seeks to recreate by (re)finding it—the object *a*—in the constellations of the world. In this sense jouissance is an oscillation between the alienating language (Φ) and images ($-\phi$) with which one identifies to fill the void ($\emptyset$), itself experienced as a "beyond" (in) meaning. Miller writes the drive as the conjunction between primary identificatory unary traits (S_I) and the "being" of the (a) that coalesce into the Ideal ego formation that demands the drive-object(s) that will fill the gap in the other of the *che vuoi?* of desire.[46] Thus, one can say that the three jouissance(s) "structure" the three orders (R.S.I.) around the (a) as three topological knots one may call,

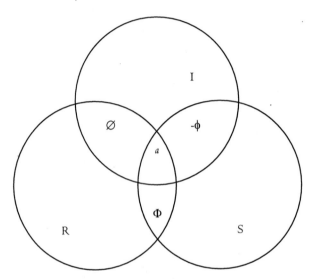

conventions (Φ), gaps between image and word ($-\phi$), and the pressure of the cut ($\emptyset$), circling around the (a) at the center of each unit of meaning.

From these perspectives, one cannot accurately describe Freud's libido as an autonomous volitional agent of drive, mysteriously animated to move toward something or someone one unknowingly wants to possess, or vice versa. Rather, one might say that the drive *aims* to mime the conditions of fantasy by making a rapport between what the subject lacks and the jouissance that will hopefully reify the ideal filler for that lack. [47] Thus, the drive concerns representational and libidinal meaning, not instinct. It is drawn by an unconscious recognition of the traits to be recuperated in the quest for something lost that *seems* to reside in the object desired.

Lacan's concept of the Freudian libido is clarified by Miller's *First Course* (1981–22) where castration is described as "the separation of jouissance and the body" by the alienating effect of the symbolic (p. 4). In all psychoanalysis, Miller continues, when Lacan found a discontinuity, a structural cut, or an erogenous zone attached to a partial object (breast, feces, and so on), he found a separation of the body from jouissance (p. 7). One might suggest that the relation of an hysteric to the ego ideal other she makes into her Ideal ego (or master signifier) is experienced by her in the real. Answering a question whose fence she straddles in fantasy—Am I a woman or a man?—its symbolic forms reflect her to herself in the social gaze as desirable (or not).

In the first stage of the Freudian Oedipus complex, the little boy wants to possess his mother to repeat the experiences of a corporal jouissance of imaginary oneness. Not surprisingly, "he regards his father as a disturbing rival and would like to get rid of him and take his place" (Freud, "Some Psychic Consequences . . . ," p. 249). Referring to other essays where he had explained the Oedipus complex as belonging to the phallic phase—that is, to the male fear of literal castration, inseparable from his narcissistic interest in his genitals—Freud, in 1925, portrays the male Oedipus complex as more complicated than the fear of organ loss, one proof being its bisexual constitution, which he calls a double orientation, active and passive. Boys not only identify with the father's desire for the mother, but also want to take the *mother's* place as the love object of the father (the feminine attitude) (p. 250).

In "the Ego and the Id" (1923), the "triangular character of the Oedipus situation" and "the constitutional bisexuality of each individual" took on a completely different meaning than in Freud's later work (*SE*, 9, p. 31). When discussing the prehistory of the Oedipus complex in boys in 1925, Freud admits to his own lack of clarity. But in 1923, he spoke of the affectionate identification of the boy with his father prior to any rivalry in regards to his mother: However, as his sexual wishes toward his mother become more intense, his father ever more perceived as a rival, the Oedipus complex originates ("The Ego and the Id," p. 32). Still, Freud questions whether the masturbatory activity of this period is *caused* by the Oedipus complex, thereby discharging the excitation attached to the complex, or whether it emanates spontaneously from the organ qua organ and only becomes attached to the complex at a later date. In any case, Freud supposed in 1923 that the *suppression* (*Unterdrückung*) of masturbation by social threats caused the onset of the castration complex. Although Strachey translated *Unterdrückung*, meaning that *something* is pressed back or pressed under, as "suppression," it is not masturbation that is suppressed but, rather, the concrete details of the prohibition that are "pressed under" as unconscious memories.

Lacan's solution to Freud's perplexity regarding the active and passive orientation found in male castration anxiety and in female "penis envy," is addressed in his sexuation graph. On the top line, he situates the asymmetrical consequences of male and female identification with castration or "no." In one sense, castration means submission to the Other's law. While the male identifies with the law of the group, attributing supreme law to an uncastrated Ur-father ($\exists x \, \overline{\Phi x}$), the female need not bow to an Ur-father. She already bears the mark of difference from men (or sameness with the mother that) Lacan calls castration: ($\overline{\exists x} \, \overline{\Phi x}$). This suggests that men submit to a leader, while women simply submit. But in a paradoxical, double negative, Lacan says on the bottom right line that all women are not all castrated ($\overline{\forall x} \, \Phi x$); each one finds a place beyond phallic law(s), as well as being anchored by it.

Given that these different positions toward the phallic law of sexual difference are epistemological interpretations of castration, not biological or anatomical ones, they produce different solutions in love. Lacan placed the lack-in-being ($\cancel{S}$) on the masculine side of the graph, under the sexuation tables. First created in the reference to the potential lack of an organ, imaginary castration ($-\phi$) is bolstered by a positive identification with the master signifiers (S_1 ; Φ) of prestigious ideals located in the Other. Later, a man may love a woman sexually insofar as she incarnates the sexual desiderata of his Ideal, thereby fulfilling his fantasies, although he may seek a marital alliance at the point where the woman's Father's Name signifier elevates him in the social group.

Reciprocally, a woman will make herself a man's object of desire insofar as his name (or knowledge) elevates her phallic position in the symbolic. But woman's experience of castration—being identified with the unquantiability of a logic of the same ($\overline{\exists x \Phi x}$)—places the demand for love prior to her demand for sex. Insofar as love is a mirror-stage construct, it gives a grounding in the real—fills the lack—prior to (the oedipal third-term) symbolic-order recognition of place. This puts woman at a loss in the universal where she encounters the void in the Other (S[∅]), rather than the male group gaze of a simulated oneness: $\forall x \Phi x$. Whereas the man's demand for a worthy Father's Name is linked to symbolic-order social prestige, the woman's primary demand is for protection from encounters with the real void of loss: S(∅). Both males and females inscribe themselves in the phallic function of the symbolic, identifying with particular master signifiers (S_1) by which they endure the lack of one signifier for a sexual rapport that would unite the sexes in a Oneness of jouissance pregiven in the Other. Both suffer from this lack, represented by the bar dividing man from woman, the masculine from the feminine.

In 1925, Freud attributed the castration complex only to boys: A literal fear of organ loss made them passive. But since such a fear was not strong enough to stop them from masturbating, Freud sought to understand what would cause an excitation greater than fear. Bed-wetting was one response to the suppression of masturbation. Such inventions, Lacan says, are mythical interpretations of child sexual excitement. But "myth," in Lacan's terms, does not mean untrue: "Myth gives epic form to that which arises from structure,"[48] structure finally being for him, in *Seminar XX*, an equivalent of the Borromean knot. In Lacan's reading of Freud, the Oedipus myth is not a tragedy, then, but an outcome of the varying fates of desire. The son can enjoy his mother if he "murders" his father. Laios must be disposed of in order for Oedipus to enjoy (*S. XVII*, p. 139). The Lacanian logic is this: Myth aims at the real, at a point beyond imaginary oedipal identifications. While any symbolic signifier can function to represent a "real father" who serves as the agent of castration; as the one who introduces the signifier "no" that causes desire, the result is not obedience to this real father. Rather, fantasy dominates the entire reality of desire as a desire to exceed law (*S. XVII*, p. 149). In this sense, myth articulates something of an impossible enunciation beyond the law (*S. XVII*, pp. 143–45). One goes from the *impossible*—that which does not stop not writing itself—of myth, Lacan argues, to the multileveled interactions of structure he defines in *Seminar XX* as a strict equivalence of topology with the Borromean knot (p. 2).

Sexual excitement is caused by the primal scene, Freud wrote. At an early age a child hears its parents copulating and this causes the first sexual excitation. Freud thus stressed an event, not a structural function: "Analysis shows us in a shadowy way . . . how that event may, owing to its after-effects, act as a starting point for the child's whole sexual development. Masturbation, as well as the two attitudes in the Oedipus complex [castration anxiety and penis envy] later on become attached to this early experience, the child having subsequently interpreted its meaning" ("Some Psychic Consequences," p. 250).

From a Lacanian perspective, the primal scene could be any memory the child attaches to the excitement aroused in him or her. It could be a thunder storm or a wild wind. The point is that it will not correspond to actual knowledge of a sexual scene. Lacan finds it striking what Freud leaves out here. The real father—interdictor of incest—is the castrator, and, as such, is attached to myths in the guise of gods, spirits, totems, demons, and so on (*S. XVII*, p. 145). Lacan recasts Freud to say that we dream of libidinal objects because the particular ones we have lost have already been sexualized as objects we desire and are, thus, under the mark of interdiction. What we obtain in desire is pleasurable because it has been forbidden to us (*S. XI*, pp. 154–55). Likewise, we desire it because we have been deprived of it.

Subsequently the child *interprets* its meaning (the meaning of the primal scene), which Freud describes with the German *Eindruck an*, meaning to "press upon." If one contextualizes Freud's biological scenario by considering the German word in a Lacanian topological sense, something is placed upon something else to create a third thing in the interval of an overlapping space. One might wonder *what* is pressed upon *what* in the interstices of the child's interpretation. In the Borromean chain of real, symbolic and imaginary categories, one might answer that real master signifiers or unary traits point to lost "objects" that first linked desire to libido, which is pressed under symbolic and imaginary associations into the radically repressed real. Desirous rememorations begin to structure fantasy in reference to the real of excitement that anticipates potential recuperation of lost jouissance.

These three orders intersect and interact in an endless signifying chain of the associational *dits* of unconscious memory,

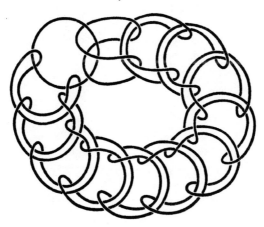

that most Western thought collapses into the whole agency one calls "mind." The idea of a static mind agency, or even the image of "mind" as brain "hardwiring" that obeys certain "rules of language" belie its dynamic, interactional, after-the-fact qualities. The "mind's" various modes follow the libidinal logic(s) of transformation whose structures are those of desire, fantasy, drive, and symptom, not those of generative grammar.

Freud was too careful a thinker to make a universal out of his concept of the primal scene; thus, it acquires the force of a myth in his work. Since this literal copulatory scene cannot be said to produce universal trauma, he evoked, instead, "primal phantasies." But Freud could not say in 1923 what caused "primal phantasies," any more than he could determine whether the Oedipus complex invariably follows the same course, or whether a variety of preliminary stages converge upon the same terminal situation in the case of the male ("The Ego . . . ," 1923, p. 22). In 1925, when Freud turned to the Oedipus complex in girls, having implied that things are not as simple for males as he had claimed in earlier declarations, he wrote: "In little girls the Oedipus complex raises one problem more than in boys. In both cases the mother is the original object; and there is no cause for surprise that boys retain that object in the Oedipus complex. But how does it happen that girls abandon it and instead take their father as an object? In pursuing this question I have been able to reach some conclusions which may throw light precisely on the prehistory of the Oedipus relation in girls" ("Some Psychic Consequences," p. 251).

But instead of throwing further light on the *prehistory* of the maternal oedipal relation in girls, he turns to a discussion of the girl's relationship to her father. His comments do not center on all girls, moreover, but only on certain kinds of women that psychoanalysts see: The ones who identify primarily with their fathers. This is in precise contradiction to Freud's discussion of male oedipal issues where he starts with a generalized concept of males and ends up referring to "a great variety of different preliminary stages."

Little girls want to have a child with their father, Freud says describing this wishful fantasy as the probable "motive force" or power (*Triebkräft*) behind female infantile masturbation. But beyond this fiction—this biological myth—Freud finds that the Oedipus complex has a "long" *prehistory* in girls prior to being recorded in the language of fantasy. He implies a structure that is described in Lacanian terms as the two-and-one-half-year "developmental" period in which a response to the object (a) establishes a basic grammar of the drives. This occurs in terms of the jouissance(s) desire seeks via sublimation of the (a) that produces the fantasy ($\emptyset <> a$) of its own return.

If one reads the references Freud makes to the theories of sucking, excretion, and so on, given by an old pediatrician, Lindner, as having the logic of the drives, then, Freud saw the phantasy as a secondary formation, the primary one being the "language" (*Lacan's la lalangue*) of *jouissance*, if one reads the references he make to the theories of sucking, excretion, and so on, given by an old pediatrician, Lindner, as having the logic of the drives. In his "Three Essays on the Theory of Sexuality" (1905), Freud linked masturbation to a *discovery* of the genital zones as sources of pleasure, a discovery that arises concomitantly with thumb sucking, said to displace the sensual pleasure of nursing. Suggesting that later fantasies of fellatio support this notion, Freud, nonetheless, leaves the cause of fantasy an open question. Since he found no "scientific" support for attributing any particular psychical content to the first genital activities, Freud focused, rather, on the first step in the phallic phase as causative of fantasy.

Lacan retained Freud's use of the *phallischen phase* to describe the relation of genital sexuality to oedipal identifications, thus keeping the notion of the phallic (genital) in connection with the libido; one libido for both sexes. But once he transformed the meaning of the phallic symbol to a positivized phallic signifier (Φ), not referring to a biological organ, several realities arose: the real of jouissance, a symbolic "no" to totalized jouissance, an imaginary separability of body parts. Equating Freud's concept of the phallic phase with a structure—a series that makes order, however minimal— not with a period of time, or a biological developmental reality, Lacan argued that an infant identifies step by step with the imaginary world of images, the symbolic order of differential distinctions, and the real effects of images and words on the flesh we call "the body," which Lacan describes as the remainder of the object (a) (*S. XX*, p. 6):[49]

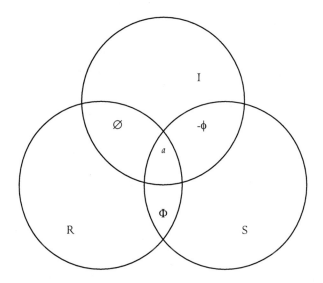

Lacan argued, then, that Freud did not locate ideal reality only in the sensuality of organ pleasure (i.e., nursing), but also in identification with a "father" signifier who could confer on one's being a guarantee of knowledge and worth. Freud's readers who reduce his theories on neurosis to biological dysfunctions miss what Lacan stressed; Freud's clinical discovery that *certain* kinds of women have an idealized attachment to their fathers, not their mothers, while certain boys do not want to relinquish identification with their mothers. Such attachments suggest that one cause of the dual nature of the pleasure principle's oscillation between joy and suffering (reality) is a real split in gender identifications (which is not a binary oscillation).

Since, in Lacan's context, an unconscious subject of desire is constituted by identifications whose principle referent for both sexes is the phallic signifier, one can say that this signifier gives rise to the symbolic-order reality principle, defined as the distance an infant takes from the corporal real of its mother. The Father's Name signifier need not be the "imaginary daddy" of contemporary conceptualization, then. It can also be a signifier such as "the outsider," or a river god, rather than the actual progenitor, or even the mother's brother. The point is that this signifier represents the symbolic order as the *effect* of difference. Both sexual difference (Φ) and distance from the drives ($\mathcal{S}$) make the social order possible.

Lacan's sexuation graph symbolizes the effect of gender differentiation by the bar drawn between the symbolic and the real. Among its other meanings, the phallic symbol (Φ) denotes the jouissance derived from real unary identificatory traits (S_1). These determine that the reality principle for a person or a group be what they "already" think. This justifies Lacan's description of the reality principle as the corporified signifier of language or thought. When the symbolic signifier is opposed to the matheme for the real—S ($\varnothing$)—it governs perception of reality as a semblance. That is, the symbolic covers over the real, rewriting the oedipal terms of the Father's Name over the mother's body.[50]

From another angle, the $\varnothing$ governs perception because it reveals that the symbolic order is not complete within itself, that a void place *in* the reality of language perforates oneness(es) and unities. Thus, Lacan's interpretation of Freud's "phallic phase" places the symbolic significations of difference from the mother over the imaginary collusions of oneness that infants of both sex experience. Yet, the real of the mother's body is separable from the imaginary or symbolic. Her body is experienced as a set of partial objects that give rise to the desire for jouissance. Her body is, thus, received paradoxically. This dual encounter with union and disjunction creates the infant's desire for (re)union with the One that will defer the fragmented realities introduced into the imaginary by the real. We might read the "one" here as the phallus that "unites" the subject in language fictions. Indeed, this is the formula—–FN/MD · MD/? → FN(Other)/(phallus)—by which Lacan first reconfigured the oedipal complex as a paternal metaphor (cf. Ragland, *EPD*, ch. 6).[51]

In a later phase of his teaching, Lacan transformed the identification with a particular phallic signifier in infancy to a broadening of identification with others (ego ideals) and finally with the *sinthome*, which he defined as the sublimation of an elaborate system of thought and beliefs built up around the Father's Name(s) one takes as a guarantee of knowledge. The *sinthome* knots the orders together in a kind of "complete writing" where imaginary fantasy and symbolic (desire) are both articulated with the real. Insofar as the knot gives the truth of the *sinthome*, the social symptom can be isolated in what Freud identified as the ideal leader in "Group Psychology, and the Analysis of the Ego" (1921).[52] Freud's hierarchy of identification goes from the base primitive disorganization of the ego by lack($\cancel{S}$) that produces the real of fragmentation (hysteria), to a group collectivity of shared beliefs and ideals—ego<—>ego<—> ego—to identification of the group with a leader thought to embody their ideals: Σ/Φ. Lacan called any leader a symptom of the group's desire to find closure and certainty in substituting an imaginary ideal father as an oedipal figure, a concrete image of the abstract Ur-father who is the, exception to the law of castration ("Group Psychology," p. 105).

At this point, let us summarize several steps in Lacan's rereading of Freud's 1925 essay. In trying to ascertain what *causes* the pleasure principle ($\cancel{S} \diamond a$), and how it differs from a reality principle:

$$\left(\Phi \leftarrow \begin{array}{|c} S(\cancel{\emptyset}) \\ \uparrow \end{array} \right)$$

Lacan redefined the fantasy as that which is not reducible to its imaginary version. This is so because the Other *is* castrated and does not want to know anything about it. In the fundamental fantasy, the subject externalizes him or herself as a real object of the Other; not of the other. Thus, Lacan did not equate fantasy with subjective thought, but showed how fantasy—like dreams—enters the subjectivity of conscious thought as a veil over the real of castration. It is not just that fantasy subsumes the partial drives— an object-relations theory—but that the form and material of fantasy show desire as parental desire that precedes and libidinalizes the infant's desire as the Other's desire:

$$\Phi \leftarrow \begin{array}{|c} S(\cancel{\emptyset}) \\ \uparrow \end{array}$$

The part-object quality of fantasy also veils the creation of an aggressive fragmented body in the time of mirror-stage identifications. Later, the child places imaginary masks—semblances—over the inadequacy of parental desire to fill the holes.

To say that an object is lost and leaves behind residual traits of its pleasurable (or traumatic) effects as the basis of thought and "behavior" does not solve the problem of how this happens. Miller implies that jouissance itself is strong enough to bind an S to other S_1s in the real of primary identifications. We remember, then, Lacan's three kinds of jouissance: the phallic symbolic one (Φ), the imaginary one ($-\phi$), and the real ($\emptyset$). The symbolic word is itself an act, Lacan claimed. The *dire* (saying) produces traces of what was said (the *dits*)that make up one's unconscious knowledge of what one will later be driven to desire. Yet neither language nor objects-of-desire can become unconscious thought until alienation and separation have transformed them into a "language of desire" spoken in reference to primary partial objects that cause desire and, secondarily, to oedipal identifications.

Lacan claimed that the libido is a "substance" of constructed meanings, a montage of the primary and secondary effects of identification with concrete things, mixing meaning, sense data, affects, and so on. Libido is a montage of itself, in other words. The question of how matter becomes mind concerns desire as it engages jouissance. As linguist Charles Pyle has pointed out, Lacan's theory differs from conventional theories of language that cannot explain markedness (or inscription) phenomena—how the real is made—much less their transformation into dreams or poetry. Theories of historical sameness (language evolution) or historical contact (borrowing) have tried, but failed. Even though markedness phenomena, as explained by Charles S. Peirce, according to Pyle, are relations between *opposites*, they are, nonetheless, related asymmetrically. The Buddhist theory of language-effects also tries to solve the problem of markedness, built up by their triadic structures similar to Peirce's icon, index, and symbol. Pyle says Peirce argues that the present is first and the second, past. While the first is not marked, a mark would be a sign of the second.[53] That the first must be marked to "count" is a paradox not explained by Peirce or Buddhist theories of language. Lacan explains the mark as a residual remnant of the real of the lost object, the loss causing the desire for its return. And he wrote this effect alternately as $S_1S_2S_3S_4$ (*dires*)/$S_1S_2S_3S_4$ (*dits*), or in an equivalence of *being* (*a*) and thinking $(S_1 \rightarrow S_2)$ as $a_1\ a_2\ a_3\ a_4$.

If one reads this problem backward, from the Borromean structure, wherein the final ordering of structure is real, symbolic, and imaginary, one can say that the first union with the object produces a shedding of unary traits that inscribe a marked real-order effect that resurfaces in the symbolic as reminiscence that responds to desire or drive. The loss binds a trace $(S_1)$of the object to empty space, thus beginning to form the holed rims described in Lacan's topology of the surface of body and thought. Lacan's trait is inscribed in a paradox, unlike Peirce's pat index of secondness. Rather, the mark denotes an affective trauma or cut whose components reflect the *real* of (dis)continuity Freud called conflict. Lacan's early distinction between identifying with *having* the phallus or *being* it turns into identifications with the knot that supports one as being what one thinks one is.

Such identifications demonstrate the asymmetrical character of desire as a dialectic between separation loss—

—and alienation—

—logical operations whose negotiable terms are the real of the object (*a*) and the S_1 (Miller, "*Le sinthome* . . ."). When the real returns to the same place, its material content in language is either that of unary trait(s), or the *semblant* of a lost object. At the base of this series, one finds desire as a paradoxical primary and secondary cause precisely because the object-*cause*-of-desire is lost, such that inside and outside are contiguous in a torus of doubleness without edges:

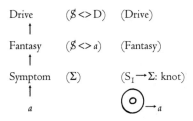

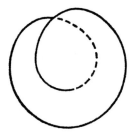

Desire is a primary and secondary cause because the torus is formed by the simultaneous interplay of having and losing (*Fort! Da!*) that Jeanne Lafont defines as a first knot or twist in the Moebius structure (8) whose hole is surrounded by the edge of a surface. But the (a) is not identical to itself, thus, it is known only in terms of its effects. Alienated effects (S_I) are left over as sublimated drive residue after a lost object sheds its binding traits. In turn, the effects are inscribed by real in-corp-oration and made functional via imaginary projection (transference) and symbolic introjection (or the associative linkages we call memory or thought).

In Lacan, when there is a question of structure, the Borromean knot or unit serves as a referent, a knot being a torus (($\circ$)); that is, a form without an edge is plunged into a torus of superior dimensions, such as:

Thus, an infant's pre-"oedipal" identification with a primordial maternal real will include the three Lacanian orders: the fleshly real is in-*corp*-orated in a proximity of enjoyment and trauma that include the unary traits of the *sinthome* as a kind of ego-envelope around a fantasmatic body. This body is, in turn, projected or anticipated both in the imaginary visual field and in reference to the symbolic signifier, which is introjected as a diacritical or differential element linked to another signifier. Insofar as the father's "no" is the referent for the dialectical development of the signifier, the incest taboo is the reality principle of differentiation. One identifies away from the object (a). The residual traits place a libidinal "substance" (marks of primary jouissance) in the unconscious as "fattened" knots of combined imaginary and real "sense."

This leads Lacan to say, "There is no other definition of the signifier than the hole" (*R.S.I., S XXII*, p. 127). That is, "sense effects" are the constructed signifieds or chimera of the imaginary and symbolic which create, while the holes in the real are impasses of the unrepresentable. With this theory, the signifier/signified binary is definitively undone (*R.S.I.,* p. 127). The real enters thought on the slope of the imaginary body, which is held in place by knots of images, later named by language. In *R.* [real] *S.* [symbolic] *I.* [imaginary], such an imaginary consistency comes third in mental development (p. 128), its mathematical structure being that of Frege's $0(1+n)$. The paternal law of "no"—$\exists x \overline{\Phi x}$—links the maternal objects to castration via the object (*a*) that translates the real and "ek-sists" in the symbolic. This transgression at the heart of any signification places a paradox in the center of prerational being: Law will always contain its own opposite. The truth it hides is that jouissance—as an absolute—will always subvert it. Thus, Lacan departs from Freud's view of feminine sexuality as a secondary formation, placing the feminine real as an a priori shadow or myth on which the masculine depends: $\cancel{S} \not\vdash a$.

In trying to figure out how the mind and body can be mutually supporting or intertwined logical structures, Freud never got beyond a reduction of "complexes" to organ realities. From Freud's many interpretations, Lacan deduced several levels of castration negation(s) that make asymmetrical logic(s) of male and female thought ($\exists x \overline{\Phi x}; \overline{\exists x \Phi x}$) whose epistemologies place the masculine or feminine in different relations to the Other. The masculine identifies with a complete Other, while the feminine identifies with an incomplete Øther. An hysteric—a girl who identifies chiefly with her father—may take a masculine or feminine position in sexuality (lover [$\cancel{S}$] or beloved [*a*]), but she will identify her *being* largely with the two feminine logics of the *impossible* and the *contingent*. Split in identification between mother and father, she holds the *contingent* knowledge that The Woman does not exist, while hanging on to the impossibility of her father's castration.

These identifications distinguish the hysteric from the normative woman who believes the Other is whole—that is, that The Woman exists. Such belief, paradoxically, means that most women accept the reality views of their local community, based as it is on the masculine sexual logic: There is a superior knower who gives the laws that others follow (via castration): $\exists x \overline{\Phi x} / \forall x \Phi x$. She has accepted the sexual difference Lacan called castration. She chooses phallic postures, deployed in deference to the Other, whether a male or female is in authority. Unlike her "normative" sister, the hysteric sees the father's lack and hides his castration in an effort to save, at least, the appearance of his "masculine" potency. While the hysteric's desire ($\cancel{S}$) seems to be the wish to make the Other complete, she sees the Other as incomplete ($\varnothing$). Thus, she places the gap or lack in the place of the agent of discourse: $\cancel{S} \rightarrow S_I$. We remember that the discourse places are: agent · other/truth · production (cf. *S. XX*, pp. 16–17 and *S. XVII*, p. 106). The hysteric knows what the Other lacks. The (normative) woman in the masquerade identifies with the Other from the S_I in the place of the agent of speech, who equates knowledge (S_2) with what the other knows. Thus, she speaks a master discourse of the *all* whose adherence to the *necessary* merely allows for the *possible* as a margin of potential divergence from the rules.

While critics of the 1930s and 1940s responded moralistically to Freud's observations about the psychology of masculine and feminine sexuality, reducing

Freud's deductions to imaginary views of good or bad, right or wrong, Lacan's interpretation of Freud's varying theories of the masculine and feminine marked a turning point described by Miller as ushering in Lacan's third period of teaching. In the chapters "God and the Jouissance of ~~The~~ Woman" and "A Love Letter" in *Seminar XX*, Lacan retained Freud's radical insight: Sexual difference is not innate, but a symbolic-order response to the injunction to break the bonds of mirror-stage symbiosis. By refining the *structure* of Freud's argument, Lacan's sexuation graph crystallizes his own thinking of over four decades on the implications of the sexual difference. While Lacan is clearly not the first to see that the difference is not simply anatomically or biologically determined, he is the first to argue that it is symbolized (or not) in an infant's recognition of the lack imposed by the perception of the separability of body parts. This refers sexual difference to a primordially corporal image $(\sqrt{-1})$ on which one's fantasies of the imaginary phallus will be built.

Sexual difference is determinative, not of sexuality in children, as Freud thought, but of the structuration of desire in relation to a cut or loss of an image whose first form is an experientially, perceptually fragmented body. Subsequent interpretations of the sexual difference establish the root cause of a subject's position within desire as the normative concern to please the Other; the neurotic's demand that the Other fill the void by proving love; and the psychotic's immutable certainty of being one with the Other, despite the unbearable anxiety the Other causes for him or her.

Secondly, whatever the orientation of a person's libidinal object choice—homosexual, heterosexual, or bisexual—Lacan's point is that masculinity and femininity are positions within knowledge wherein one (who is not psychotic) thinks he or she knows it *all* or does *not [know it] all*. As such, these categories are irreducible to gender, although the *all* is a masculine logic and the *not all* a feminine one.

Given that masculine or feminine identifications arise first as a symbolic interpretation of a real lack, not as an organ reality per se, organ reality plays its role, rather, in the real of sexuality and trauma and in the imaginary conception one has of one's body. Freud wondered why we need to invent "fantasmes" and Lacan replied that the fundamental one concerns the place where the subject consists as an object of the Other (Morel, *"La différence des sexes,"* p. 102). Moreover, insofar as the lack-in-being is not innate, but an interpretation of an abstract third "term" concerning sexual difference, it is logical that Lacan remind us that the facts of human psychology cannot be conceived unless one defines the function of the subject as the effect of the signifier (cf. *S. XI*).

But, how does the subject become "the effect of the signifier?" How do unary traits (S_1) bind with jouissance (a)? Lacan answers that the subject is constituted by two lacks that overlap within the logical vels (vel meaning "the place of") of alienation and separation (cf. *S. XI*, p. 43). While alienation is correlated with representations of the subject, separation names the experience of the cut between the object of satisfaction and its loss. Within the space of the overlap, master signifiers (i.e., unary traits) that are left over from the loss of the object (a) coexist with traces of the object. The

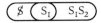

of alienation is complimented by the

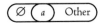

of separation. That is, loss of the object from the Other not only does not exist as such, but cannot even be "supposed" to exist until traits of the object fall away, thereby, decompleting the seemingly whole subject and giving birth to basic fantasies: $\emptyset \leftarrow | \, \rule{0.5em}{0.4pt}a$ (*S. XX*, p. 16).

In symbolic logic, the vel of either/or is called the exclusive vel. One chooses one thing or the other. Or, one can go to one side or the other, but one always loses one element by choosing the other. The consequence of this kind of choice—not characteristic of classical logic—is the creation of a neither/nor category. When one chooses the lack ($\emptyset$), one has *neither* the pleasure of S_I/unary traits of identification, *nor* identification with the Other's knowledge S_1S_2. That is, in a place where sets of elements are joined together certain elements seem to have disappeared, although they continue to "ex-sist" in the overlapping part. The primordial S_Is are what Lacan called the lost elements of the unconscious (*S XI*, p. 211). The logic is paradoxical: Priority is given to consciousness or the second. One can only know firstness (the real) once secondness (the symbolic) has disappeared. Thus, the operation of alienation or joining creates the first apparent lack of evaporating—the lack of a presence of "self"—while it also produces language as a covering over of lost knowledge.

Intersection, or product, produces separation that alternates between the Other and the void ($\emptyset$). Indeed, one experiences the effects of the cut that causes this operation only when the object falls from the Other, showing the face of angst that decompletion produces as $\emptyset$. Thus, Lacan's decompleted Other ($\emptyset$) has a special relation to proof insofar as only the sudden revelation of the Other's not being whole or complete triggers anxiety. Lacan calls anxiety the pure real that he considers the only true affect, the only one that does not lie. If one identifies with one's jouissance being (a) in the fantasy, one makes a false choice because a part of being has already been subtracted or lost (for most people) from the Other by its very constitution. But if one chooses the Other as the basis of subjecthood, one also makes a false choice insofar as a part of meaning (S_I) has already been subtracted as well.

That some part is always already taken away from the object of libidinal being or the subject of representational meaning, determines that *neither one nor the other* will ever be fully definable in its own terms. This double lack marks the subject as divided; never whole within itself. For Lacan, such a view of the subject places a great importance on the categories of the masculine or feminine, for not only are they structured according to the logic of alienation (masculine) and separation (feminine), they also bear the weight of linking meaning (S_1S_2) to sexuality (a) via the lost elements of each category, loss leaving an empty place to be filled.

Although the losses are not symmetrical or correspondent, the object (a) holds the central place in Lacan's Borromean unit, representing alternately the real cause of desire, the aim of the drive in the symbolic, and the imaginary fantasmatic forms that fill the lack-in-being. Separation, the second logical operation of the two vels joined by the object (a),

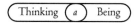

explains the first operation of alienation concomitant with secondary-process thoughts, in terms of traits that constitute the particular conditions of jouissance for any person as a kind of primary process. In this context, Lacan speaks of the incomplete Other ($\varnothing$) on the feminine side of sexuation as the reality principle and the phallic signifier of symbolic anchor (Φ) in masculine sexuation as the pleasure principle.

Thus, although the elements of *being and meaning* belong first to the Other, they cannot make their presence known to consciousness directly, but only through the transformations effected by alienation and separation. The metonymy of desire works by evocative displacements of the real object (a) to which substitutive metaphor gives the "solid" form of meaning (*S. XI*, p. 213). Insofar as Lacan connects desire to the metonymy that anchors metaphor—displacement leading to condensation—the objects one seeks for enjoyment belie what one can "translate" of metonymy's "form(s)." One's jouissance of objects makes of fantasy that which covers over the void place in being (*"La différence des sexes,"* p. 100). If desire has the structure of the subject of the unconscious, taken as a repressed knowledge about jouissance, this suggests that the phallic law not only prohibits transgression, it also occasions guilt and constitutes a superego. But, more enigmatically, the incest taboo is causal of phallic prohibitions. The symbolic Father's Law makes of castration the paradoxical Ur-paradigm of society, forcing the brothers to invent the myth of an Ur-father in repressed explanation of the trauma caused by losing the mother to someone else.

Lacan's is a radically different theory from those which reduce the masculine and feminine to oppositional gendered positions. Not only do oedipal interpretations of the phallic signifier show sexual difference as an enigma—thereby, traumatic—and castration as its interpretation, these interpretations result in different structurations of desire, each being the outcome of negotiating two lacks—the symbolic lack of being whole (*castration* or alienation) and the real castration of the cut that makes the hole concrete and, thus, necessary to fill. Marc Darmon writes in *Essais sur la Topologie lacanienne* that the necessity of inscription—real effects that become causes in the Other—introduces the topological dimension in Lacan in the first place. That is, the Lacanian cut is not a geometrical space separated by a union of circles that do not intersect one with another.

Rather, Lacan starts with the hole made by the cut of loss to deduce the surface of the body, and not the inverse.[54] In arguing that the hole can be reduced to point zero dimension, or to the englobing of a sphere, Lacan concludes that the interval between the hole in the symbolic and the surface of the body is a subject function. It is not the visible universe that directly causes desire, that is, but the *time* of desire that animates the relation between cause and effect. This relation is also animated by the "logical" time it takes to understand the hole as an "intersubjective" space among persons, whose desire each one tries to fathom or anticipate. Insofar as desire is the desire to have the object (a), the desire of fulfillment, the masculine and feminine find a way to join within the particular conditions of jouissance for each, even though the relation of every subject is first and foremost to his or her unconscious Other and not to his or her partner.

Lacan defined neurosis as a denial of castration, which means responding to the Other by demand, not by desire. Unfortunately this places the neurotic within a repetition of impossible demands made to an Other who knows nothing of the unconscious denials in play. In perverse fantasy, the sexual difference, while negated in the unconscious, is nonetheless played out through the paradox of fetishistic replacements for the lost object(s) fantasy seeks. In consequence, the feminine is often clearly marked by the fetish—by stiletto high heels, bound feet, lacy garters, blue velvet, and so on. And insofar as the signifier for difference is foreclosed in psychosis, this subject retains the illusion that all objects and words are real, not substitute representations of a veiled object (a) one must continually replace to restore the illusion that nothing has been lost by the first cuts of real loss, or later, by the sexual divide.

While Freud finds the sexual difference necessary as a basis for finding harmony in love and pleasurable sex between the two sexes, Lacan rereads Freud's *Totem and Taboo* (1913) as a "structural" reinterpretation of sexual difference as disharmonious. The myth of a primal hoarde of sons who murder the father explains sexuation, in part. Freud's myth sought to find in the sons' jealousy of the father the basis of the beginnings of cooperative society. Although the myth of the murder of the father is rendered necessary by the constituent presence of the Oedipus complex in every personal history,[55] "the armature of the Freudian edifice," Lacan says,—and its law, as well—are, "namely, the equivalence . . . of the imaginary function of the phallus in both sexes . . . the castration complex found as a normative phase of the assumption by the subject of his own sex. Using the existential quantifiers for function (the x), along with the philosophical symbols for existence ($\exists$) and the universal ($\forall$), the top portion of Lacan's graph of sexual desire formalizes them so they can be transmitted by the logic we have examined from the beginning of this chapter. Indeed, this graph marked an end-point to Lacan's second period of teaching.

In the third and fourth periods of his teaching, Lacan used the Borromean knot as the base unit of meaning in a topological demonstration of the ways mind and body are joined. The cosimultaneous functioning of all the orders, knotted by the symptom, produces three different kinds of jouissance at each point of overlap, different elements being primary according to the desiring structure (hysteric, obsessional, and so on) a person has evolved in resolving the oedipal conundrum. Again, Lacan depicts the masculine and feminine as orientations toward the phallus and castration and not biological categories. In the certainty of psychosis, for example, the *sinthome* finds its equivalent in the necessity that the phallus (Φ) function as the law of reality: $\Phi \cong \Sigma$. In perverse fantasy, the object (a) eroticizes all knowledge. The conflation of mother with a myth of The Woman who exists knots the orders $(R.S.I.)$ together in the obsessional's myth. For the hysteric, the Father's Name signifier is equated with the possibility of a

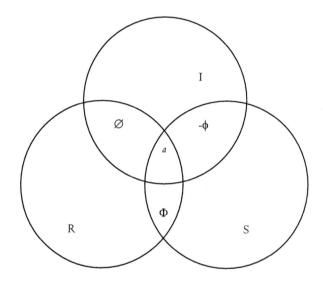

phallic signifier that will make the orders cohere, the identification with the father or brothers pointing to an imaginary confusion about her own sexuation in the Ideal ego formation ("On a Question Preliminary to Any Possible Treatment of Psychosis," p. 191).

Lacan argues that the masculine/feminine distinction does not obtain in psychosis, referring to Ida Macalpine's study of Schreber and her substitution of the word *unmanning* for Freud's use of *emasculation* (*Entmannung*) in volume 3 of his *Collected Papers*, as well as in the authorized version of his texts, *The Standard Edition*, he suggests that perhaps Macalpine had guessed that the real organ—not its imaginary representation—was in question in the castration complex of this subject. Lacan praised her for noticing the ambiguity in Freud's effort to make equivalents of *Verweiblichung*, meaning the transformation of becoming a woman that marks Judge Daniel Paul Schreber's delusion, and what Freud called Schreber's *Entmannung* (unmanning). But, since Macalpine takes the confusion to be a terminological one, Lacans says that Macalpine does not really see that the ambiguity in question is that of subjective structure itself ("On a Question," p. 206).

As is often the case, Lacan looks to the psychotic impasse in sexuation to better understand how the other structurations of desire function. Insofar as the psychotic subject encounters a hole in the signifying chain at the point where the symbolic law of the father appears for others, the sexual difference is not marked for this subject. He or she may "decline from any heritage from which it may legitimately expect the attribution of a penis to his person. This because if being and having are mutually exclusive in principle, they are confounded, at least as far as the result is concerned, when it is a question of a lack . . . [a]s one realizes in observing that it is not by being foreclosed to the penis, but by having to be the phallus [the symbolic parity *Mädchen = Phallus*] that the patient [Schreber] is doomed to become a woman" ("On a Question . . . ," pp. 206–207).

Freud's 1925 equation of female manliness with psychosis comes from this error: By having already established equivalency relations between male identification with a visible organ and "reality," he eschewed philosophical and aesthetic concerns with representation. In Lacan's teaching, most men identify their masculine being (their machismo) with some semblance of "having" the imaginary phallus at the unconscious level where the real of fantasy is the measure of reality. Not only did Freud oppose fantasy to reality in his 1925 discussion of castration anxiety, he widely missed the mark of evolving any viable theory of differential distinctions between the masculine or feminine, taken as different responses to the question of what reality is.

Lacan clarified Freud's confusions between neurosis and psychosis by proposing that if the signifier that gives meaning to the sexual difference is foreclosed—not negated or denied—it is not actually the organ qua organ that is at issue. It is, rather, a failure to evolve a mental idea of what constitutes the reality of one's being for the Other. Images and language appear as enigmatic to the infant long before they are interpreted as organs. And so powerful are the effects of language that it "creates" imaginary organs by naming them. It then assigns "mythic" attributes with properties and values of meaning to their biological functions. As Geneviève Morel puts it, language provoked the phallic symbol—Φ—which cannot exist for [other/non-human] animals and which, at its base, polarizes jouissance in such a way as to interdict the sexual rapport. There is, then, this equation: "Sexual nonrapport" [is] equivalent to the 'phallus'."[56]

On page 235 of his 1925 essay, Freud again concretizes a literal link between organ reality and mental reality by analogy, not by logic: "A girl may refuse to accept the fact of being castrated, may harden herself in the conviction that she *does* possess a penis, and may subsequently be compelled to behave as though she were a man" (p. 253). Lacan argues, rather, that the phallus masks the sexual asymmetry, or nonrapport, even to the point of seeming—in the imaginary—to be a sign of reunion between the sexes (Morel, p. 21).

The psychical consequences of the anatomical distinction have far-reaching consequences, Freud writes. If female narcissism is wounded, the girl has an inferiority complex. Thus, a first consequence of penis envy is that once the little girl gets over believing that the lack of a penis is a personal punishment and realizes that it is a *universal* occurrence, she, like men, comes to share their contempt for women and in that respect, if no other, "insists on being like a man" (p. 253). Despite his attempts to understand the relation of similarities and differences between the sexes, Freud has been read as prejudiced against women—and thus dismissed. One can only be surprised by Lacan's view of Freud as having discovered that the representation of difference qua difference from the same is what accrues high desirability in the social realm. It is not a separate point from Lacan's argument that the privilege of the symbolic lies in its covering over the traumatic real.

If society—that is, exchange among people, recognition of one another—might be defined as the gradual distance one takes from the corporal jouissance of proximity to the maternal real, such distance would be seen as necessary to an order(ing) of symbolic material. From this perspective, contempt would be an unconscious phenomenon, an attraction/repulsion that emanates from the pull of the familiar, the tug of the intimate, the nostalgia for, and fear of, the same. For the tug of the primordial real—the bedrock of us all—is the confusion between woman as sexual and woman as mother. Moreover, the mother is taken as a guarantee of being and celebrated as such, is essentialized as The Woman in the symbolic by myriad myths and figures. This view of distance implies a paradox of the real: Eros and Thanatos have a contiguous base. We want to *repeat* the familiar, which has the odor of Thanatos, but only the familiar gives us the comfort of the known, which dovetails with *Eros*.

In his discussion of the phallic phase, Freud discussed only autoerotic pleasure. When he returned to the Oedipus complex with its subtle twists and turns, he suggested that the little girl's libido takes a new position in the oedipal phase. Masturbation takes on less importance once she unconsciously equates the penis with a child: "*With that purpose in view* she takes her father as a love-object. Her mother becomes the object of her jealousy. The girl has turned into a little woman. If I am to credit a single analytic instance, this new situation can give rise to physical sensations which would have to be regarded as a premature awakening of the female genital apparatus" (p. 256). Although he errs in considering the source of genital awakening to be the father, at least, he associates genital awakening with the real father of jouissance, a man who conveys both sexual desire for the mother and prohibition for the infant.

Geneviève Morel points out in her course *La différence des sexes* (1996–1997) that Freud's expression "to have the phallus" takes on a logical meaning only if one understands that his references are to the libido (or jouissance) that typifies what he calls the "phallic phase." Borrowing Gottlieb Frege's propositional function, Lacan wrote phallic sexual jouissance as Φ (x), "x" representing the subject as a function of being sexuated by the signifier. Yet, even though it is the signifier that "sexuates," a sexuated being is one whose object is the (a), or whatever remains to him or her of the positive jouissance left over from a maternal (a) $[a_1a_2a_3a_4a_5a_6]$, jouissance that is never negated; but is always a "plus" (pp. 21 and 33). The new element Lacan advanced in the Φ (x) is the positive function of libido, elevated over all the prior negative functions of castration. Indeed, which can only be dropped one by one in traversing the fundamental unconscious fantasy (Morel, p. 33).

In one sense, the awakening of the libido is an interpretation of lack made by both sexes. Thus, Freud might be read as trying to coordinate the phallic signifier to masturbatory jouissance. Lacan's rereading of this Freudian approach is to be found in "For a Congress on Feminine Sexuality" (1960).[57] There, Lacan maintained that post-Freudians failed to see that the phallus was, for Freud, a signifier, one which permitted him to order things; especially psychic "development" ("Guiding Remarks . . . ," p. 48).

Lacan encouraged his interlocutors to read Freud's "Inhibitions, Symptoms and Anxiety" (1926),[58] taking account of his order of the symptom. This is the fourth order of the knot where the fate of the paternal metaphor—Lacan's restructuration of the Oedipus complex—plays itself out in the destiny of a life (*Joyce avec Lacan*, p. 45):

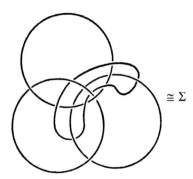

$\cong \Sigma$

In "Painting," Gerard Wacjman writes: "As for real space, its representation supposes that one will promote, along with the graphs and the schemas, the notion of a picture which presents *sites* . . . one could define as pure real places . . . (The graphic representation of the Borromean knot would, then, be a picture) . . . a picture [being] that which shows . . . [and] always supposing a knotting of the three [orders] . . . Topology, then, is not a metaphor. . . . It does not represent the subject. Neither signified or figured. It presents the structure, the site where the subject emerges as effect" ("Painting," 143–44).

In 1925, Freud adds that when a little girl gives up her attachment to her father—that is, accepts that he cannot be her husband or the father of her child—she may return to her masculinity complex and remain fixated there. Choosing to identify with her mother means, in one sense, finding a substitute for Daddy quickly. The sexual masquerade is a logical dance around the ramifications of castration interpreting the phallic difference. Its history would be that of the stereotypes common to any historical, sociological moment. That is, at the level of sexual jouissance, one finds endless variations of response to a minimal drama: "Compulsory heterosexuality," homosexuality, bisexuality, wife-swapping parties, *ménage-à-trois* relations, and so on, rather than the supposed sexless Victorians of Freud's day. That is, sexual mores are appended to history as a sequence of events, not to sexual types versus asexual types. The picture Lacan paints of the normative masquerade concerns, first and foremost, an avoidance of the lack-in-being (i.e., castration) in order to please the social Other and win love by fitting in with a given standard of its ideals. This concerns public behavior, not libidinal pleasure. But it also concerns libidinal pleasure insofar as the "normative" desire is to do what pleases the Other.

Both Freud and Lacan imply that most women are not hysterics. But neither does the "norm" mean normal. Lacan called it *nor-mâle*. Nor can one reduce the feminine to the performative, sociological power referred to by Foucauldian historical constructivism. Rather, the desire *cum* power Lacan invoked, is a matter of wanting—not truth, but—love; wanting to be desired by the Other, thus, wanting to conform.

The later Lacan developed the "father" signifier to distinguish the masculine from the feminine, thereby equating sexuation with his proposal of 1971 that the feminine is *not all* castrated—*not all* under the phallic function. From this he deduced that one of the consequences of the *not all* is a feminine doubling of the libido (Morel, p. 171):

$$\swarrow \begin{matrix} S(\varnothing) \\ \Phi \end{matrix}$$

The S($\varnothing$) means, not only a lack in the Other, but also a jouissance without inscription or reference (Morel, p. 33). This supplemental enjoyment of the entire body is susceptible of applying to all women (and to some men, such as mystics) precisely because the phallic identification with "law" is *not all* under the law of phallic jouissance.

The *pas toute* (S [$\varnothing$]) (*not all*) placed over the *pas tout* ($\exists x\overline{\Phi x}$) in the phallic function (*S. XX*, p. 81), means that in feminine sexuation the phallic function is already *not all* (*pas toute*). It is *contingent* ("What ceases *not not* writing itself"): $\overline{\exists x\Phi x}$. If a male is on the feminine side of sexuation, his relation to the phallic function is also *contingent*, unbarred by the prohibitive symbolic phallus. But, if he is to be located on the masculine side, the father must (have) serve(d) as a symbolic castrator, causing subject division ($\$$), not acting as the real jouissance phallus (Φ), which eschews castration or lack. Paradoxically, this paternal interdiction is required to confer a phallic identification on a male (Morel, pp. 172–73).

As far as the feminine *contingent* ($\overline{\forall x\Phi x}$) relation to the phallus is concerned, Lacan says the S($\varnothing$)—the hole and the Other—evoke the real in such a way as to cause acute suffering "beyond the phallus," or ecstatic pleasure, insofar as the feminine is also identified with and as the object (a) (Morel, p. 173). If she is further beautified as the imaginary phallus desired in the scopic field—Marilyn Monroe, Grace Kelly—she is elevated in sublimation.

We remember that in his sexuation graph, Lacan explained the logic of the masculine and the feminine, not only as epistemological positions but also as asymmetrical logics (Morel, p. 73). On his graph, for example, he acknowledges four points of split: A tension in the formulas on the top line—$\exists x \overline{\Phi x} \mid \overline{\exists x \Phi x}$—leads him to place a gap between the masculine conditions of existence, the *necessary* and *possible* and the feminine ones of the *impossible* and the *contingent*. Gilson points out that Lacan's feminine *impossible* ($\overline{\exists x \Phi x}$) is based on Freud's article "The Taboo of Virginity," where he argued that men place this taboo on women out of fear that women are different from them. The taboo is one signifying effort to make them different or Other (Gilson, pp. 167–68). Since the *impossible* is, by definition, unfeasible, Gilson suggests that it gives way to the undecidable, which arises from the oppositions of $\overline{\exists x \Phi x}$ qua/Other to $\forall x \Phi x$ qua/object (a) on the feminine side: $\mid a \longrightarrow S(\varnothing)$. Gilson also finds a contradiction between the masculine *necessary*—$\exists x \overline{\Phi x}$—and the logic of the *possible* it produces: $\forall x \Phi x$, the contradiction coming, partly, from the order Lacan places in the masculine quadrant. Lacan reverses Aristotelian logic by making the particular ($\exists x \overline{\Phi x}$) both negative and that which gives rise to the universal ($\forall x \Phi x$) as positive (p. 168). However, Lacan explained his logic of the *possible* in *Le Sinthome*, *L'étourdit*, and . . . *Ou pire* as concomitant with recognizing and accepting rules that allow the social to exist.

Lacan said in *Seminar XX* in a sentence he repeats in *L'étourdit* in *Scilicet*: "What one says remains forgotten behind what is heard in what is said; this *énoncé*, assertive by its form, belongs to the modal [logic] of what it emits concerning existence" [59] (cf. *S. XX*, p. 111).

Modal logics:	
Masculine	Feminine
(the *necessary*)	(the *impossible*)
$\exists x\ \overline{\Phi x}$	$\overline{\exists x}\ \Phi x$
$\forall x\ \Phi x$	$\overline{\forall x}\ \Phi x$
(the *possible*)	(the *contingent*)
$\not{S}$	$S(\varnothing)$
$\Phi \longleftarrow$	The Woman

Lacan stresses that each person is *divided* by signifiers, images, and objects of drive and desire. These create sexual identifications that constitute particular conditions of jouissance. These identifications are not random, moreover, but follow a strict modal logic depending on how one has been "fixed" in the real at the level of the knot, which functions as the truth of the subject's *sinthome*. There the structures of desire keep repeating an identificatory sexual crisis in a person's life or a trauma assumed by the subject from a beloved (or hated) parent. At a general level, girls identify with a logic of the *impossible* (that which "does not stop not being written") insofar as they are radically in the symbolic order of difference and just as radically out of it, in the real.

This means that for females there is no exception to the rule of being born a woman to a woman (the mother) whose own unconscious desire imposes her story of the trauma caused by the sexual divide. Women are traumatized in one way and men in another because the split is not natural, but culturally defined. No sexual relation can be written as a oneness, in this purview; rather, there is a relation of thoughts and feelings to body parts, fantasies, and images that identify an infant first with object(s) he or she desires and, ultimately, with a symbolic posture vis-à-vis the phallus and castration (*S. XX*, p. 59).

To say that boys identify with a logic of difference is equivalent to saying they identify with "the necessary . . . which doesn't stop being written as a reference to the phallic function" (*S. XX*, p. 59): $\exists x \overline{\Phi x}$. Morel informs us that Lacan started writing these sexuation formulas in 1971 in *Seminar XX* (Morel, p. 45), proposing there that in sexuation, the phallic function determines how a subject is signified in a culture: $\Phi / \cancel{S}$ (Morel, p. 51). But insofar as femininity means that all are "castrated"—$\overline{\exists x \Phi x}$—not one being an exception to this rule, one also confronts two voids: The Woman does not exist as an essential being for she is not signified in reference to difference, but by Otherness. Her primary referent is not her place in the symbolic, but the void in the Other that is imposed by the castrating symbolic order.

The resulting "feminine" knowledge is that one element is lacking or excluded in each meaning ensemble each time it is put forth or evoked. Denoting this epistemological turn by the matheme $\varnothing$ (the barred Other of the *not all*), Lacan adds that even if one tried to equate nonidentical elements, $a = A$, "a" does not equal "A" (or "0") because a heterogeneous element—one which likely differs from itself—has been introduced by castration, that is, the sexual difference as cause and effect. A logic of the "same" would, thus, be impossible for women since the phallic function gives rise to a logic of *not all* (*pas toute*) under the law—$\overline{\forall x \Phi x}$—but partly under it. This feminine logic leads to an identification outside social law—beyond the phallus." Paradoxically, the logic of the same characterizes—not women, but—the male group who are universally in thrall to obeying the rules of the one whose is not castrated and, thus, can make the laws. The exception is the signifier that marks the law of a group as one: $\exists x \overline{\Phi x} / \forall x \Phi x$. Women can act on the masculine side in the symbolic, or man, on the feminine side, in the real. The point is simply that the effect of the sexual difference gives rise to the symbolic as a set of laws (and transgressions) "structured" by the phallic signifier as the referent of any differential that marks a negation, and so on.

The man loves the object (fetishistically) that elicits his desire: $\cancel{S} - | \rightarrow (a)$. The woman loves the evidence—$(-\phi \rightarrow \Phi / $the organ fetishized$)$—that the man desires her. Here, Morel distinguishes the imaginary phallus and the real phallus as the desired objects (for example, girl, or an organ) from the propositional phallic function $\Phi(x)$ (Morel, p. 47): At the level of knowledge about jouissance, men mistake The Woman at the level of sexual essence with their phallus qua organ that desires precisely because She veils castration for the man. His demands of the "veil" add up to the particular conditions of jouissance for him—the ones that will counter the castrating potential in his desire.

Surprisingly, Freud's conclusions in "Some Psychic Consequences" are not altogether incompatible with Lacan's logic of castration. Responding to Freud's idea that the Oedipus complex is destroyed in boys by the castration complex—that is, how can a male compete with other males when he *fears* their retaliation?—Lacan says he bows to the law of the group, laws, instigated in the name of the leader, exception to the rule of castration, who is nonetheless a myth. Such acceptance of castration is Lacan's definition of a man. By contrast, Freud says, the fact that girls rival with males in the Oedipus complex is made possible by, and is led up to by, their undergoing a castration complex: $\exists x \overline{\Phi x}$. Freud does not like the castration complex, while Lacan finds it necessary for becoming a subject and for having a society. In Freud's picture, the castration complex inhibits and limits masculinity when it leads to the guilt occasioned by a rigid submission to a tyrannical superego or strong leader. For Freud, this complex encourages feminine rivalry, or feelings of inferiority. For Lacan, women do not escape identification with lack and loss, but by not identifying only with the phallus, they are free both to assume a symbolic identity and to not be *all* under the thumb of phallic values: $\forall x \Phi x$. For women, if there is no exception to not being identified with castration in the real—$\overline{\exists x \Phi x}$—then, paradoxically, there is no universal (i.e., symbolic) castration for women—$\overline{\forall x \Phi x}$—insofar as the two negatives on the top line yield a positive on the bottom line.

Put another way, Woman is not signified as such in the unconscious, while man is signified there by the mark of difference from woman. And although women are not castrated in reality, they are castrated culturally by masculine signifiers that seek to interpret the sexual difference, and, even more profoundly, by the male confusion between woman as sexual and mother as asexual. One could also add a third castration upon which Freud remarked: Woman are also denigrated by their daughters at the moment of grasping the denigrations surrounding the sexual difference. They want to identify with a value of difference or symbolic Otherness, rather than the similarities and samenesses of their mothers. What Lacan stresses in the feminine, as apart from the masculine, is the asymmetry of the impossible—"There is not one who is not"—on the top line leads to different solutions on the bottom line. If for women, there is no law of exception that gives rise to a leader who valorizes difference, inscribable as unconscious castration ($\cancel{S}$), each woman is, paradoxically, like every other ($\overline{\forall x}$) and— "discordentially"—like no other (Φx).

In . . . *Ou pire*, 66 Lacan concluded that in speech men and women refuse the sexual distinction based on anatomy, and "recognize one another only as speaking beings by rejecting this ["natural" anatomical] distinction [replacing it] by identifications" (Morel, p. 52). The difference plays itself out in the real of jouissance. Freud finally called the difference between male and female sexual development a psychic castration that has been accomplished in the case of the girl and only threatened in the boy's case (p. 257). From the start of his teaching, Lacan rejected Freud's idea of a female castration complex, arguing that never having had the organ in question, girls have never had the fear of losing it. One can speak of the castration complex for both sexes, he argues, only in the sense of a lack of their being One:

No rapport also means no androgyny. Not only does no organ signify what constitutes a *relationship* between man and woman, the logic of choice—alienation and separation—forces one to choose between one or the other, however much one vascillates between the two. In gender politics this means that one is never "both/and" of the two sexes. One is at any given time only ever "either/or." Other signifiers supplement this impossible gap in meaning, signifiers that belong to the imaginary realm of semblance, the symbolic realm of narrative, and the real domain of fantasy and unary traits.

In his seminar on *Hamlet* (1958–59) Lacan described the phallus as a signifier that could *supplement* the *lack* of a signifier to mark a relation between the sexes.[60] Proposing that the feminine form of love is erotomanic and the masculine form fetishistic, Lacan depicted the masculine subject as loving his partner "insofar as the signifier of the phallus constitutes her [for him] as giving in love what she does not have" (Lacan, "The signification . . . ," p. 290). In other words, what she *lacks* is what she *has* to give. Her particular "lack" enables him to take her as the "phallic" object that will fill his own lack-in-being ($\cancel{S}$—| $\rightarrow$ *a*). As early as the 1950s, Lacan emphasized this point: The lack in question is not the lack of a penis, but the particular lack-in-being that marks the feminine partner's demand for love and a particular man's desire for this demand. In a more general sense, insofar as the male confuses *having* the penis (the real organ) with *being* the phallus—that is, an object of desire—the partner's lack assures him of being the phallus. Insofar as he is loved and desired, such assurance "gives" him the gift of "having" the penis.

Girls encounter a different problem from boys in regard to the phallus. While both sexes relate indirectly to the phallus through the mother for whom the father (or his substitute) *represents* the phallus, the boy is invited to identify with his father by the symbolic, while the girl is not. In *"Le désir au féminin,"* Sol Aparicio stresses the structural logic of the feminine by looking at the different words Freud used when grappling with varying nuances of the sexual asymmetry in the constitution of feminine sexuality. At a level of infantile precocity, some little girls want what little boys *have*—the penis—not because it has any innate superiority, but because boys *display* it manifestly in the seeming fullness of the imaginary, where a visible image is often mistaken for *das Ding*.

Aparicio writes that little girls explain away that seemingly important difference by substituting other things, a bicycle, a baby sister, a new doll, and so on. In describing such a phenomenon, Freud used the word *Penisneid*. In tracking the little girl's love as she becomes increasingly attached to her father, Freud speaks of *Peniswunsch* and *Wunsch nach dem Penis* (Aparicio, 1993).[61]

Lacan lets us see that the valorization of the male, in any context, marks symbolic difference over the real of the drives, associated, as they are, with sameness or intimacy. Difference starts the count of value itself. Lacan points out in . . . *Ou pire* that the mathematical operation between zero and one is not demonstrable by a diagonal method that depends on the decimal (Gilson, pp. 216–17). Thus, he focused on the logic of Frege's discovery that "O" grounds one and implies something more: O(1+n). When he emphasized in his *Hamlet* seminar that one is "sexuated"—as masculine or feminine—but also castrated ($-\phi$) insofar as one "has" or does not "have" the attributes desired by a given symbolic order, it is the logic of excess or jouissance he is depicting, not that of organs. The compensations for the installation of a lack-in-being are the remainders of jouissance each subject accrues from the object (*a*), whose status is real insofar as it is the metaphor of the subject of jouissance. That is, an object must fall—like an averted gaze or a verbal slight—in order that it be subjectivized (Gilson, p. 101). The jouissance(s) an object leaves behind as associations with the breast, gaze, voice, feces, oscillate in fantasy between the body and the word, translating themselves into a seeming copula of union Lacan called the phallic mask.

Given the paradox that loss and supplemental jouissance are primary in the constitution of *being*, Lacan argued that Aristotle was deceived by envisaging logic as based on grammar and language (Morel, p. 21). Rather, the sexual masquerade emanates from loss, lack, splits, and divisions, as well as from the comings and goings of jouissance. And these subtend grammar and language as positive data, evoking disguise, deception, and comedy—not information or communication—with the effect of "irrealizing" the relations between subjects and between the sexes. Would-be "relations" are linked, rather, to fantasmatic notions of one's body and the phallus (Morel, p. 22).

Unlike boys, a girl is required to give up her identification with being the phallus, to give up the father, if she wishes to find a man to whom she can give herself sexually. Pierre Naveau capsulates this dilemma in *"La Querelle du Phallus,"* as female grief that mourns the loss of the phallus by stressing that it does not concern an organ. Mourning the loss of the phallus refers to a little girl's feeling that she must find a man other than her father because, although he loves her, he has dropped her. He makes love to someone else.[62] Lacan tries to show ("monstrates" [demonstrates]) what Freud could not enunciate: The problem in the constitution of male or female sexuality is not the organ qua organ, but the dialectic of desire.

In "Some Psychical Consequences" Freud concluded that the Oedipus complex differs from the castration complex. Decades later, Lacan sought to validate the importance Freud gave the Oedipus complex by showing how its "resolution" (or not) structures the destiny of each human subject in an interplay between desire and lack. The Oedipus complex and the castration complex are intertwined, Freud argued. Indeed, the castration threat causes the Oedipus complex to be smashed to bits for boys, "its libidinal cathexes . . . abandoned, desexualized and in part sublimated; its objects . . . incorporated into the ego, where they form the nucleus of the super-ego" ("Some Psychical . . . ," p. 257) that replaces the Oedipus complex. Nonetheless, the penis escapes superego dicta and continues to be "cathected" narcissistically. Following the biological explanations of his day, Freud agreed with Sandor Ferenczi (1924) that the boy's investment in his penis has an "organic significance" (*organischen Bedeutung*) for the propagation of the species.[63]

Lacan's logic of sexuation seeks to demonstrate how archaic are Freud's imaginary biological explanations. Insofar as biology works positivistically to delimit two precise classes which it then constructs empirically, at the level of logic, Freud's theory does not differ from Aristotle's classificatory logic, be it the Viennese doctor's "biology is destiny" argument, the more recent right brain/left brain distinction, the hormone/steroid-causal argument, or evolutionary theory described by Theodore Roszak as a "macho science" that leads to bizarre fictions like the "selfish gene" or "cannibal-cell galaxies."[64] All accept the imaginary proposition of reducing sexuality to gender. Biological organs are presumed to know, a priori, and naturally how to function in order to propagate the species, be it as "organ," "gene," "hormone," "selection of the fittest," or intuition.

Lacan demonstrates an entirely different kind of knowledge caused by the sexual difference, one based on narcissistic identificatory investments that have nothing to do with the reproductive function of organs. While Aristotelian logic relies on the attributes of ten categories (substance, quantity, quality, etc.) to describe classes, not until the nineteenth century did a major cut in knowledge appear: the introduction of modern logic on which Lacan depended to formulate his theories.

Postulating an ideal, a resolved Oedipus complex, Freud praised the superego replacement of the Oedipus complex in males, explaining the male narcissistic investment in his penis as necessary to the survival of the species. But in the same sentence, Freud changes tone, referring rather, to "the *catastrophe* [done] to the Oedipus complex (the abandonment of incest and the institution of conscience and morality) [which] may be regarded as a victory of the race over the individual" (p. 257). If the boy's abandonment of sexual desire for his mother and sister(s) is a victory for the human race, Freud seems to have assessed the incest taboo as the sacrifice of libido required to maintain society via difference and exchange, via exogamy. In the next sentence he implies that "neurosis [i.e., "hypersensitivity"] [arises out of this forced separation] . . . based [as it is] upon a struggle of the ego against the demands of the sexual function": The ego bears the burden of mediating between the superego and the id. Surprisingly, Freud defines neurosis, here, as the persistence of sexual desire.

Lacan gives another definition: The "mental" (the "mind's language") or psychic suffering that Freud called "neurosis" comes from identifying predominantly with the split in gender in hysteria ($\mathcal{S}$) and from substituting knowledge (S_2) for the phallus in obsession. By denying the "castration" that gives rise to the sexual masquerade of the "norm," neurosis, paradoxically, obviates the "envy" of the opposite sex Freud ascribed to a "normative" oedipal resolution.

Geneviève Morel argues that no one could even "think" the concept of "gender," except in terms of binary oppositions, until three nineteenth-century logicians developed the basis for modern logic by ungluing grammar from its "attributions," even to the point of showing grammar to be a mask for a more fundamental proposition: The propositional function. To introduce the *phallic function* as a proposition, Lacan referred to the work done by Morgan in 1846, George Boole in 1854, and Gottleib Frege in 1879. Although Lacan hypothesized that the abstract effect of difference is the third-term referent of sexual division: Φ/a, his thesis is that the subject as such nonetheless, is empty ($\mathcal{S}$) and, thus, must cover him or herself with language and image attributes that are never completely identical with his or her being in jouissance. Even "gender," then, is simply a conglomerate of attributes or signifiers, not a biological fact. Modern logic is derived from this fact: What is "written" or inscribed in differential references differs from what is said (Morel, p. 21).

Freud argued that boys overcome the Oedipus complex by evolving into morally correct citizens, whereas girls have no motive for overcoming the complex. Castration fear *causes* the Oedipus complex in boys at a literal level of organ reality, but since girls, are, in his view, already castrated, they have no real motive for escaping this complex. "It may be slowly abandoned or dealt with by repression [*durch Verdrängung erledigt werden*], or its effects may persist far into women's normal [adult] mental life" (p. 237).

Focusing, rather, on a new logical idea of "the writing of the concept," Lacan followed Frege's text from 1879, "*die Begriff Schrift (The Concept of Writing).*" Lacan refused both familiar translations of the term as "ideograph" or "writing," in favor of a new way of thinking about memory or wish displacement. Insisting that the signifier, since Saussure, has been characterized by the fact of always being different from itself—"I am doing this"—means something else two minutes later, even though one uses the same words. He stressed that in this sense, it is not the same or identical "I" in question, or the same "this." Saussure discovered that the signifier opposes itself to itself: $a \neq a$. But while the signifier depends on context, the letter is different from it. Aware of this, Frege opposed his logic to Aristotle's, who thought of Language as sufficient to itself (Morel, p. 30). An immobile, constant, invariable function is something different from Aristotle's static prime mover, said Frege, and wrote it as: Φ (Morel, p. 31).

In borrowing the capital phi from Frege, Lacan proposed sexual phallic enjoyment as the hypothesis of a propositional function, and the consequence as a further argument (Morel, p. 33):

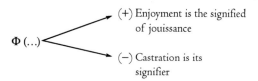

$\Phi\,(\dots)$

(+) Enjoyment is the signified of jouissance

(−) Castration is its signifier

In this way of thinking, language can never directly describe an organ, as Freud thought. Language can only ever describe the interpretations of an enjoyment as linked to thoughts about an organ. These thoughts have fixed values in fantasy, only insofar as there is sexual difference. Otherwise, one is enmeshed in a psychotic's chaotic delusional system where there is neither difference, distance, or perspective. While difference marks the masculine imaginarily, sameness is equated with (feminine) intimacy and oneness—with being connected. This is because the feminine overlap of motherhood and sexuality has interpreted "The Woman who does not exist" as a whole essence. Paradoxically, Woman can be seen as whole only insofar as she is represented as a semblant of the object (a) that fills the real hole of the void ($\varnothing$), the incomplete Other.

In 1925, Freud's thesis was that since women do not have to resolve the Oedipus complex, they have a weaker superego than men: "Their super-ego is never so inexorable, so impersonal, so independent of its emotional origins as we require it to be in men. Character-traits which critics of every epoch have brought up against women— that they show less sense of justice than men, that they are less ready to submit to the great exigencies of life, that they are more often influenced in their judgments by feelings of affection or hostility—all these would be amply accounted for by the modification in the formation of their super-ego which we have inferred above" (pp. 257–58).

Lacan interprets Freud's ideas here thus: In identifying with the proposition of difference itself (Φ), males (heterosexual or homosexual) identify predominantly on the masculine side, equating their thoughts with the reality of a particular symbolic order set of mores such that their "certainties" have a superego rectitude. In identifying with a jouissance point beyond superego or symbolic injunctions—$\forall x \Phi x$—women show less rigidity and greater tolerance and flexibility than men, precisely because complete identification with the phallic "rule" is not required of them: $\overline{\forall x}\Phi x/S(\varnothing)$. Rather than make of this phenomenon a "relational feminine essence," Lacan depicts it as a subjective logic "beyond the phallus," with ramifications for feminine jouissance and epistemology.

We have seen that, in his sexuation graph, Lacan returns to Aristotle not Freud to construct a new logical picture of existence, considered via universals and exceptions: masculine and feminine superegos are formed as different kinds of relations to the phallic signifier. Insofar as a man identifies with the Ur-father, exception to the law, who, paradoxically, gives laws their basis, his relationship to the "reality" of a particular symbolic is a "resolved" Oedipus complex—that is, a normative identification with a cultural superego—where every one is under the phallic function ($\forall x \, \Phi x$) of pleasing the Other.

Woman, by contrast, does not find her identification culturally affirmed by the law of the signifier, except insofar as she is interested in the stake she has in the symbolic camp:

M	W
Φ	$S(\emptyset)$
	~~The Woman~~

Given that there is no universal covering of her existence as woman from the position of mother (*Encore*, p. 94), women are thrown into this existential dilemma: There is no Ur-mother exception who gives rise to the existence of women as a clan or group who identify with an Ur-mother they have overthrown. Insofar as every woman is a mother, or was born of one, the mother is already a signifier in the symbolic. Thus, the problem of Woman's existence relies on a double negative (an impossibility in classical logic). There is no exception—no woman qua woman alone—in whose name social law is pronounced as a symbolic-order (local) universal, although there are figures and myths of such women in literature and in history.

In Lacan's logic, one of the names of the Father is "Woman" insofar as she signifies difference at the level where myth copes with inexpressible facts of the real, such as birth, eros, death, kinship perpetuity.[65] Thus, all women are under the law of there being no individual woman—like God or Buddha or Mohammed—in whose name a social order can be founded. There is, rather, the generic category of mother. The reason the signifier "mother" does not solve the problem of woman's existence, is that law itself is established on the basis of the logic of difference, difference not only of the brother from the (Ur-)father, but of males from females. Thus, a male is, by definition asymmetrically opposed to the impossibility of oneness or sameness. Sameness cannot give the basis of law anyway, insofar as the one is a grounding base whose negative referent is "O": $O(I+n)$.

Having warned against the feminist view of women as completely equal to—that is, the same as—men, Freud says that most men, nonetheless, are far behind the ideal. Moreover, sexually speaking, all individuals are bisexual, making of "pure masculinity and femininity . . . theoretical constructions of uncertain content" ("Some Psychical Consequences . . ." p. 258). It is not a great leap from Freud's conclusion here in 1925 to Lacan's statement in *Encore* (1972–1973) that men and women are signifiers (p. 34) whose attributes are given them on the bias of language, a bias on which they must continually identify as either one or the other.

5

The Place of the Mother in Lacanian Analysis
Lacan's Theory of the Object, or Castration Rethought

Lacan's Theory of Sexuation as It Relates to "Gender Identity"

In Freud's "Little Hans Case" (1909), two particular relations of Hans to the object—his fetishization of the object and his phobic experience of it—bring his father to Freud. Lacan interprets Freud's case in *Le séminaire, livre IV* (1956–1957): *La relation d'objet*,[1] arguing that by dismissing the theory of a castration complex, as analysts have often done since Freud's day, impasses in Freud's work have remained unsolved. Moreover, the nugget of truth buried precisely at the point of an impasse has, unfortunately, been thrown out as well.

Before taking account of what is new in Lacan's rereading of the Little Hans case, let us look at some of his ideas regarding the end of the pre-oedipal period, the moment when any small child is first presented with the challenge of assuming a sense of being or identity in terms of gender. Although contemporary feminist theories, as well as the American clinic of psychoanalytic psychology, conflate the two terms, saying "gender identity," Lacan used the word *sexuation* to argue that childhood interpretations of the sexual difference as lack, in relation to the phallus, structure "mind" in normative, neurotic, perverse, or psychotic epistemologies of desire. Rather than a binary either/or, Lacan's sexuation means that castration structures mind out of an interpretation of sexual difference, not the reverse.

While the American clinic of gender identity writes of causality as oppositional—either a biological, psychological, or sociological base to gender identity—[2] Lacan's theory obviates any binary as explanatory of cause. There is no mind versus affect, or body versus mind, or society versus a *developmental essentialism*. Indeed, Lacan's enterprise might be described as his carrying forth Freud's efforts to elaborate an adequate theory of mind as tied to sexuality. Lacan taught that what we call mind or thought or reason is, rather, the way an individual's language negotiates the real of his or her desire which, moreover, is inseparable from the (partial) drives. And both drives and desire materialize language with a *real* portion of affect—with jouissance—which emanates, in the second period of Lacan's teaching, from a fundamentally *unconscious* fantasy—which he describes as "sexuality in function."[3]

Lacan's notion of a contrapuntal unconscious knowledge, interwoven with conscious knowledge and speech, has little in common with Freud's idea of a hidden, instinctual combustion chamber, or Jung's notion of the shimmering underside of a dream world of symbols and shadows. Lacan argues, rather, in the last period of his teaching, that "the unconscious is the impossible to know, which is what one constructs with language, in other words, it is a swindle. The association of ideas is the delivery to the little happiness"[4] which subtends the cognitive components of one's "being-for-thought." The mental and the affective are cojoined, as in the contiguity of a Moebïus band (8), making *identity* a totalizing imaginary concept whose multiple components, enigmatically arranged in a continuous movement of points at the surface of thought, are much more complex than any binary feedback paradigm would let one think.

This is a *new* turn in thinking about gender identity and its link to sexuality in that it obviates the age-old opposition between biological sexuality—whose bases are found in affect or "feeling"—and identity, which has generally been seen as a mental construct. Moreover, such a view retains the mind/body split so central to Anglophone theories. Instead, Lacan's theory draws attention to the particularity of desire and fantasy—and, henceforth, of symptoms—rather than to object relations wherein gender identity holistically conflates sexuality and sexual object choice. Adding the symptom as the fourth order constructive of the "mind/body" join—the order of the knot that ties together the real, symbolic, and imaginary—in 1975 and 1976,[5] Lacan argued that each person is a *symptom* of his or her shaping in the oedipal trajectory.

We remember that the Oedipus complex was recast by Lacan as early as 1938 in *Les complexes familiaux* where he presented complexes as concrete constellations of familiar images.[6] He recast the notion of a "complex" again in his first theory of the paternal metaphor advanced in the 1950s. There, it meant the unconscious part of the mother's desire, referring itself to the signifier for a Father's Name, whose signified is the sexual difference itself taken as a third term.[7] Later, in the third period of his teaching, Lacan stressed the *specificity* of signifiers and identifications that make up each person's symptomatology. This path of inquiry led him to borrow the French medieval spelling of *sinthome* to focus on the particularity of the *unconscious* knots of words/images/affects that constitute each subject as *subject* of and fixated to singular desire whose real associations are myriad and nonlinear.

In Lacan's theory, one sees the *dawn* of the oedipal *unconscious* nexus as a secondary formation, erected in the assumption of sexuation. Thus, rather than focus, as did Freud, on identification with the same-sex or opposite-sex parent, with attendant feelings of jealous rivalry, Lacan points out that the encounter with difference, which is first experienced as *sexual* difference, gives rise to a differential, symbolic order axis he calls a phallic orientation. Identifications are ordered in reference to this pivotal signifier for difference in a dialectic that oscillates between law and jouissance. Although reified imaginarily in relations with others, in Lacan's reformulations, drive affects, signifiers, and images coalesce in fixations (*fixions*/fictions) of being he called an unconscious Ideal ego formation—which is, surprisingly, a symbolic structure. Repetitions create such fixations as the guarantee of imaginary ego stability. Such stability serves as a defense against the concrete losses whose effects on being go from slight worry or doubt to acute anxiety. In Lacan's theory, the Ideal ego, although "acted out" narcissistically on the imaginary axis of relations with others, is, nonetheless, formed from symbolic identifications with the outside world imposed on the biological organism. But how would Lacan's theory constitute an advance over the idea of gender identity, taken as a selection of masculine and feminine identifications and resulting in the choice of a bisexual or a heterosexual or homosexual partner?

To answer the question just posed, one would need to understand that Lacan's is a clinically based theory of logical, even semiuniversal, structures, not a predetermined theory wherein persons operate good or bad effects. Rather than focus on a good or bad (totalized) mother, his insistence is, for example, on the importance of the phallic third term, or the signifier for the Father's Name that create an obstacle to Oneness. This imposes the necessity of achieving a distance from the maternal objects that first caused desire in order that the infant develop the capacity to defend against the overpowering force of the real of incestuous drive identifications and trauma. He maintains that the series of pre-oedipal identificatory "introjects" or unary traits constitutive of *being*— which always includes something real of the living organism—are an intersection of *imaginary* transferential material (on the o′/o narcissistic axis of the Schema L) with the *symbolic* order of language (on the Other/subject axis).[8] Lacan showed the interweaving of mind and body out of the buildup of imaginary and symbolic material that links and overlaps to form elementary signifying chains. These, in turn, become the particular knots or *sinthomes* that join meaning to being and body in the energetic field of the partial drives Lacan called oral, anal, scopic, and invocatory (*S. XI, The Four Fundamental Concepts*, chapters 13 and 14).

In this topological picture, the Ideal ego formation is built up element by element, moment by moment, out of pieces of the concrete world. These ever-accreting signifying units reproduce themselves as Borromean knots that are the links of body to language. Their referents are the object (*a*) as lost, or the other of oedipal identification as absent. The multiple-layered associational memory bank we call *mind, self, identity, or imagination* is formed in this way. The real is that part of the "mind" which *ex-sists* just beyond the graspable meaning of precise images, signifying words, or desired objects. Another way to describe the real is as the particular Other, or unconscious, one equates with one's true feelings, or with the interior or inside of one's being.

Lacan argued, moreover, in *Seminar XX* that the assumption of *being*—or the coalescence of the symbolic and imaginary in the Ideal ego unconscious formation—as preponderantly masculine or feminine makes of an identificatory position an epistemological one as well.[9] And although any person's identification with masculine or feminine signifiers and images *necessarily* implies an identification with both, Lacan does not take that to mean that identity or being is bisexual, either inherently or constructively. Since masculine or feminine concern different positions taken vis-à-vis lack—as lover or beloved—; not sexuality per se, there is *approchement* as well as non-rapport. What, then, links jouissance to masculine or feminine knowledge? The answer Lacan gives refers to the particular jouissance traits that elicit love. Their early foundations lie in one's "resolutions" (identifications) of the oedipal matrix.

Rather than resort to arbitrary agents such as "chemistry" or "kismet," Lacan speaks of concrete conditions that evoke identificatory unary traits (S_I). This distinguishes them from the imaginary love one has for movie-star stereotypes, placing them, rather, in the lineage of one's own family. Indeed, this is the opposite of the theory that says opposites attract in love.

In linking the masculine to the feminine with Freud's notions of active and passive, such that active characterizes the position of the lover found on the masculine side in sexuation, Lacan depicts a paradoxical "active" since it depends on the lover's being lacking, wanting. While passive marks the place of the beloved on the feminine side of sexuation, again, there is a paradox, for the feminine assumes the garb of a seductive "object," thus manifesting action, activity. As such, active and passive are sexual and epistemological, as well as interchangeable, stances. They arise out of the fact that sexuation is taken on in reference to a tertiary oedipal structure wherein "active" and "passive" define castration as well as desire. Although we know that by oedipal Lacan did not mean, as did Freud, that the child wants to have sexual relations with its opposite-sex (oedipal) parent, we also know that both sexes are sexually drawn to the (pre-oedipal) mother. Since sexual feelings mark any subject's relation to the object (a)—goal of the drives—within the family, the reality of sexual feelings is not Lacan's point.

At the point where "identity"—and its masculine or feminine forms in *sexuation*—comes into play, one confronts the particular fantasy that marks *subject* identity as necessarily sexualized, not only in terms of the jouissance satisfied in the drives, but also in terms of that which cuts into jouissance, forbidding it. Lacan calls this the fourth order, where the subject is the *sinthome* of his or her relation to the object (a)—cause of desire—at the point where the Father's Name signifier has placed a prohibition. Its effect is that of knotting a residue of jouissance to language and images. Lacan learned this, empirically speaking, in his work with psychotic patients who lacked this prohibitory knot.[10] Lacan's insistence that most infants take on the images and signifiers of fundamental fantasy, not only in reference to the *two* sexes of their universe, but in an asymmetrical way, allowed him to advance a new analytic theory of the mother's role in the construction of her child's drives. In *The Seminar IV*, he maintains that identifying with the mother connotes an identification with the drives in the real; with the gifts of love she prefers in the symbolic; and with the images of Woman she projects in the imaginary.

One might think Lacan's theory here is similar to Nancy Chodorow's or Carol Gilligan's.[11] Unlike Chodorow or Gilligan, however, Lacan's theory posits mother plus father, a *structure* of the masculine (and feminine) wherein the masculine means that the logic (of difference itself) creates a given symbolic content that takes itself as *all* there is to know or be. That is, a wholistic identification with an historical symbolic moment's set of conventions is taken as reality. The feminine, by contrast, is constituted by a logic of *not [being] all* enslaved within a symbolic order. A woman is tethered to the real wherein the same is not identical to itself, while a man is anchored by the symbolic that exists only to define differences. Consequently, any woman has the "right" to emotional excess—through tears, laughter, gossip, religious fervor—as defined by her symbolic context.

Lacan, unlike Freud, does not link the logic of the masculine or feminine to the distinction between the biological sexes. Although Lacan retains the logic Freud was trying to get at in speaking of the male as the standard or norm, Lacan stresses the valorization of difference as castration to explain why a masculine identified subject would speak a master discourse. The answer is for the purpose of closing up gaps or silencing questions. "Having the penis" does not mean being the representative of the largest number of people who are "standard," or in some way, superior or preferable, Lacan reiterated. But knowing the answers does. In separating the master discourse from the analyst's, Lacan showed that Freudian psychological arguments actually replicate the errors made by the imaginary "master" insofar as he or she appeals to the realm of the immediately visible, which seems full and adequate to itself, even seeming to *be* itself. Imaginary delinations between the masculine and feminine clearly make up the multicultural history of how the sexual difference has been variously represented in a given society.

Lacan, unlike Chodorow or Gilligan, is neither sociological or psychological. Whereas psychological and sociological refashioning of the terms of the masculine and the feminine take the sexual differences as created by silly mistakes, susceptible to easy restructuring by modification of the language and role models given an infant, Lacan was struck by the persistence of an early fixity of the ideas underlying any "behavior" once they are the language bedrock from which unconscious associative memories are drawn, from *la lalangue.* Lacan's theory would not claim that sociological modifications of gender constructs do not occur. The symbolic order continually restructures its definitions of the masculine and feminine. Rather, Lacan measured the difficulty of changing one's *sinthomes* given the impasses that make up the order of the real. Meanings that are unsymbolized in conscious thought ex-sist in the real and contain information precisely about the trauma of taking on sexuated being in reference to a sexual difference that is neither inherent or natural.

Lacan's point does not concern role behavior or sexual object preference, then. His is, rather, a bare-bones argument about the causes of individual suffering that transcend the moral prescriptions of cultural or subjective realities of a given historical moment. Whatever her personal identifications or sexual preferences, the girl, as an *anatomical* female, will be defined by the symbolic and imaginary as *not being all within* the order of the symbolic that marks the male *as* male (symbolic/patriarchal) precisely *because* he is not female. Being in the "symbolic" means differing from the first Other, the mother. These first imposed descriptions will become a part of the Ideal ego. Even if the girl is told from birth on that there is no difference between her and a boy at the level of aspiration, brains, professional future, and so on, it will be her mother's *unconscious* desire regarding the phallus—the difference qua difference—that determines the "content" of that daughter's Ideal ego, not the conscious politically correct language of the child's symbolic order, or her mother's.[12]

As one works with Lacan's dense teaching, it becomes clear that his is not a biological essentialist argument, as many feminists have believed.[13] One could even say that Lacan's implicit theory that the sexual difference is the basis for all subsequent differential judgments has been confused with Freud's misogynist view of women that argues that biology is destiny and, thereby, militates against any equality of the sexes in the many spheres of human potential. Lacan's point is, rather, that the symbolic and imaginary *orders* arise as interpretations of a forced awareness of a difference that exists at the level of the body. He inadvertently, although logically, connects Freud's theory of psychic trauma to his own mirror-stage moment in which thought first becomes coextensive with the body. He argues that taking cognizance of the sexual difference is experienced by a young child as traumatic—particularly for the male—since both sexes identify first with the mother.

Along with the myriad cuts of separation, the oedipal "identity" cut is the basic one on which an order of the real is constructed as a knowledge of contradictions and paradoxes that, nonetheless, remain truth-functional at the level of repressed meaning.[14] If the real of flesh links imaginary body to symbolic language via extremes of affect, then the real will be avoided and covered over at all costs. Since the fate of the anatomical male is to identify as *being all within* in an order of the symbolic Other's power, he experiences a paradox. This group dynamic denies the castration attendant upon his recognition that girls—and ultimately his mother—are Other to himself. Lacan calls these structurations of sexuation *masculine* and *feminine* to stress that their causation is not biological. That is, as soon as the biological level is interpreted, it is *mentally* represented. But insofar as representations can never completely cover over the real cuts of separation and the attendant desire for completion, one cannot call Lacan an idealist thinker.

To emphasize this, Lacan removes the value-laden meanings of virile and active, versus subtle and passive, that Freud had ascribed to the terms *masculine* and *feminine*. Opting for lover and beloved, Lacan places these terms within a moebian transformational configuration, not a binary oppositional one. That is, such traits are on opposite sides of a surface, ever moving toward the twist in the center of the band, and all the while oscillating between two poles. Sexuation—that is, masculine and feminine traits—subtend all identificatory structurations of desire: In the (oedipal) sexual masquerade Lacan calls "normative," the split between the sexes. ("Castration") is accepted as a regulatory axis for social relations. In the neuroses, the split between the masculine and feminine is denied, thus causing neurotic suffering. This is not to say the normative subject does not suffer. One could argue that "normative" suffering often takes the shape of somatic symptoms. The point is that such suffering comes from a different placement of the lacks and splits that characterize obsession and hysteria, (the neuroses) in their denial that the sexual difference makes a difference. While the denial can be proved true in the symbolic, it remains, nonetheless, as a residual weight in the real that appears in the imaginary as an inert burden.

Insofar as the psychotic subject identifies as being One with the primordial mother, as such, he or she is not psychically marked by the difference of sexuation, with its implicit loss or lack of the other gender. Lacan stressed not only the psychotic's fantasy Oneness with the primordial mother, but also the lack of an inscription for loss of the object in the real. Paradoxically, Lacan finds a whole ego only in psychosis, even if that ego has reorganized itself into a delusory construct such as Schreber's wife of God. In his discussion of the Schreber case, Lacan elaborated his Schema I to describe the psychotic's jouissance as transsexualist insofar as this subject experiences himself or herself as one with the other of address, be it a woman or a man.[15] By transsexualist jouissance, I understand Lacan to mean that the subject experiences himself or herself as one with woman qua mother ("Subversion," Schema I, *Ecrits*, p. 202).

In the sexuation of nonpsychotic subjects, the "mother-object" is lost detail by detail—the breast, the voice, the gaze: That is what Lacan means by "The [essential] Woman does not exist" (*S. XX*, ch. 7). And these losses are interpreted by signifiers that build up a system of dialectical reasoning based on lack (or doubt); $\$/S_1 \rightarrow S_2$. In his third theory of psychosis, Lacan implies that the object can be partially lost, but that this loss is not dialecticized in thought. Thus, James Joyce, for example, uses a reified, purified form of the voice to fill the void place in being created by object loss (*Le séminaire, livre XXIII* (1975–1976): *Le sinthome*).

Lacan's kind of thinking runs counter to the International Psychoanalytic Association's (IPA) psychoanalytic thought in which ego splitting is said to accompany fetishism, or psychosis, or borderline conditions. Lacan maintained that IPA adaptive models prefer a master discourse of duplicity and misrecognition over any encounter with the real of truth and the ego splits that follow in the wake of an encounter with the real. Here, Lacan developed a germ of thinking present in the later Freud which made sense to him in light of the work being done in the 1940s on the phenomenon of imprinting in animals and the observation of a normal period of transitivism in young children. Lacan brought all these phenomena together in his theory of "a mirror stage" of would-be "normative" development, characterized by a splitting of the ego between self and other. Lacan placed this relation on an imaginary axis of narcissistic mergers, intersected by the symbolic prohibitions and expectations that language and Otherness bring into the imaginary consistencies individuals develop as a defense against the real void place that carries anxiety in its wake. Indeed the imaginary conflates inside and outside much like Descartes handled the body as a *res extensa.* One can find a hint at such a conceptual alignment with Freud on Lacan's part in Freud's 1937 piece "Splitting of the Ego in the Process of Defence," where he says: "I have at last been struck by the fact that the ego of a person whom we know as a patient in analysis must, dozens of years earlier, when it was young, have behaved in a remarkable manner in certain particular situations of pressure. . . . It occurs under the influence of psychical trauma."[16]

The psychical trauma par excellence, in Lacan's theory, is the assumption of an ego via identifications with Other (i.e., alien) images, language, and drive affects, all of which organize themselves around the central lack of being all one sex: $\Phi/-\phi \rightarrow \varnothing$. Given that one of Lacan's innovations for psychoanalytic theory and practice lies in his idea that the structurations of desire culminate in four different epistemological orientations toward the sexual difference—normative acceptance of castration or the central lack-in-being; neurotic denial of the sexual difference; perverse repudiation of it; or its psychotic foreclosure—these structures recast Freud's concepts of normalcy versus psychopathologies. No one is whole. We are all subjects of our "pathologies," which one might call our interpretations of castration. By adding a category of the real, Lacan acknowledges traumatic knowledge as inscribed, but not symbolized in language. He argued that psychoanalysis can, however, enable one to symbolize bits and pieces of this real as the "truth" of repressed suffering that resides at the points of impasse in knowledge and in inabilities to change.

For purposes of gender theory and psychoanalysis, his argument is that no matter how role models are given in language and images—portraying boys and girls as radically different, as totally equal, as interchangeable, and so on—a child takes on its sense of being gendered or sexuated in response to loss, as well as in response to the mother's *unconscious* desire concerning castration vis-à-vis a signifier for the Father's Name. The unavoidable and imperfect coordinates that constitute each child's experience in the particular—in the *sinthome*—are, then, a combination of the mother's *unconscious* desire and the Father's Name.[17] Analytic practice, in this context, will *not* be a matter of the patient's (re)telling his or her story to the point of resolution or being reparented in the countertransference, but rather, will place upon the analysand the responsibility of changing his or her relation to his or her jouissance.

Lacan's Concepts of the Phallus and Castration

Lacan gave the name phallus to the space between the mother's desire and the Father's Name where the sexual difference is interpreted. When Lacan says that the phallus or phallic signifier have no readily discernible signified, he means that the interpretation of the division between the sexes will always constitute the enigma of a subject's desire as signified responses without any apparent cause, albeit within the normative language of the masquerade, the neuroses, perversion, or psychosis. That the third-term *signifying* sexual difference is the basis of the development of a potential dialectical movement (except in psychosis) in thinking means that one first goes from a question mark ($\cancel{S}$) about the gaps in one's life, to whatever "object" filler(s) (a) one finds to suture this lack-in-being. This is the formula for fantasy—$\cancel{S} <> a$—that collapses lack/desire and the desired object along with alienation and separation ($<>$). This gives greater precision to a term like *subjectivity*, making sense of Lacan's claim that one's reality is one's fantas(ies).

In the sexuation graph Lacan set out in *Seminar XX*, chapter 7, we remember that he reread Freud's *Totem and Taboo* (1913) to deduce a logic of the "masculine" as a denial of castration—that is, a denial that the sexual difference requires one to lose anything—based on the premise that there is one supermale, a kind of Ur-father, who is not castrated and in whose name the brothers join together as a body committed to the cooperation based on group law (see also "A Love Letter" in *Feminine Sexuality*).

Unlike the logic of masculine sexuation, the logic of "feminine" sexuation, does not identify woman with sexual difference such that she need evolve a myth of The Woman exception-to-the-law—an Essential Woman or Ur-mother—which would sustain the same kind of mythical lie touted by men in order to ward off the threat of phallic castration. Although women generally identify with an exception to the rule, be it God or some powerful figure in the symbolic, Lacan's hypothesis is that at the point of the "feminine" in identification, woman has a direct rapport with the lack in the Other such that she cannot entirely sustain the phallic lie of there being no such lack.

When Lacan terms *castration* the effect of the phallic signifier—to create lack— and unveils the oedipal triad where the mother and father define the baby-phallus in reference to what each has and each lacks—*castration*—he designates the child as a dual interpretation of the sexual difference insofar as *lack* marks the being of both parents. In human relations the lack of the female penis in the imaginary register gives rise to a *Fort! Da!* perception wherein both sexes have unconscious fantasies regarding having or losing an organ. The representational interpretation of this imaginary difference creates a hole in the symbolic of each sex that is experienced as a lack-in-being. As we know, this secondary lack, which one might call the first oedipal cut, has a referent in a prior cut between the objects that first *caused* desire and became associated with the promise of pleasure based on their being refound after having been lost.

In the third period of his teaching, Lacan formalized the gap between the imaginary object and the symbolic name that interprets it by a matheme denoting imaginary castration, the negative phi ($-\phi$). Because the image and the name for it do not correspond inherently, Lacan argues that meaning immediately becomes paradigmatic of deciphering the basic sexual riddles. Language itself takes on the charge of jouissance (*jouis-sens*) because—public or private—*it* becomes responsible for closing up the concrete effects of a difference that, at the very least, produces doubt or worry, and at the most, anxiety.

Lacan clearly does not mean emasculation by castration, nor masochism, nor an inferiority complex, or any other such literalist interpretation. Castration refers, rather, to the particular effects on each person of (potential) loss. One might speak, then, of loss in the field of the partial drives, which arises primarily in response to the loss of the objects-cause-of-desire and, secondarily, in response to the loss that organizes identification in an oedipal trajectory. Although, Lacan used Freud's terms *Verneinung* (denial/neurosis), *Verleugnung* (repudiation/perversion) and *Verwerfung* (foreclosure/psychosis) to describe unconscious stances taken toward the real of sexual difference, more foundationally—although Lacan is not a foudationalist precisely because the phallic signifier is neither innate nor always socially constructed (as in autism or psychosis)—analysis unveils the trauma each child undergoes in interpreting himself or herself as castrated in reference to the mother. Finding no kind of mental, spiritual, or psychical superiority in being a male, Lacan was perplexed by any privileging of the sexual difference until he understood that *mental* acceptance of this difference could be foreclosed and, indeed, was the hallmark of psychosis.

Put another way, Lacan argued that knowledge is itself a defense against the *trauma* of taking on being in reference to an unwelcome (phallic) intrusion into the experienced oneness of mother and child. One represses, denies, repudiates, or forecloses knowledge of this difference, thus establishing particular differential criteria as the basis of mentality, as well as of the jouissance desiderata of sexuality. In psychosis, the *Verwerfung* is of the real Father's Name, the real father of jouissance being the one who "normally" imposes castration (Φ) on his children by introducing a "no" to the child's wish to have the mother all to himself or herself. This no begets symbolic castration as the basis of social law, and creates the foundation for the possibility of dialectical thought.

While Piaget, for example, took dialectical thought to arise in response to developmental normality, Lacan allows us to see it as the outcome of the oedipal route by which one "develops" as a subject who lacks a fullness of being or a whole ego, since one *mentally* accepts losing the primordial object(s) of satisfaction and replacing them with substitutes. The psychotic subject eschews lack. In consequence, he or she becomes mentally conflated with his or her own ideals. Lacking the distance from images, objects, or words to represent himself or herself by images or signifiers, this subject feels One with the images and signifiers of her world. They are real—not metaphorical—for the psychotic subject. It is in this sense that Lacan says there is no lack-in-being in psychosis; no $\emptyset$. There is no subject of fantasy, nor of dreams; only a subject of delusions and nightmares. Freud's "psychopathologies" have become Lacan's structures of desire whose referents are the phallus and castration. We remember that of the many meanings Lacan gave castration, the lack-of-being all one sex, is the concomitant denial found in any myth or dream of androgyny, harmonious union, or hermaphroditic oneness.

Rather, Lacan referred to the object—or, more precisely, its lack—to interpret Freud's idea that object *Refindung* can only be *imagined* via desire in reference to an object that has already been lost. In Lacan's recasting of Freud, the four possible interpretations of castration bear on the overall sense he gives to Freud's notion of object *Findung* as a refinding. The initial loss of the object—be it of the mother's breast, the infant's own feces, a voice, or a gaze from the Other—places loss at the beginning of the constitution of being or identity or self. Thus, loss causes the inscription of jouissance effects Lacan names drive affects or unary traits.[18] Losses are not forgotten, are not just nothing, are not altogether lost, but leave behind indivisible traces of the real that Miller has described as "divine details." And these unary traits both create and bind the holes that ex-sist in the imaginary and symbolic to void space, bringing unconscious material into conscious life as the hole and its mark or unary trait.

While the cuts of primordial castration—that is, the loss of the primary objects that first *caused* desire—underlie the jouissance ups and downs of affect, in secondary castration a child is confronted with the necessity of interpreting the sexual difference. Thus, Lacan recasts Freud's content-specific narrative as the triadic structure of the oedipal experience, a topological structure. Lacan focused on the fact that neither the boy nor the girl *has* the phallus. Its "thirdness" is powerfully registered as its potential separability, its signified being the lack-of-being all one sex. Here we are confronted with a symbol that is neither an image or a dual meaning. It is more like a metaphor. That is, something is first substituted for an invisible effect that Lacan localized on the axis of gender identity. The substitution in question is the structural outcome of the oedipal identification where what is signified is the loss of one's other half. Thus, here phallic "symbol" does not indicate a duality of meaning whose referent is explicable by Greek philosophy, theology, biology, Chomskyan linguistics, or any other supposedly primary meaning system, or any other metalanguage.

Rather, Lacan uses *symbol* to mean the base unit of experience that is transformed into images of identification, signifiers of nomination, and inscriptions traced on the body that become Eros or Thanatos.[19] The symbol's signified, in other words, is not some deeper or truer meaning, but the epistemological nexus of image/word/affect that composes knowledge itself. And speaking *enacts* this knowledge in the real. It seems almost incomprehensible that much of a person's knowledge is an elaboration of his or her first interpretations of the phallic signifier's producing the effect of castration. But Lacan argues nothing less.

In *Le séminaire, livre IV*, written in the 1950s, Lacan reconceptualized the "object" away from then popular psychoanalytic concepts of it, elaborating a theory whose relevance lies not only in a new way of conceptualizing the subject/object distinction that has worried theologians and philosophers for centuries, but also in a logical explanation of what causes *disorder*. These revisions of knowledge are based on a new understanding of the differential signifier (the phallic one) in reference to which *order* is constituted. That is, oedipal identification becomes the pivotal construct—gender difference is learned (or not) as a third term between two others—out of which a dialectic constitutes the law of the symbolic order as an interplay between Freud's reality principle and the jouissance of the real (Freud's pleasure principle).

Prior to his first "formal" period of teaching in the 1950s, Lacan argued in "The Mirror Stage as Formative of the Function of the I as Revealed in Psychoanalytic Experience" (1949) that a child's sense of *being* a being is taken on imaginarily—that is, in reference to images, imagos, or gestalts that merely reduplicate his or her body in a virtual way ("The Mirror Stage . . . ," pp. 281–91). Even though such a theory is rooted in Husserl's phenomenological idea of the body as the source of knowledge in its immediate, intuitive, subjective experience of the world, Lacan argued that the body can only be experienced as existing—beyond the real—insofar as it is first named or represented to itself. Lacan's first theory of identification shows what the Freudian concept of the *complex* owes to the imagos that anchor one's first sense of "self" in a matrix of signifiers. This new theory of identification gave rise to his subsequent topological theory of the imaginary body as the doubled representations by which one makes realities mentally consistent.

In the 1970s, Lacan argued that the image is *more* than mere appearance, semblance, or lure "object." Indeed, the image-object functions with all the force of the-thing-itself.[20] Just prior to this period, Lacan had located anxiety in the imaginary order. When an image is perforated or subverted—either a simple image or an elaborate picture of one's life—the real of anxiety appears as a hole in being that an image cannot completely cover over. This hole rips into the comforting consistency the imaginary generally offers as a buffer against encountering lack or loss from the unconscious.

Lacan's Theory of the Real and the Object (*a*)

Insofar as an infant's *first* awareness of a concrete lack- in-being refers to the cut between the *object* that offers satisfaction and the *void* created by the loss of that object, the cut itself is invested with positive traits of the objects, as well as negative traits of the loss. Lacan explained this dialectic in *Le séminaire X* (1962–1963), where he claimed that anxiety has an object. That object is an *encounter* with the void place *in* being. This is an entirely new picture of anxiety from Freud's notion of it as a response to fears in face of which one is helpless, or as a reaction against sexual excitement.[21] At stake in anxiety, Lacan argues, is the imaginary illusion that typically marks the mirror-stage logical identification with the belief that one is a whole body appended to a whole "self." This misconception imagines a total, unperturbed self as representative of a complete body. Lacan placed consciousness in the imaginary, which is anchored in jealously, agressivity, fantasy, narcissistic exchanges, and subjectivity.

Working by a logic of the "whole," the imaginary projects the ideal traits with which an individual, in turn, seeks to identify. In the last phase of his teaching, Lacan called the imaginary the order of the body as projected onto the real of the flesh, word-pictures simultaneously taming and exciting the real at limits and impasses. Although the *real* is the order of the disruptions of trauma, Lacan taught in this final period that it appears within logical thought as enigmata, as intrusions, or as absolute densities of affect, unlike imaginary repetitions that seek to keep "reality" consistent by avoiding any encounter with the void place located between the imaginary and the real:

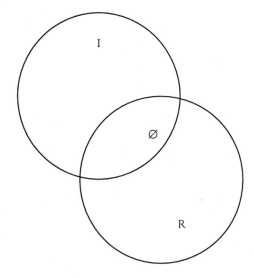

By the third period of his teaching,[22] Lacan had formalized many of his ideas, which he simplified by reference to a basic topological unit—the triadic form of the Borromean knot that arises from simpler toplogical forms such as the Moebius strip or the cross-cap—whose loops he called the real, symbolic, and imaginary. These orders, each discrete within itself, are knotted together (or not, as in psychosis) by overlapping one with another. In a larger sense, the overlappings themselves constitute what Lacan called the order of the knot, a fourth order whose referent is the signifier for the Name-of-the-Father, or the order of the Symptom, which knots the other three together around belief in a guarantor of a knowledge's correctness. Lacan explained how the excluded middle—the place of the three jouissances—in the space of the overlaps are constituted out of elements of any two interlinked orders and, thus, also form their own logic, even if it seems nonsensical or irrational.

Jacques-Alain Miller has developed Lacan's use of the term *extimacy* to describe the "outside meaning" (*horsens*) nature of the concrete details of the real that enter conscious thought as enigmata or impasses: "The traits of the real are symptoms which have the property of agalma—an outsideness and insideness coalesce—as more than you." They are like a distant interior that seems to be both outside and inside at once (*Extimité*). In the "development" of the "exigencies" of the real, symbolic, imaginary, and the symptom—which constitute mind/body as a vast interlinked network of signifying units—myriad associational chains *fix* premirror-stage fragmentary identifications with the real of partial objects that caused desire prior *to* the mirror-stage illusion of unity. These, in turn, subtend the oedipal experience of disunity where an effect of thirdness divides a pleasurable, albeit illusory, symbiosis. This concrete account of how the mind/body intrication is disassociated and interwoven by accretions of Borromean units—

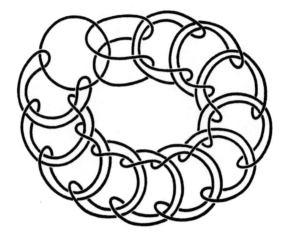

—gives quite a different picture from Freud's conception of mind as an a priori unified agency, perturbed in certain cases by uncontainable conflicts. Where Freud places conflict, Lacan placed the real as traumatic. One might say the oedipal encounter with sexual difference is traumatic precisely because the child must interpret it in terms of castration—that is, in terms of his or her primordial experiences of *the object as lacking*, the cut already serving as an initial encounter with loss.

Jacques-Alain Miller has stressed Lacan's concept of "extimacy" in describing the organization Lacan gave to the void place whose positive existence is proved not only by the fact that all life is structured so as to avoid experiences of isolation or aloneness, but also by the very negativity of the affects that life activity avoids. What *object* fills a void place in being, then, giving its structure to the hole: $\varnothing \leftarrow a$? In 1960 Lacan listed eight objects that *cause* desire. Characterizing Freud's "mamilla, faeces, the phallus (imaginary object), the urinary flow" as "an unthinkable list, if one adds, as I do, the phoneme, the gaze, the voice—the nothing"[23]—Lacan made it clear that insofar as desire is causal, by *phallus* he does not mean penis, except as an imaginary form. As early as 1958 he had used the term *phallus* to describe this image or representation of a difference between the sexes as that on whose basis each sex forms a relation to the symbolic order as himself or herself lacking (or not lacking) this semblant.[24]

Since the image is real for the psychotic subject, it is not a representation. For all other subjects, it marks gender imaginarily. So strong is the psychotic subject's conflation of organ with being that the mere confusion of his or her name with the opposite sex name can shake the fragile link between the real and symbolic, held rigidly together by an absolute belief that the word equals the thing.[25] "Mistakes" in language risk exposing the psychotic's lack of an imaginary, which one might describe here as an order of distance from the jouissance of the real, something the psychotic subject lacks.[26] Where Freud found conflict, Lacan implied that the cause of conflict is the real of loss. In the "Names-of-the-Father" seminar, Lacan wrote that anxiety comes from not knowing what you are for the Other. One might say the encounter with sexual difference is traumatic precisely because the child must interpret this difference in reference to the loss Freud called castration—$(-\phi)$—that is, in terms of his or her experience of an imaginary organ as potentially *lacking* in the eyes of the Other. Since the image is real for the psychotic subject, it not a representation. For all other subjects it marks gender imaginarily, as we have already noted.

We remember that Freud first used the word *phallus* when seeking to show the relations and distinctions that mark "reality" by a split between biological reality and psychic reality, while Lacan took this to mean that the interpretation of sexual difference is the first abstract concept—the axis of dialectical thought—which children normally grasp around age five. The first oedipal moment, in Lacan's teaching, occurs commensurately with the acquisition of language as a viable grammar base for thinking. The significance of this for cognitive studies lies in Lacan's discovery that language functions differently in psychosis, neurosis, perversion, and the normative masquerade. If sexuation is an epistemological affair which determines that individuals deploy language in *reference* to the phallus and castration, the *referent* is the real father of jouissance. One could say that the psychotic, over-burdened by the real father, finds the ideal imaginary father outside his Ideal ego which is maternal, mythologizing some ideal father figure or institution. Normative subjects—those who accept to embody an equation of gender identity with biological sexual difference—reify the internalized father signifier by repeating cultural rituals organized around an idealized leader. Neurotics deny that they need any father—or leader—around whom to organize their questions, while the imaginary father must exist for the pervert to subvert insofar as the law of jouissance is, for him, the antithesis of the inherently vacuous representations that "normally" stand in for law, giving a false and duplicitous basis to the Wizard of Oz social masquerade.

Empirically speaking, then, the control "variable" in terms of which Lacan came to understand the oedipal axis as the standard referent against which to measure a differential relation to the object(s) one desires was the relation of the psychotic subject to the foreclosure of the phallic signifier that usually marks sexual difference by symbolic castration for other subjects. Lacking the *lack* on which dialectical reasoning is based, the psychotic, perforce, uses language rigidly and rigorously because the representational distance that continually interprets differences as *imaginary distances* between desire and the objects meant to fulfill it, is lacking. Having never lost the object(s) of desire, having never registered the cut of loss—$\emptyset$—the psychotic is not individuated or separated from the primordial mother, to use object-relations theorist Margaret Mahler's terms. But unlike Mahler, Lacan elaborates the rationality of the logic that ensues from this rejection of castration, not the fact of inadequate separation.

Based on Freud's description of the object as present only insofar as it is absent in his "Three Essays on Sexuality," Lacan put forth a theory of the object—which he, at first, called the *quod*, the thing—that differed radically, not only from psychoanalytic concepts of the object current in his time, but from today's theories as well. At that moment, in the mid 1950s, Lacan was not concerned with the properties of the object qua object-*cause*-of-desire, objects he named in 1960. Nor was he concerned in 1957 with the object (*a*) as a denotation for the present/absent structure of "objects" one pursues in fantasy—$ \rlap{/}{S} <> a$—with the aim of filling a structural lack-in-being. However, in *Seminar XI: The Four Fundamental Concepts of Psycho-Analysis* (1964), Lacan described the object (*a*) as an algebraic variable, denoting that which responds to lack and can be called into presence as a function of lack.

The earlier theory of the object developed in *Seminar IV* argues that its dialectical nature is not a matter of whether the mother is present or absent, or whether she offers her infant a good or bad breast. Rather, castration—defined by Lacan, at that moment, as the object as lacking—gives rise to a different subject *function* in each of the three registers, the imaginary, the symbolic and the real (except in psychosis where there is no lack). The lack operates cosimultaneously, but differently, in each of the three registers that *constitutes* the subject. Given that there is no "personality" in Lacan's teaching, there is, rather, a double-sided subject/object relationship of desire and lack that necessitates the quest for satisfaction outside oneself. In *Seminar IV* Lacan argued that the dialectical nature of the object does not come from a transitional space, as proposed by object-relations analyst Donald Winnicott, where the mother is present or absent, nor from the transitional object between mother and infant. Rather, insofar as castration creates a lack between the object and the desire for it, one can pinpoint three different *functions* of lack in each of the three registers, functions where the lack of the object concerns the subject.

Lacan's point is that objects are present in fantasy only because they have already been lost within the outside world from which they first came. Thus, fantasy objects are constituted of multiple, *concrete* details—unary traits (S_1) as master signifiers—that make any fantasy partial and particular to each subject.[27] Nancy Chodorow does not say, as does Lacan, how traits constitute objects as qualitative aspects of place (*topos*) wherein the traits are inscribed as the basis of a differential between continuous and discontinuous processes. The traits appear as the minimal resemblance(s) of difference between an object and an image, for a word and a sound. Chodorow does say, however, that biology cannot explain the content either of cultural fantasy or private erotism.[28]

By contrast with other subjects, because the psychotic has never symbolized the object-cause-of-desire as lacking, this subject experiences the objects of the world through a grid of chaotic delusion, not as integrated fantasy.[29] Rather, a retention of the jouissance connected with the first experience of objects organizes psychotic language, not the desire that responds to the lack or loss of those objects.[30] The psychotic's refusal of object loss (Freud's *Verwerfung*) *shows* up imaginarily as an affirmation (*Bejahung*) of particular traits for most subjects.[31]

In *Seminar IV*, in his concern to say what creates lack in the first place, Lacan listed three objects that correspond to three lacks that constitute the subject, in reference to three different agents. In chapter 16 ("How Does Myth Analyze Itself?"), he put forth the fully developed form of this table (*Le seminaire IV*, p. 269):

AGENT real father	LACK symbolic castration	OBJECT imaginary phallus $(-\phi)$
symbolic mother	imaginary frustration	real breast $(\varnothing)$
imaginary father	real privation	symbolic phallus (Φ)

Having lost the actual object—both a real organ and an image of it, the breast, for example—the infant's desire for a return of the real organ-object turns on a pleasure that is paradoxical, overlapping as it does with the imaginary frustration experienced at its loss. Lacan describes the frustration as imaginary, not because it "is not real and true, but because it is the step of jouissance. At the same time, it is what gives its [pseudo]consistency to the symbolic, it is precisely that there is no Other of the Other" (*R.S.I.*, March 18, 1975). Unlike Freud, who thought conflict arose at the site of psychic disturbance, Lacan posited conflict as the real that makes imaginary frustration a discontinuity. An infant's first task of symbolizing the world starts in disharmony, Lacan argued, not in union or harmony.

Given that the forces that structure being for subjectivity are not stages or developmental sequences, they are, rather, "topological" logical "passages" that organize the real of the partial *drives* in reference to the symbolic mother. This is the mother who *gives signifying* responses from the Other—Lacan often calls the symbolic order.[32] The other two lacks of the object are organized in reference to a real father, agent of symbolic castration insofar as he forbids incest, that is, a totality of jouissance between the infant and mother. The real father of enjoyment deprives the infant of the imaginary phallus—"You don't have it," he implies to the girl; "You are not it," to the boy—which creates the symbolic castration Lacan equated with a lack-in-being. In the second case, when an infant loses the real object—the breast, for example—his or her desire to have the organ-object back gives rise to a pleasure that is paradoxical. Since loss begets desire in a dialectic of imaginary frustration between the real loss and the agent, the symbolic mother, Lacan describes the cause as frustration, as imaginary, creating confusions of corporal responses with symbolic identifications.

The material that structures fantasy (subjectivity) from the start of life is not stages or developmental sequences, then, but the confusion between the real of (organ) satisfaction and the symbolic mother whose *signifying* responses are the first gifts or givens taken from the Other. The third agent of lack, the imaginary father, is seen as the cause of real privation in the guise of images that lead a child to configure him in representations of authority. The imaginary father does not really have the symbolic phallus of authority, Lacan argues, but insofar as the child believes he does, he can occasion responses of despair, such as the Young Homosexual woman's throwing herself over a bridge when her father deprives her of his approval in a scalding gaze of derogation.[33]

Insofar as lack is *organized* in reference to actual parents who simultaneously serve different functions in different orders, the range of responses to lack can not be uniform. One response to early experience in the drives is autism—the extreme pole of psychosis in which an infant identifies entirely with a negativity of the partial objects. In autism, there is no object loss, which is another way of saying that there is no pleasure of the object, merely a negative, oppressive presence of it. In Lacan's teaching, autism is structured prior to the mirror stage and prevents the mirror stage from occuring (cf. Ragland, *Essays on the Pleasures of Death*, Ch. 6). Normally objects cause desire because they are repeatedly lost and, hence, traces of them must be refound outside. In this sense, transference onto others constitutes the hope of recouping object satisfaction. It is set up from the beginning of life as a dialectical relation between the infant and the world, an exchange the autistic infant never has.

In the psychoses, schizophrenia and paranoia, an infant remains identified with the illusionary (dyadic) Oneness of mirror-stage moments. These are governed by the voice, most particularly, in schizophrenia, while the gaze is paramount in paranoia. These objects attempt to substitute for the missing dialectical or tertiary nature of the oedipal structure. While the teleology behind object relations in psychosis is that of a literally identical mirroring, most people who are not psychotic seek others and things to close up the structural lack-in-being. Lacan argued as early as *Seminar IV* that no object, person, thing, or activity, can ever finally or permanently fill up a structural gap, or close a set. This is a logical (and tragic) fact he symbolized in the third period of his teaching by placing a bar over the Other itself (Ø).

Lacan's Interpretation of Freud's "Little Hans Case"

In *Seminar IV* Lacan developed his theory of the object as lacking by referring to Freud's "Little Hans Case," as well as to Freud's 1924 essay on "The Dissolution of the Oedipus Complex," written a year before "Some Psychical Consequences of the Ana-tomical Distinction between the Sexes" (1925).[34] These two essays in which Freud developed his theories of the castration complex and the phallic mother were crucial to a reconceptualization of the *object*, Lacan argued. Individuals seek objects to fill the emptiness whose constitution places a concrete *place* of suffering in being. The point many readers of Lacan miss is that the void is so unbearable that one rarely encounters it. Indeed, we structure our lives so as to avoid it. For most people, the void shows up anyway in various permutations of affect, all focused on the details of the lost objects that are supposed to fill the void. Although this is a reversal of Plato's theory of ideal forms in which all forms imitate a perfect invisible and indivisible form, Lacan gives a concrete explanation of what forms "form," trait by trait. Given that the unary traits of concrete details are "transformed" in all four orders—real, symbolic, imaginary, and the symptom—primordial experiences are the bedrock of all signifying chains of mind and memory, the bedrock even of the most abstract endeavors.

Lacan's concept of the *object* in *Seminar IV* does not harken back to the 1920 Freudian object of *pare-excitations*, then, or to Freud's 1933 concept of the pre-oedipal mother who produces in her infant a sense of conflict between herself as seductive and herself as offering a protective barrier from id excitement. Insofar as a subject's relation to the other, be it mother, love partner, or analyst, is only ever mediated in reference to lack, this is the aspect of the object relation Lacan takes up in *Seminar IV*. Although, Lacan finds Freud's 1924 comment on the resolution of the oedipal experience helpful, he emphasizes that it is not a literal fear of castration that defines the castration complex, but the mystery regarding why the "self" suffers.

If an infant's "intelligence" and emotionality are not predetermined to develop in biological stages, nor in reference to the mother's mothering skills, but primarily as jouissance responses to the partial objects that cause desire—and only secondarily as an interpretation of gender via oedipal identifications—one can understand Lacan's claim that frustration by the real results in an imaginary attempt to control it. Freud's conflict model would be an imaginary effort to represent the forces at play in the real of the drives. Thus, the *dialectic* of anticipation and retroaction of meaning, desire, and enjoyment places diachronic temporality *in* language as a kind of logical time, referring to associations surrounding the loss and refinding of traces of the mother's breast, her gaze, her voice, and so on, all harkening back to disruptions of the imaginary infant-mother dyad. At those originary moments, the mother acts as agent of the symbolic order, the giver of real gifts—the breast, the gaze, the voice—objects-*cause*-of-desire, whose dialectic concerns presence and absence, having and lacking/wanting, love and hate, all of which elicit frustrations.

Within Lacan's topological framework, the identifications of imaginary frustration are situated in the turn of the curve where desire begets lack and lack begets desire. The object at issue is occulted in the twist. Such a logic is best represented by the continuous structure of the Moebius strip: 8. Lacan's view of conflict as a temporal tension in the present that makes contradiction logically truth-functional, clearly differs from Freud's who saw it as a behavioral regression to the past and not as a structural dialectic of contradiction between categories; that is, in the spaces of overlap between orders. For Lacan, conflict is the insistence of a real component in the signifying chain, one that oscillates between narcissistic identification and aggressive rage or anger at being thwarted in an experience of primary jouissance. That is, conflict comes from the real of the drives. Later, conflict will blame the Woman-supposed-to-exist. The very first experience of frustration arises when the desire for the real breast (or bottle) is disrupted, for example, by a telephone call that breaks the infant's perceived unity of a moment. Perception is defined by Lacan here as a gap between what is and what is not (Groome, p. 84). Lacan's point is that the infant's relation to the object is not to the mother as a person, nor even to the breast qua object-thing, but to the sudden *lack* of an object he or she thought was his or hers, one with him or her.

Although the organ-object appears to give rise to *imaginary* frustration, *seeming* to belong to the mother or to exist on its own as a piece of flesh, the agent of the first frustration(s) is the *symbolic* mother/Other (*S. IV*, p. 199) whose "symbolic" gifts are the primordial material of love. The breast "symbolizes" nurture just as the voice "symbolizes" calm or joy, and so on. Lacan writes in *Seminar IV:*

> The mother exists as a symbolic object and as object of love. . . . The mother is first a symbolic mother and it is only in the crisis of frustrations that she begins to become real [for the infant] because of a certain number of shocks and particularities that are produced in the relation between the mother and the child. The mother, object of love, can be at each instant the real mother insofar as she frustrates this love. The relation of the child with the mother, which is a relation of love, opens the door to what one generally calls, for lack of knowing how to articulate it, the first undifferentiated relation. (p. 223)

But even though frustration surrounds the aim of the drive for a primordial object— for the breast (or bottle), the gaze, and so on—the aim is not the goal. The goal seeks a oneness of continuity with these objects. Frustration is readily expressed as a cry. In this sense, frustration is quickly caught up in the law of the signifier, which tries to translate it into verbal meaning. The naming of the frustration—be it hunger, a wet diaper, a wind pain, or any other true or false cause—places symbolic alienation over the real of the experience.

Lacan advanced his theory of the object after decades of work with psychotic patients who mentally foreclose the dialectic created by loss. By foreclosing symbolic castration—law—psychotics try to incorporate the mother as the sole object of satisfaction. For other subjects the lack that ordinarily ensues from a loss of primordial objects becomes the differential in reference to which a libidinal order of the drives is created and determines, as well, what causes *disorder*. The effect of an object's prevailing mode—be it hunger, an earache, a wet diaper, a sore throat, or any other true or false cause of discomfort—annihilates the *phallic* signifier as the agent of organization which means rejecting the signifier for the symbolic Father's Name, be the signifier of a mother's brother, a river spirit, or a Woman representing the symbolic. The significance of this key signifier—the Father's Name—in psychic development lies in its calming the lack-in-being by the imposition of a no which places the real of jouissance under the law. In this sense, the father is not a person, but a *function* of language.

The paternal function, by which Lacan redefines the Oedipus complex as the interdiction of a psychic oneness between infant and mother, gives the child an injunction to individuation. The Father's Name signifier acts as a fourth term—a form of the knot—which, paradoxically, denotes the pleasure of a Oneness in jouissance that is simultaneously forbidden. Another name Lacan gives this signifier is the *sinthome*. One *sinthome* of repressing the unconscious shows that most people use language casually, accepting its lacks and gaps and haltings as normal and natural. Psychotic language is, on the contrary, used rigidly. But no matter how astute, accurate, or poetic its use may be, its referent is always *la lalangue* circling around a drive object, not the sexual difference taken as the dialectical base of a lack-in-being[35] that opens onto the social domain of exchange and reciprocity.

To summarize, in the logic of the object Lacan set forth in the first period of his teaching, he described three different experiences of the object as lacking, which he called symbolic castration, imaginary frustration, and real privation. Each relation to the object, linked to a corresponding agent and lack, led him to speak of a "*symbolic* debt, an *imaginary* displeasure, and the hole, or *real* of absence" (*S. IV*, p. 37). Symbolic castration—the lack of being (or having) the phallus in the symbolic that affects both sexes—refers to an *imaginary* object. Lacan symbolized the inscription of this castration, this negation, by the (−φ), which marks a cut between language and the images to which language assigns a value, thereby creating a subject's narrative of identity. The image at issue in symbolic castration would be the little boy's penis. For a little girl, it would be any visible image in which her narcissism is invested—a doll, a bottle, a part of her body, a teddy bear, or whatever. Some clearly visible image will be taken as the phallus, defined here by Lacan as that which has positivizable value insofar as it is visible and stands in as a semblance for one's sense of "being." Certain clearly visible images—a toy, an article of the mother's clothing, even the imaginary phallus—will become problematic when the "reality" of a sexual difference, not perceived before, intersects with the "demand" (drive) to interpret it, or act upon it.

In 1960 Lacan had called the imaginary phallus a nonspecularizable object-*cause*-of-desire ("Subversion . . .," p. 315). By non-specularizable, he did not mean that which lacks an image, but that whose "ex-istence" is absolute, basic, and indivisible in its effect(s). In *Seminar XX* (1972–73), he equated the imaginary phallus with appearance, taken as *the thing itself* (*Encore*, "Knowledge and Truth," ch. 8). In the seminar (*livre IV*) on "the object relation" he still took the image as a representative of the thing and argued that the agent held responsible for the lack of this imaginary object in the symbolic is the real father of jouissance as carrier of the incest taboo. Lacan stresssed that it makes no difference whether the imaginary incarnation of the real father is the Daddy in a contemporary monogamous family, or the signifying function of the outsider or stranger in certain tribal cultures described by Freud in *Totem and Taboo*.[36] It is the divisive effect that is at stake in Lacan's teaching.

"In [symbolic] castration there is a fundamental lack which situates itself as a debt in the symbolic chain," Lacan says early on in *Seminar IV* (p. 55). Something sanctions the prohibition of incest and gives it its support, and its inverse, which is punishment. The debt is owed, in other words, to society. This makes a certain sense of the myriad forms of sacrifice rituals practiced throughout societies in history. "Castration," he says, "has been introduced by Freud in a way [that is] absolutely coordinated with the notion of the primordial law, what there is of the fundamental law in the interdiction of incest and in the structure of the Oedipus" (*S. IV*, p. 37). Thus, "[symbolic] castration—whose object is imaginary—can only be classed in the category of symbolic debt" (p. 37).

But *what* is owed to whom? The answer can only be love insofar as the other interdicted by the real father is the primordial Other, the mother.[37] While Lacan made sense of the notion of an intersection between the visible, a lost object, and the drives, starting in *Le séminaire X* on *Anxiety*, he links the anal (partial) drive to imaginary castration and to the scopic field of the gaze. But he never developed the logic of the relation between love and the primordial mother of the drives. Miller takes up this challenge in *Silet*. His reading of *Seminar IV* gives a logic to the place of the pre-oedipal mother in psychoanalysis that differs from the place she has been given by object-relations theories.

In *Seminar IV* Lacan emphasized the fictional guises given the real father by the imaginary father as figures of the superego that represent the symbolic phallus. He stresses that these are functions and not individuals. Moreover, the functions concern the object and its lack. In *Seminar XX* he set forth the theory that there can be no law except in reference to a superman—a real father, exception to the law of castration or lack—above the law who is, at the same time, excluded from the law and thus, paradoxically, gives it its foundation.[38] But in *Seminar IV*, Lacan was still somewhat Freudian. He portrayed symbolic castration as the experience of the object as lacking, and the agent of this lack as the real father of jouissance. Yet he is clearly not Freudian when he describes the *object* in question here as the imaginary phallus $(-\phi)$, one of whose names might be Woman. Indeed, Fenichel made the equation *Mädchen* = phallus. Another way to understand the imaginary phallus is as a *semblance*, an "object" sign of the visible world, residing between the real and the symbolic. It could be the mother's breast, the little boy's penis, or a new baby. The special privilege accorded the penis above other objects or organs is simply that it visibly symbolizes difference for both sexes as sexual difference. Its transformational forms—baby or baseball bat—are interpretations of this symbol.

After symbolic castration (the incest taboo) and imaginary frustration (loss of the breast), Lacan named *real* privation, as the third relation to the object. Identifying the agent of real privation as the imaginary father who appears in myriad *figures* of the superego, he taught that the *object* to be valorized here is the symbolic phallus (Φ). In *Seminar XX* Lacan developed his theory of the symbolic phallus, arguing that the reality a given subject experiences comes from that subject's master signifiers (S_1). Another name Lacan gave the master signifier was the symbolic phallus: Φ. That is, a subject accepts his or her lack-in-being, which he or she then supplements or replenishes with "master signifiers" already inscribed in his or her Other. They give a precise meaning to his or her life. But what has all this to do with analytic practice?

When the threatened object is the *imaginary* phallus, as in the case of "Little Hans," the person held responsible for the threat is the "real father" of jouissance, a function of the mother or father or anyone else who says no to phallic enjoyment. Lacan's point is a structural one. The basic no is that of the real father whose feelings of desire for the mother automatically forbid a oneness of jouissance between the mother and child. Hans's father brings him to Freud. Lacan attributes his symptoms of phobia and anxiety to his refusal of symbolic castration. At age five Hans is still under the influence of a "phallic mother." But by "phallic mother," Lacan does not mean maternal virility. He means that Hans has not yet substituted the father's law for the desire to be the object of his mother's jouissance. In interpreting Hans's desire to be *all* to her as her desire for him to be *all* to her, Hans makes of his mother a "phallic mother."

Having repudiated the castration that installs a *psychic* lack-in-being during the typical oedipal experience at around age five, Hans is burdened by the imaginary phallus. Lacan says he is encumbered by it, obsessed with it. Lacan retains Freud's term *Verleugnung* (repudiation) here—the mechanism proper to the structure of perversion— arguing that Hans repudiates maternal castration. At age five, Hans is caught in a moment of perversion. The cause of Hans's suffering, Lacan argues, is his inability to renounce *having* the imaginary phallus in order to drop it, lack it, and, thus, assume a *repressed* part that opens up a position within the group structure of his social world.

Lacan's point is that Hans's imaginary father is not adequate to separate Hans from the symbolic mother whose gifts are of the *real*. Such a division can only be accomplished at the level of the real father, at the point when the child understands that his or her mother is the jouissance object of someone else's desire, and someone else is the object of her desire. In his interpretation of the "Little Hans Case," Lacan argues that the *true problematic* of the oedipal experience is in full view here. Even though Freud saw the oedipal experience as a normativizing development, ending in a heterosexual object choice, Lacan points out as early as *Seminar IV* that the most heterosexual of choices can, upon analytic investigation, appear in a truer light as a homosexual desire (*S. IV,* p. 201).

The psychoanalytic problematic does not concern the outcome of object choice, in Lacan's opinion, but how a boy or girl is situated in reference to the function of the father; that is, one can change libinal position only if the signifier for difference is inscribed such that a lack-in-being makes it possible to exchange out of the family romance and make substitutions. Since the function of the father does not mean the actual father, but the structural necessity—lest one be psychotic—that there be a strong enough mechanism to deflect a child from the compelling power of the drives that bind the child of either sex to the pre-oedipal mother, accepting the sexual difference is, perforce, the basis of law itself (cf. the sexuation graph).

Freud reports what Little Hans's father recounted and had written down in meticulous details. Hans is obsessed with his *Wiwimacher,* his *faire pipi,* his penis that he describes by its organic function of "going pee-pee." He asks everyone whether they have this organ too, including his mother. When his father takes him to the zoo, Hans's interest in the lion centers only on whether his father has seen the organ with which the lion makes pee-pee. Lacan viewed Hans's comparisons as efforts to form the image of an absolute object—*the* imaginary phallus—that he can understand in reference to a real bodily function—the urinary function. At age five, Hans confronts the ordinary oedipal task of trying to link his anatomical sex to a "formula" for being. In "To Interpret the Cause: From Freud to Lacan," Miller argues that the oedipal challenge of taking on an identity in terms of one's sexuality is complicated by the child's efforts to "picture" his or her being as male or female in reference to a parental couple (M <> F), which is not the same as the sexual couple (M <> W) (p. 36). But Hans has an extra problem at this moment, an excessive concern with who actually *has* this particular organ. And the psychoanalytic question is why such a question can be so pressing.

At this same period, a little sister is born to Hans. Shortly after his sister's birth, his phobic fear of horses appeared. One could say that Hans's symptoms are, quite literally, a response to his losing his usual place within the field of the familial gaze, a place that had given him an imaginary sense of a consistency of being in terms of the honored position conferred on him there. In response to his sister's birth, he adopts a bunch of imaginary babies—dolls—and plays with them in every way imaginable. Around the same time, he informs his mother that if she has an organ like his, she should show him. In any case, he deduces, her *imaginary* organ must be as big as the *faire pipi* of a horse. Competing with his sister and father for *all* his mother's gaze, he tries to make his mother aware of himself as *having* the organ, Lacan argues.

In 1959 in *Le séminaire VI: Le désir et son interprétation*, Lacan argued that males confuse having the penis—that is, the visible image that first marks difference as a sexual difference—with being the mother's phallus, with being that which she desires.[39] Lacan's theory is that Hans's five-year-old concern with the imaginary phallus shows the point of anxiety between an image that seems stable in itself, that seems to anchor being in a consistency of the body at the level of a wholeness of sexual reality, and the actual failure of the imaginary to provide a grounding precisely because it is made of illusions. That is, the imaginary is perforated by the $\emptyset$, the a, and the $-\phi$.[40]

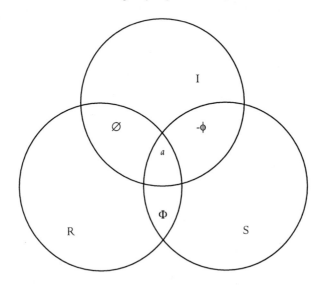

Because the imaginary phallus ($-\phi$) is a perceptually separable organ—a partial object, if you will—because the Other sex does not have it, Little Hans must anchor his sense of being in reference to a visible image that troubles him. He tries to do this by equating being with his penis. He is, thus, a *"sexuated"* subject who is not calm since he has not been able to place his imaginary phallus under the law of castration. That is, he must first have seen the Other as lacking the difference that allows sexuated individuation if emotional calm is to occur, according him a place within that social sphere.

Not only is a foreclosure of the sexual difference the cause of psychosis in Lacan's teaching, the typical acceptance of castration as a lack-of-being-all actually pushes one to find or create a *place* in the symbolic order. In Hans's case, at age five he is implicitly asked by his social order to accept the position or place of son or brother. His (psychic) symptoms come from the *conflict*—that is, the real of what is known, but not symbolized as conscious knowledge—of his inability to identify himself with these figures. He identifies, rather, as his mother's baby, as well as her potential husband. His identificatory confusions show up as attempts to solve the oedipal riddle ($M <> W \cong M <> F$) by threading together an associational series where a bodily function in the real—the penis with which he urinates and masturbates—and an imaginary phallic organ, which he attributes to one and all, give a formula for identity. Rather, he is overwhelmed with the anxiety attendant upon a too-great proximity to the object-*cause*-of-desire (*quod matrem*). If he had remained "psychically" locked in this moment of the oedipal interrogation, Lacan says, he would have been fixed at the level of the Ideal ego unconscious formation in the "forced" choice of realizing his "object" relations with a double of himself, a larger double (*S. IV*, p. 206).

Lacan's position is that, in the oedipal development of the little boy, no mother can answer her son's question about the sexual difference, his "Do you have this imaginary organ?" Only a father can solve the little boy's perplexity. It must be the real father of jouissance who "castrates" the little boy by a *symbolic* interdiction against *having* (being) the imaginary phallus. In other words, the real father makes symbolic castration possible by placing a signification on the imaginary phallus. In Hans's case, such an act would be tantamount to giving him a signifier at the point where he is troubled by a lure image: "You do not have the *imaginary* phallus," would mean "you are not the one who has the means of filling your mother's desire, of giving her jouissance." Although Lacan seems to imply that the penis is the agent of such fulfillment, a careful reading shows that he means by *phallus* the one who desires. When the real father desires the child's mother, his is the place of the lover—$\emptyset$—waiting to be filled by her. In this case, being takes sexuation as its base, in a particular stance vis-à-vis the other, not of organs.

The real father's no to the infant's desire to "own" the mother at the level of jouissance introduces a *lack* into his or her image of "self." This lack-in-the-image ($\sqrt{-1}$) is, in turn, interpreted as a castration in the symbolic. And, paradoxically, in turn, symbolic castration gives both sexes a position in the order of the social exchange where he or she is defined by the family myths—the career girl, a perfect mother—Lacan called the *fixions* established in the oedipal drama. At age five, Litte Hans has not yet found his place in the social world of exchange, in part because his mother is a phallic mother, the phallic mother, Lacan insists, he is designating as an imaginary figure. She is hypothesized as such by Little Hans in his dialectical efforts to decipher the meaning of the sexual difference. Further, Lacan claims that Hans had not yet symbolized his mother as different from himself because his father had not yet acted as a real father, one who indicates to the child his jouissance relation to the mother. And indeed there are rumors that Hans's father could not fulfill this "paternal" function because he had a mistress. Put another way, no little boy can interpret his biological penis for psychic meaning (sexuation)—except insofar as it is given a meaning by the Other—the secondary Other of the symbolic order. The organ must be interpreted and its future trajectory named. This is another way of saying that unless the real of sexuality is represented, a child is disoriented within the chaos of the drives.

In Lacan's view, that is precisely what the phobic object means. Such an object— a horse who bites in the case of little Hans—is a signified stuck somewhere between the (symbolic) signifier for castration and the sexual drives that render an object real. Whereas Freud called this signifier the masculine superego, Lacan tried to ascertain precisely what concrete, real event precipitated Hans's phobia. The penis stopped functioning as an imaginary lure, Lacan says. It stopped being an imaginary object in reference to which Little Hans could interrogate the lack-in-being whose first interpretation ordinarily establishes meaning as dialectical, on the basis of an *imaginary* presence or absence. After his sister's birth, the phallic organ became real for Hans, confronting him with the anxiety that always accompanies the traumatic character of the real (*S. IV*, p. 225).

Yet Hans's phobia was cured, Lacan argued, because his father became a real father; that is, one who finally says a no that enabled his son to interpret the penis as an imaginary phallus that incurs lack, not endless jouissance. Lacan argued in *Seminar XVII* that the male wish to retain the primacy of the imaginary phallus, nonetheless, causes him to repress or deny his perception of castration, thus creating, in males, a failure of the oedipal resolution to which Freud aspired for his analysands.[41] At the start of his analysis, Little Hans was caught in the male refusal to acknowledge that having the penis did not make him the imaginary object that will fulfill his mother at the point where she lacked (and, thus, desires). Lacan says Hans's father became capable of "laying down the law"—disrupting the excessive fixation of Hans to his mother—so to speak, once he was backed up by a strong symbolic father, Freud himself (*S. IV*, p. 230).

In "The Agency of the Letter in the Unconscious, or Reason since Freud," delivered in 1958, Lacan argued that "one has only to read the 'Three Essays on Sexuality' to observe, in spite of the pseudo-biological glosses with which it is decked out for popular consumption, that Freud there derives all accession to the object from a dialectic of return."[42] In Freud's essay, he states clearly that the object is present only insofar as it is lacking, moreover, making this a theory of castration. Lacan's choice of the words *dialectic of return* is crucial to his meaning here: To wit, that the object can only return because it is absent. As one sees here and in *Seminar IV*, Lacan did not use the word *object* in the sense Freud did, even from the start. Nor does he use it as it has been developed in object-relations psychoanalysis.

Because of a dialectical movement of temporal tension in language—the anticipation of meaning which only becomes clear retroactively—an absent object can return into the present *as if it were there*. And Lacan found the basis for such an interpretation of the dialectic, not only in Hegel, but also in the work of linguists contemporary to the 1950s who had discovered that not only can meaning be made diacritically (oppositionally and relationally) in the reference of one signifier to another, be it in the relation of black to white or man to woman, or in the differing phonemic sounds of "i" and "e," but moreover in the logical time it takes to make meaning in the space between primordial repressions and the associations drawn from them.

Lacan's Reinterpretation of Freud on Repression

With the idea that the object-cause-of-desire is implied *between* signifiers, Lacan reinterpreted Freud's theory of repression in which the drives or id are repressed. Lacan sees repression as occuring in a temporal tension. If something can be repressed, it is only because it has already been constituted in a *first logical moment*, then pressed under (*Urverdrängt*) in a *second logical moment*, and it will return in a *third logical time*. The infant's *desire* for the breast is constituted by the loss of the gratifications it affords and the desire for its return is "re-pressed" in the time of deferral. The return of desire as drive, or demand, constitutes a third moment, attesting to something lost or re-remembered to the point one can ask for a substitutive form of it. Thus, the something repressed is not a biological id pressure, not a primordial hallucination of pleasure, but the concrete details of libidinal *meaning* Lacan called *jouis-sens*.

This experience of the cut or loss creates the real. The fantasy of the object's return takes some *imaginary* forms while the demand for the object requires *symbolic* articulation. Thus, the sense of an unconscious meaning appears between the imaginary and the symbolic. The constitution of temporal tension is brought about, then, by three different castrating operations: (1) the primordial loss that marks the cut ($\varnothing$) between the image of a thing and the real of its bodily effect; the imaginary castration or deferral—Derrida's *après-coup*—that plays on the instability between images and words ($-\phi$) from which all kinds of *décollages* ensue; and (3) the symbolic castration of the incest taboo, which links the real father of jouissance to the symbolic father of language and law.

Insofar as jouissance meaning is constituted in three different orders—the real Other ($\varnothing$); the "phallic" reality of a particular symbolic (Φ); and the negativized image of a gap between word and thing ($-\phi$)—Lacan had begun to sketch a logic of the intersecting parts as early as *Seminar I*. This logic portrays how body functions are intertwined with "mind." From 1974 on, Lacan argued that jouissance meanings are first experienced and then repressed by three different castrating or negative operations: (1) The primordial loss that marks the cut as a gap between the object and its image, [$\varnothing$] that is, between the image of a thing and the real of its bodily effect; (2) the imaginary castration that plays on the instability between images and words from which gaps ensue ($-\phi$); and (3) the symbolic castration of the incest taboo, which links the real father to language as a law of interdiction (Φ), placing a fourth order of the symptom or knot in language itself (Σ). The symptom is the point where sublimation and the real coalesce, placing drive in language. These three castrations all circle around the object (a) at the center of the Borromean unit, the object that first causes desire and that one seeks in subsitute forms to close the gap between drive and desire.

At the level of *experience*, however, repression makes itself known in a disconcerting if not unwelcome way, which Lacan called the return of the real into the symbolic. That is, repressed memories return from the past into the present as enigmas or unwelcome awarenesses whose affective modes bring discontinuity and disharmony. But to grasp Lacan's theory of repression—conscious language represses the real—one must understand the category of the real he first began developing in *Seminar II* while trying to grasp what really was at stake in the Wolf Man's dreams.[43] As a result of this critique, he redefined the Freudian category of conflict as an order of significations made up of traumatic knots that appear as concrete knots or impasses in conscious language. In this sense, knots are truth-functional paradoxes or contradictions that can be untangled to yield up logical meaning that was previously thought of as nonsensical or illogical.

Lacan insisted that it is possible for repression to function as the dialectical return of the real into the symbolic precisely because "the signifier [has already] install[ed] the lack-of-being in the object relation" ("The Agency . . . , p. 164). In other words, repression is inseparable from the *lack* of a pregiven or innate internal object. But if the object is internally lacking, how can it be repressed? This is a paradox Freud never solved. In other words, repression proves that the object is external, rather than pregiven or innate. It nonetheless constitutes affective memory out of traces or traits of itself at the moment of its loss. In this way, the void place in being and meaning is positivized by traces of an Ideal ego formation that becomes susceptible to interpretation within a transference relation. Although the real cannot be remembered as thought, or reminiscence, its details repeat as a writing that symbolizes the signifying chain and reappear objectively as *sinthomes* of rememorations. Jean-Paul Gilson calls this a real ideational reliving, as opposed to an imaginary reminiscence.[44]

Miller's Return to Lacan's Theory of the Object in Psychoanalysis

From his first course on, Miller argued that insofar as the symbolic order, by its very definition, represses jouissance, it may succeed in putting it under erasure, but does not actually destroy it. Thus, although whatever is repressed in the real will, de facto, return in the symbolic, repression does not work very effectively.[45] *Sinthomes* continue to write a double of the signifying chain. Since Lacan's death, Miller has continued Lacan's exegesis of Freud's theory of the object. In *Extimité*, his course of 1986–87, Miller developed the structure of the Lacanian object (a)—the notation by which Lacan symbolized the object as lacking—to explain how an object that has no positive features or actual existence can ex-sist anyway in the symbolic. In *Donc*, his course of 1993–1994, Miller linked his explanation of how an absent object can be present *in* the symbolic, to the *place* of the pre-oedipal mother. Although Lacan's object (*a*) denotes absence as a concrete place *in* language and being, he never answered the question of how an absent object can have the positive properties of present effects within the symbolic order.

In *Extimité*, Miller referred to Lacan's logic of alienation and separation from chapters 16 and 17 of *Seminar XI* to depict the object (*a*) as acquiring unary traits at the point of intersection between one thing and another:

In setting forth the structure of the object, he stressed that it shares properties of insideness and outsideness, the object itself being, nonetheless, neither inside or outside. It floats somewhere between and, in this sense, is extimate. Topologically speaking, then, the object (*a*) has the tridimensional structure of a torus:

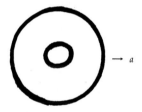

Locatable between being and thinking, between mind and body, Miller says the object (*a*) is structured in internal exclusion to itself. As a consequence, one seeks in the other of object relations and in the Other of the symbolic order the traits that have already structured one's own Ideal ego from the outside, traits that have been distorted or transformed by the operations of substitution (metaphor) and displacement (metonymy). These operations appear quite clearly in dream language. To attain the other of object love—the beloved partner one takes for one's soul—one must seek him or her in another, in a separate body, bringing a quality of strangeness into the experiences of love and sex. And, this is of a piece with Freud's saying that the object can be found only *because* it has already been lost.

Although these ideas may seem to have little to do with feminine sexuality or with the pre-oedipal mother, they are the basis on which Miller put forward a new theory of feminine sexuality in his reading of Lacan's *Seminar IV*. Developing Lacan's idea that the symbolic mother's relation to lack concerns imaginary frustration, while the object in question is a real organ (the breast), Miller elaborates the logic of the interlinking of objects that cause desire and the master signifiers later caught up in the drives that coalesce around these objects. Having translated Freud's *Einzeger Zügen* as *unary traits*—that is, a single identificatory "stroke," detail, or "letter" that binds language to the body via the various experiences of the object as lacking—Lacan gave new meaning to Freud's concepts of identification. With his work on insignia, the divine details, and the symbolic mother's "gifts"—the first "givens"—Miller shows how the unary signifiers that structure the field of the real in the drives, the symbolic in words, and the imaginary in images, join soma to language and images in a way that produces three discrete but interlinked orderings that build up mind as criss-crossed signifying chains.

In Lacan's return to Freud, nothing is innate in "mental" life. Even the partial drives, by which Lacan reconfigures the Freudian id, are constituted as montages of associated forms and sounds as they eroticize the biological organism around the objects that cause the desire for the repetition of lost pleasures. The drives are neither instinctual nor natural, then, but are made up of a coalescence of language, images, and the senses as they cluster around oral, anal, scopic, and invocatory experiences. It is this *material*—the primordial givens (which philosophy questions)—that Miller calls the first gifts of love given by the symbolic mother.

Lacan adhered to the untenable thesis Freud could never prove: That all a person's later thoughts have their roots in the first experiences of primordially repressed material, the *Urverdrängt* or *la lalangue*, which is organized into ever more complex accretions of signifying units. But since the link between conscious meaning and the real is disassociated in thought, the roots of meaning in memory disappear when one uses language consciously. Yet they reappear in fantasy, symptom, and sublimation if one knows how to decipher them. In the first period of his teaching, Lacan presented language as a kind of mask over jouissance or libido. In his final period, *jouissance* had become a formalized meaning system, placing libido in language as a sublimation of the drives and a *décallage* between language and the fantasy object of desire. In trying to prove that jouissance is repressed in the real of the *sinthome*, or knot, and sublimated in language around an Ideal, Lacan defined a logic in *Seminar IV* that showed jouissance as derived from three different relations to the object as lacking: symbolic castration, imaginary frustration, and real deprivation. Castration or the lack-in-being supports the social link ($-\phi \rightarrow \cancel{S}$), while frustration and privation show the extremes of distress occasioned by lack and loss (cf. the graph on page 269, *Seminar IV*).

Addressing this aspect of Lacan's work, Miller returns to the first teaching of the early Lacan who made statements such as "the letter killeth while the spirit giveth life" ("Agency . . . , p. 158). Miller argued as early as 1981 that language represses jouissance. Not only do we not enjoy in language all the time, we are, generally speaking, dead within it—alienated from jouissance. Still, some traces of the primordial, or pre-oedipal, mother remain *in* language, building a riverbed (*la lalangue*) of fantasy. In a very large sense, *any* demand for satisfaction subsequently calls for the repetition of a prior state of pleasure, known as such only in reference to the object first implicated in the interplay between desire and the lack Lacan called symbolic castration, or the internalization of a no whose first objectal referent is the imaginary phallus ($-\phi$). It is not the father's imaginary phallus that is in question, however, but the imaginary phallus in question between boys and girls. At the level of "object relations," the real organ is the mother's breast, which is offered or not, in one way or another, as the infant's first symbolic gift. Miller's focus is not on the breast as good or bad, a metonymy for the quality of mothering, but on the symbolic love in question.

The fixities that mark the real as countable unary traits (S_Is) or *sinthomes* (re)appear as the infant's demand for the return of the symbol—the base element—quickly turns into the demand for consistency, which Lacan calls the repetitive imaginary. The infant confronts a paradox: Pleasure is linked to the rigidity of ritualistic demand from the start. We are confronted with a startling notion of the pleasure principle. The *lack* of an object constitutes the demand for pleasure, not an ideal or idealized union between mother and child. In this context, pleasure always contains the seeds of displeasure within itself. Put another way, any infant knows the pleasure of an object only in terms of the loss of that pleasure. Moreover, the real appears as *sinthomes* (S_I ; *a*) that circulate around the organs engaged in seeing, speaking, eating, defecating, and so on, where images, sounds and libidinal effects weave together the particular conditions of jouissance (in Borromean units) that later govern a person's sexuality in terms of libidinal response, as well as a person's thought, from the concrete pieces that compose ever-flowing fantasy (as reality) matter.

Early in his teaching, Lacan had argued that all language is built upon the *jouis-sens* of *la lalangue* or a primordial maternal murmuring. In *Donc*, Miller presented this primordial language as constituting the first gifts of maternal love to which Lacan referred in *Seminar IV*, saying that a child does not depend on its mother or even its experience of her at the level of partial object, but rather on her love. In Miller's reading of *Seminar IV*, maternal love is not a mystical essence, nor is it equatable with good physical care, a good enough breast, or adequate mirroring. The concrete signifying associations that surround the first objects given in love—the breast, care of the feces, the voice, and the gaze—program the infant's "brain" with concrete information subsequently communicated as affective messages through the synapses. This material composes the primordial givens that phenomenological philosophy has either taken for granted as a priori, or sought to define, as did Merleau-Ponty, by an a priori natural.

Although it was Lacan's position in *Seminar XX* that belief in the existence of an essential Woman cannot be divorced from the natural fact of the mother, he advanced no theory there, or elsewhere, of the pre-oedipal mother. Rather, he argued that there was no pre-oedipal mother, there being no mother prior to the language that one uses to describe her. Yet, insofar as the imaginary frustrations attendant upon interaction with the real of the maternal breast are quickly subsumed by language as it seeks to represent and, thus, negotiate the real, Lacan argued that the mother is subsumed by language: *la lalangue*, a maternal *llalation*. Although religions and myths and psychoanalysis believe in *the* mother as the ground beyond and beneath language, Lacan proposed in *Seminar XX* that there is no essential Woman, not even as mother.

Describing *Seminar IV* as a seminar on feminine sexuality, in *Donc* Miller described the feminine as constructed around the Lacanian object (*a*) which he had presented in *Extimité* as the *signifier* for the lack of an essential Woman, a profound lack which places loss at the heart of the symbolic (Ø). Although Lacan had conceptualized the object (*a*) in 1964 as denoting a place of lack one seeks to fill, and had begun at the time of his death to elaborate the meaning system of jouissance around this pivotal matheme, showing this system as equal in complexity and organizational force to the representational meaning system of signifiers and images, Lacan never linked the object (*a*) to the mother per se, except in reference to the real breast. And even though he placed the object (*a*) on the side of the feminine in sexuation in *Seminar XX*—where feminine and passive become the position of the beloved in love and sex—a position that can be occupied by a man or woman, he did not give a logic to the relations among Woman, mother, and the partial drives.

Lacan's insistence that there is no *essence* of the feminine, no signifier for Woman qua Woman in the unconscious, has often been misinterpreted by feminists to mean that he is a phallocrat who disdains women. As we have seen, Lacan's axiom advanced in *Seminar XX*—"There is no *the* Woman"—(p. 68) means that Woman dwells in the real, beyond the symbolic. In other words, there is no whole Woman who would be equal to the various figures of Woman. But Lacan does not, then, equate Woman, mother, jouissance, and the drives in an explanation of what it means for women to be proximate to the real, although he implies in *Encore* that Woman is identified with the real polymorphous perversity of objects that cause desire.

Freud viewed the task of becoming feminine as more difficult than that of becoming masculine, given the girl's additional challenge of turning away from the mother and toward the father. Lacan implies the opposite: *Being* a man is an *unnatural* identification with the difference he equates with the symbolic, itself an abstraction derived from an asymmetrical veering away from Woman. In other words, a boy becomes "masculine"—takes on attributes of manliness—through asymmetry, rather than through an oppositional identification, as Karen Horney, Karl Jung, Jacques Derrida, and countless others, have argued. In "A Love Letter" (*S. XX*, ch. 7), Lacan argued that the real part of Woman does not exist *in the symbolic order* whose governing principle is the differential feature of being named and counted. With no opposite-sex parent to cause a conflict between identificatory loyalty and the masculine jealousy that wishes to remove a rival, the feminine evolves as an identification with a "law" *beyond* the symbolic order laws that maintain masculine group cohesion. Thus, Woman is Other to the phallic law of the symbolic by which the masculine bonds under the law of obedience to group rules and a out of debt of deferred jouissance given to the Freudian oedipal father whom Lacan renames the real father.

In relating Lacan's concept of Woman to the mother, Miller implied in "Matrice" that if Woman, whom neither sex can ever conceptualize apart from the mother, is radically Other to the symbolic order of language and social law, not only because she is the first *all* (the *tout*) against which any differential (the *rien*)—*all* and *nothing* lying at the base of any dialectical intersection (of numbers, traits, etc.)—is measured, but also because Woman will always elicit jouissance responses that come from the primordial part objects that cause desire.[46] *All*, in this context, is used mathematically to mean infinity. Nothing limits infinity. Yet, the *all*—a line of points—must be intersected at junctures along the line for meaning to exist. The points break infinity into parts, in other words. Lacan gave meaning to this structure by giving the point a dimensional value of zero whose dimension is of the unary trait(s) that bind a hole to a trait; the line, one; the surface, two; space, three; the knot, four (*Seminar XX*, p. 122). In other words, the (re)presenting of words, images, and drives, as they inscribe themselves on the biological organism, *form* the psyche topologically in a double ternary structure, rather than in the imaginary or binary one to which conscious thought conforms. One can argue that the primordial layer of being Lacan called an Ur-lining of the subject might be equated with a pre-oedipal mother.

Insofar as Woman is identified in the unconscious of each subject with the silence of the drives—jouissance being an absolute density which, as such, is not empirically measurable—Woman dwells in the nondialectical field of sameness or Oneness that Miller has described as the extimacy of a distant interior. And this distant interior is the first criterion by which any infant judges difference from the mother in reference to distance, to the loss of objects that forms the primordial layer of being one might equate with *la lalangue* or "primary process." Moreover, these identifications in the real will always be confused—for both sexes—with the engimatic meaning of the mother's desire, such identifications directed, as they are, toward her jouissance.

The pre-oedipal child takes on its first layer of "gender identity" or sexuation, then—which Freud called the active or passive part and which Lacan calls the masculine or feminine, or the positions of lover or beloved—by confusing gender with sexuality at the level where primordial repression is not gendered, but is, purely and simply, a *relation* to the objects of the world that cause desire. Perhaps Melanie Klein misread Freud, who argued that adult fantasies arise out of primordial experience of the objects, the breast, and the feces, Klein pushing fantasy back into an "innate" prebirth phenomenon. Since the object can only ever have the value of unary traits, Lacan describes infant (and adult) experience of the object as experience of the trait(s) and the holes they bind themselves to. While the object is a correlate of the real, which can be recognized in imaginary lure, symbolic fixations, or traces of the real, the signifier that demarcates the symbolic order—the phallic signifier for difference—has no signified, except insofar as the structures of psychosis, neurosis, perversion, or the masquerade are signifieds that interpret this signifier.

Lacan placed Woman, by contrast, in proximity to the palpable hole in the symbolic that pushes individuals to seek a consistency in jouissance through imaginary identifications, lest they encounter the void place at the heart of language and being where anxiety speaks as the only *true* affect, the only one that cannot lie. Life's quests, then, are for unity, consistency, and a guarantee of stability, not for truth or knowledge or justice. Although Woman as mother is generally taken as the guarantee of an ideal stability, a buffer against the anxiety that emanates from a void place in being created by myriad losses and traumas that insert a concrete ordering of gaps between words and things, Woman *as mother* is also identified with these losses. And Lacan argued that this constitutes an epistemological (rather than ontological) *place* in language that both men and women avoid touching upon. Men are uniquely traumatized by an encounter with a void place in being insofar as they are unconsciously fearful of "losing" the male organ, in addition to their very *being* being equatable with *difference* from the mother. Being a man means always being subject to castration anxiety. In this context, male identification with the law—be it the law of the social group or the superego—is a defense against the void in the Other. The masculine superego formation would not be a response to oedipal guilt as Freud thought, but identification with a reality principle linked to the name of some ideal father who would be whole, impervious to loss, and whose rules are to be followed.

In *Extimité* (1985–1986) Miller first elaborated the meaning of Lacan's matheme for the barred Other (Ø), or the hole in the symbolic, and, in so doing, gave another meaning to the object (*a*) he called the *extimate* object. Miller's clarification adds an extension to Lacan's proposition that "Woman does not exist." Insofar as Woman exists as mother in the real, she is, indeed, the primary cause around which the meaning system of the three jouissance(s) of the Borromean knot circle. Lacan's formula— Woman does not exist—would be incorrect. If Woman is represented by the object (*a*) around which the real, symbolic, and imaginary circle, and is inseparable from the Ø (the cut between the real and the imaginary that occurs at the moment of object loss), then Woman does, indeed, exist as the embodiment of the only substance to which Lacan would admit: positive jouissance. That is, woman exsists as object (*a.*)

Miller asked in *Extimité* what Lacan meant when he said there is no metalanguage, no Other of the Other. Put another way, what does it mean to say that Woman is linked to a void in the symbolic order? Arguing that the "signifier" of the barred Ø— the Ø being the signifier denoting a void place in being—is the object (*a*) (p. 238), Miller suggested that Lacan felt a certain repugnance at writing such a formula that he qualified as "unthinkable." For from the moment one considers the signifying order as based on the object (*a*), taken as a *quod* that the signifier lacks, the *names* of the father can only be taken as improper names.

Lacan never articulated this. And, indeed, he considered it an argument without possible orientation, Miller says. In some sense, Lacan remained a nominalist. He could not, therefore, elaborate the theory of affect implicit in the logic of jouissance he had begun to map in the mid 1970s, a theory that can only take on its fuller sense in light of Miller's demonstrations of truth-functional conditions of the real that can be pin-pointed, formalized, and studied and, thus, serve as guides in analytic treatment.

Miller gives a clear answer to Lacan's impasse. Lacan's matheme for castration means simply presence or absence, but insofar as the barred Other is mathematically equivalent to an imaginary value—$\sqrt{-1}$—it can also be written as imaginary castration $(-\phi)$. A symbolic-order value can be given to the logic of the cut. That is, a symbolic-order value can be given to the experience of loss because some real trait inscribes itself as an effect of loss or separation. From this equivalence, Miller says, one finds "a way of approaching *jouissance* based on its interdiction" (p. 241): Absence structures presence via precise traits in the drives.

Although Lacan located Woman in the real of the field of the drives, he never specified precisely how the real can make a hole in the symbolic. Miller's 1993–1994 interpretation of *Seminar IV* enables us to describe the hole in the symbolic (the Ø) as the signified of the phallic signifier (Φ), which conflates the mother of the drives with Woman *placed as a limit on infinitude* at the level where sex and love intersect. Thus, if Woman exists in the real and ex-sists in the symbolic, even though there is no *spirit* of Woman, no biological or psychological essence of the feminine—the "eternal feminine" poeticized by Dante and Goethe—anymore than there is a pregiven essence of man, Woman still exists as the interface between language and a primary jouissance that surrounds the nondialecticizable object (*a*) that refers all bodies to the mother's body which, throughout recorded history, has been the site or matrix around which the partial drives are constituted, giving a base to desire and fantasy.

Miller has clarified Lacan to show that since the real of the object (*a*) is clothed in imaginary guises of semblance and consistency that the symbolic tries to name as *das Ding*, one can dialecticize the object in analysis by subverting semblances and using language to work on the impasses and excesses in jouissance. These impasses index fixations in the real that have acquired all the inert power that Freud characterized as the death drive. Operating from the site of the unspoken real, that which cannot be said, the analyst occupies the place of Woman. But that has nothing to do with a "would be" better mother. The analyst serves as a stand-in for a place outside symbolic order strictures and alienations and outside imaginary order narcissism and mirror identifications. He or she, thereby, enables the analysand to try to symbolize the real material which, by definition, is the not-yet-spoken. Treatment does not bear on whether the patient had good or bad parenting, then, but on the real of suffering that comes from the ways in which a subject becomes fixed in lethal jouissance. By pushing language— that is, thought—to its limits, a person can challenge impasses in his or her jouissance and begin to unknot the rigidity of old signifying units whose marks appear in the symbolic as impasses from the real. Thus, Lacanian analysis works at the intersections between the real and language and the real and the imaginary where an analysand's symptoms show up.

One *could* argue, in conclusion, that if Woman as real mother does exist in the drives, then the referent of all language is corporal. Such an argument, moreover, would not be the essentialist view of woman as reduced to her body or her biological destiny. Rather, the real is inscribed, detail by detail, as a knowledge in the moments when the enjoyment of an object, such as the breast (or bottle), or the objects of the world, is lost. From the start, desire is constituted in dissonance with jouissance, or Oneness with the object. But the unary trait that remains in the real attaches a remnant of lost jouissance to language. That trait is incorporated as a mark that belongs to the set of meanings constituted around loss itself. And insofar as the trauma of the real equates the primordial loss of the object with Woman as bearer of the drives, analysis will always focus on this place. It is not Freud's Woman as giver of unity that one finds here. For Freud's Woman as mother is asexual. Nor is it Lacan's Woman who does not exist as Other in the symbolic. Miller gives us, rather, Woman as the mother who was first experienced as sexual and erotic. This is neither Lacan's theory that Woman does not exist as a signifier for difference in the symbolic because she is radically Other to man, nor that Woman only enters the symbolic as mother, agent of frustration. Miller portrays Woman as entering the symbolic as the giver of love at the point where love and Eros are inseparable.

In some sense, Lacan's formula—The Woman does not exist—does not advance beyond Freud's pre-1931 theory that man is the standard or norm. Although Lacan postulated the real as itself a limit to the symbolic, as a point of impasse at which the unspeakable demands of jouissance constitute an ordering of the meanings of jouissance, he did not, as has Miller, attach this theory to the position of the mother who stands in as signifier for the object (a) within the drives. Not only are the first "gifts" of this symbolic mother the real gifts of love—be they made of gold or brass—this primordially repressed material also serves as the basis of the philosophical givens (forms) out of which thought weaves itself.

Miller's threading together of Freud and Lacan around the paradoxical meaning of the pre-oedipal mother could well enable psychoanalysis to exit from the impasses of object-relations theories in which the mother is taken for the whole object in a variety of phenomenological equations of the visible with the person, or in which some part stands in for an imagined whole. Such theories restrict analytic practice to the behavioral task of reparenting or repairing a defective ideal which was never One at all.

Conclusion

Since there is no one who is not concerned with gender and gender studies, a book on sexuation—the logical development of the cause of gender—is of interest to everyone. Lacan's theory of sexuation argues that men and women are sexuated psychically, not biologically. That is, there is a psychic asymmetrical logic at work in differentiating biological woman from biological man. The goal of this book has not been to offer an alternative logic to those theories that claim that the sexual difference makes no difference, or that gender studies have switched to a brother/sister model, or any other such dismissive argument. I wished to challenge the essentialist roots of theories of gender as they are taught in fields such as biology, sociology, psychology, and so on.

Lacan's rethinking of sexuation concerns the conditions of jouissance that rotate between pleasure and pain. He argues that the masculine and feminine are particular psychic identifications. The masculine identifies predominantly with the symbolic order of language and social conventions, while the feminine identifies with the real of affect, loss, and trauma. Whether one identifies as masculine or feminine does not concern one's biological sex, but the postion one occupies in reference to the masculine *all* of knowledge, or the feminine *not all* of knowledge.

Lacan's basic question is: What is woman's nature insofar as it differs from man's? He approaches this question by considering how jouissance conditions are logically inscribed in the unconscious as an interpretation of the sexual difference. That which we seek in everyday endeavors, as well as in abstract tasks connected with the intellect, emanate from the precise real of what one will also seek as enjoyment. These conditions are "written" in reference to the phallic signifier—that is, that which denotes difference qua difference—and the consequent "castration" or lack that follows upon learning that the difference has the effect of subtracting something from an imagined whole. Lacan argues that not only does the phallic signifier have imaginary visible properties, it has abstract and affective properties as well.

The central thesis of this book has been an explication of the overwhelming effects of the sexual difference and their ramifications. Not content with wholistic imaginary models, Lacan took up Aristotle's modal (qualitative) logic and combined it with the existential quantors of the universal ($\forall$) and the particular ($\exists$) in order to arrive at a rethinking of impasses in Aristotle and Freud, impasses that could be brought together to offer a new way to think about the ramifications of the sexual difference. Whereas Aristotle was concerned to explain the cause of an act as necessary, efficient, material, or instrumental (that is, as representable or quantifiable), Lacan's interest lay in uncovering the causes of different libidinal (qualitative) modes of response to the discovery and interpretation of the sexual difference. Whereas Aristotle sought the source of cause in things or in the "know how" of technique, Lacan evolved the logical modes of the *possible*, the *impossible*, the *contingent*, and the *necessary* as effects whose cause is the interpretation made of the primordial phallus and its part-object character of being absent or present. He maintained something as profound as this: The base of mind lies in the varying outcomes of the interpretation of the sexual difference, an experience that is initially traumatic for little children. Moreover, two of the modes—the *necessary* and the *possible*—describe a masculine way of being in language, while the other two—the *contingent* and the *impossible*—take up a feminine epistemology.

Lacan claimed, moreover, that the loss of the primordial objects that first cause one to desire (the breast, the feces, the urinary flow, the imaginary phallus, the voice, the phoneme, the gaze, and the nothing) simultaneously makes of them causal "objects" at the moment they are lost. Lacan makes these the threads of connection an infant has to his or her immediate world. As each object is lost, the desire for its return begins to build up a signifying network of real, symbolic, and imaginary orders—trait by trait—loss signaling that something present is gone and that the return of a part of the object *is* desirable. Loss sets forth the dialectical mechanism by which particular jouissance conditions are laid down, singular trait by singular trait. Launching the innovative hypothesis that loss is the prime mover in the genesis of any act, Lacan demonstrates how Aristotle ended up in the impasse of a static *primum mobile*. In Lacan's theory, the leap to a "metalanguage" lies in the "meta's" seeking *in* language a way to establish his or her enjoyment. In this, any act of language is an act in and of itself, not a metaphorical duplicity. Not only does knowledge later become a *savoir* that is enigmatic, it is enigmatic because it is replete with the primordial material of gaps, holes, and doublings by which one seeks to repeat seemingly stable jouissance conditions. Instead, the quest for jouissance conditions always meets an instability between subject and object. The object one finds is never quite "it," *das Ding* of ultimate pleasure. "The unconscious is [thus] a savoir faire with *la lalangue*, *la lalangue* meaning the primordial layer of maternal murmerings and sounds of an infant's world given by the mother before the infant can begin to shape these sounds into the words that name things.[1] Lacan made the word for spoken language *la langue* into a direct object, *la lalangue*, to challenge the linguistic notion of a natural language.

In the later years of his work, Lacan presents topology as that which structures the sites where the subject emerges, not as a self or an ego but as a redoubled effect of having to represent itself as meaning, both representationally and libidinally. Put another way, individuals are representationally identified with a signifier for being x, y, or z—identified with the phallic signifier for difference from the mother as the condition of identity—or with its lack. Such identifications make of the necessary, the possible, the impossible, and the contingent, modes of jouissance whose referent is castration, or a lack-of-being whole. In other words, insofar as the phallic signifier marks a place in the symbolic, a subject *is that place*, as a signifier representing a subject for another signifier. Put yet another way, the phallic signifier denotes alienation by representations that make of fantasies the fourth-order *sinthomes* (symptoms) or knots that sustain a kind of pseudowholeness in being and thought, despite the constant interplay of the falseness of an alienated identity—the gap between the image and the word (−ϕ)—and the cut between the desired object and its loss (∅).

Alienation into language accompanies separation from the object—two logical operations—such that libidinal and representational meaning move by a constant metonymic and metaphorical rhythm of deferral and substitution. We have gone from Aristotle's inert prime mover, Freud's biology, to Lacan's Other—the outside world that imposes itself on us, making each person a concrete accretion of signifying units that build into vast signifying necklaces we call mind or memory. We do not "remember" within this conception of mind, Lacan says. Rather, "rememoration" is the process of repression whereby we continually draw upon associational meanings from the three orders to enable us to move within secondary-process language.

Insofar as negation links fantasy to meaning vis-à-vis four potential interpretations of the phallic difference and its lack, one ends up either foreclosing the sexual difference (psychosis), repudiating it (perversion), denying it (neurosis), or repressing it (the normative masquerade). These four possibilities denote precise logics, each of which marks particular attitudes toward law, as well as toward desire. Lacan argues that the problem in the constitution of male or female sexuality is not the organ qua organ, then, but the dialectic between desire and jouissance. While desire cum lack will be foreclosed, repudiated, denied, or repressed, at the level of jouissance, the masculine *necessary* and the *possible* logics believe that *all* knowledge can be included in one space, while the *impossible* and *contingent* logics know that *not all* meaning can be enclosed within a space. Geneviève Morel demonstrates this in her work on compacity.

Aligning sexuality with the real—that which is palpable, while remaining unsayable and unrepresentable—Lacan argued that the conditions of enjoyment write these four modes: In the *possible*, some symptom ceases writing itself, while in the *impossible* some symptom or effect does not stop not writing itself. The *necessary* concerns what does not stop writing itself, while the *contingent* stops not writing itself. Fittingly, the *necessary* and *possible* modes of jouissance are on the masculine side of sexuation, describing that which must be known about law for a group to cohere as social. Lacan deduces this logic from a rereading of Freud's *Totem and Taboo*—as a defense against not being allowed to remain one with the mother. Having set up the dialectical logic by which society comes into being—by contrast, psychosis evolves no dialectic, no reciprocity with another, and, thus, no social grouping—Lacan has also given a logical way of reading the sexual difference (which the psychotic forecloses).

Having returned to Freud via Aristotle, Lacan is able to show how Freud's 1925 biology yielded a few logical insights that are viable only outside the biologism in which they are wrapped. Lacan claims that Freud proposed the pre-oedipal as a response to the impasses he had run up against in his efforts to elaborate a theory of the Oedipus complex. He also claimed that Freud's theory of a phallic phase was one and the same as his concept of an oedipal identity. Lacan took us from Freud's biology to a notion of the world outside where the Other names the infant in terms of its own unconscious desire. Thus, an infant starts life under the aegis of an alienated identity. From the start, mind and body are intertwined.

Moreover, by *Seminar XX* Lacan will say that the body is thought. While jouissance depends on the universal of how an infant assimilates the exception to the rule of difference with its particular consequences for any singular subject, masculine or feminine—$\exists x \overline{\Phi x} / \exists x \Phi x$—the phallic signifier demonstrates three different ways of negating these terms: Φ, $-\phi$, $\varnothing$. The exception is marked by two negations on the feminine side of sexuation. *Lacan's is a complex logic of the phallus, taken as the differential in reference to which thought evolves as dialectical, or not.* The phallus also marks a jouissance relation to desire as representational (*necessary, possible*) or libidinal (*impossible, contingent*). Because representation is shot through with jouissance, this determines that one is never whole (except in psychotic delusion) and that mind and body are never disintricated (except in a psychotic split).

The logics of the *necessary* and *possible* enjoyments are contiguous with a belief in the *all* of the completeness of knowledge that equates what one knows with what there is to know. When one is *not all* under the phallic sway of tallying reality with language, jouissance has not completely been anesthetized. Feminine subjects are *not all* under the phallic conventions and can, thus, take a certain distance from the *all* of the master discourse. Thus, alienation falls on the side of masculine knowledge. The master knows it *all,* is identified with a totalized jouissance, and substitutes knowledge for truths of the unconscious. On the feminine side of sexuation, separation from the object of satisfaction is of a piece with a supplemental bodily jouissance that ties diffusion to the interrogatory *not all* in symbolic-order knowledge.

These positions—*all* in the symbolic or *not all* in the real—are marked as well by primary identification either with the real maternal Other of the drives, or the symbolic father of the group, of language, and of a local (universal) law of reality, while *la lalangue* marks the feminine side with maternal murmerings of *jouis-sens* (an enjoyed meaning). When Lacan argues that such logics are epistemological ways of knowing, he supports his claims by the topological that is not necessarily visible. He is, thus, positing a structural way of linking truth-functional contradictions by dissimilars. While Freud "read" imaginarily, taking the thing to be itself, Lacan reads topologically, taking primary functions to be, paradoxically, made up of secondary functions that construct the primary one. In other words, the hole is constructed by the unary traits which bind themselves to a void, making it a hole. Topologically speaking, the hole comes first, not second.

Masculine knowledge is positivized, then—countable, visible—while feminine knowledge, refusing closure, is negativized—the qualitative, the invisible. The object-cause-of-desire that builds up the primordial *la lalangue* becomes language in constructing fantasies and the Ideal ego of unconscious formation, from which people, in turn, act and know. The depiction of the most complete unit of mind is the Borromean knot that Lacan later called a *picture in the real,* or that which shows a site from which something is given to be seen, or heard, or known. The three circles that interlace the Borromean unit are intersecting parallels that mark the topological—the logic of place—dimensions of a surface as imaginary (as in the schema), inscribed (as in graphs), or presenting real places, as in a *picture.* These are joined, not only by the knot—the Father's Name signifier raised to the second degree—but also by three kinds of jouissance: the capital phi of alienation into language (Φ), the negative phi of a gap between word and thing ($-\phi$), and the cut in the Other that makes all sets, at least partially empty ($\varnothing$).

While Freud insisted on the harmony of the masculine and feminine, Lacan discovered a universal disharmony and attributed that to the logical structure of difference between a boy and a girl. While Freud believed that difference as a difference from the same—both for boys and girls—results in sociological roles, Lacan argued that the symbolic is identified with boys who are defined in asymmetrical disharmony from the first one with whom they are the same, the mother. There is no superiority of sex or organ, in Lacan's teaching, only a superiority of the symbolic insofar as it is the place of difference and Otherness. Indeed, it belongs to both sexes. The symbolic is valued insofar as it starts a count, ushering in the realm of the social, of others, while the real remains intimate and replete with secrets of agony and ecstasy, a realm of conflict, excitation, discontinuity, and disharmonious impasses.

But, finally, Lacan and Frege, whom Lacan followed in certain areas, manifested themselves as anti-Aristotelian. One of the paradoxical consequences of all women's lacking the totalized phallic injunction is that all are *not all* ($\overline{\forall x \Phi x}$) under the sway of its requisites. This logic of the all *not all* is what Lacan called a discordential feminine doubling of the libido, not a double foreclosure of Woman as some readers have misunderstood. The point is that Lacan reverses Aristotelian logic in feminine sexuation by making the particular ($\overline{\exists x \Phi x}$) both negative, as well as that which gives rise to the universal ($\forall x \Phi x$) as positive.

Chapter I maintained that identifying with the phallic signifier, for Lacan, does not mean identification with an organ. It means identifying with difference as an abstraction, an invisible thing. It means taking a position vis-à-vis difference. This is one reason Lacan talks about subject position as being a concrete lack in a chain of referential meanings. By introjecting the Other, absolute kinds of identifications are represented as the fragments Lacan called unary traits. Their ordering is real and chaotic, not developmental and smooth. Such real material reenters the symbolic as discontinuities, or as "privileged moments," or as epiphanic revelations. At the least, one can say that the real distorts any cohesive or consistent symbolic-imaginary narrative by bringing loss, lack, or negation into the smooth flow of narrative or vision. Such cuts into the symbolic give the phallic signifier a paradoxically strong superegolike quality and yet, a fundamental instability. Perhaps we could say the phallus is an *omnium-gatherum* word for *Realität* (psychic reality) and *Wirklichkeit* (sense-data reality) combined. The point is that the phallus starts the count of an order, of the serial (1,2,3; a,b,c), not because it is the object observed in the sexual difference—observed as an imaginary object by both sexes—but because the sexual difference is the first difference that impinges on human consciousness.

Borrowing Frege's symbol for the proposition—Φ—Lacan makes the (phallic) proposition itself a signifier without a signified. Its logical function is to evoke difference, to serve as a differential basis for thought that arises in reference to concrete lacks in our perceptions and identifications. The phallic differential, in other words, postulates a lack between signifiers that Lacan calls the subject. This is a radically different theory than that feminine and masculine attributes are simple oppositional binaries. Rather, sexuality takes on nonbiological specific masculine or feminine epistemological assumptions. Moreover, sex is not what or where we think it is. The reconceptualization Lacan gives us of the feminine and the masculine has the utmost to do with the terms and questions posed by feminist debates. Indeed, Lacan's logic of feminine sexuality demonstrates an epistemological position, not a one-down place in society. Constituted in a combinatory—by the law of the signifier that represents a subject for another signifier—masculine and feminine sexualities are redefined in terms of conflict, not pleasure. Further, Lacan makes no one-to-one equation of sexuality—which resides in the field of the drives (oral, anal, invocatory, and scopic)—with jouissance. While sexuality is fixed in fantasy, jouissance is lost in bits and pieces through alienation into language and separation from the primordial objects-cause-of-desire. At another level, jouissance tries to maintain a consistency by equating itself with imaginary wholeness, with semblance.

In the third period of his teaching, Lacan argued that the unconscious is sexuality in function, secondary-process representations being riddled with remnants of primary-process fantasy and desire. Moreover, he argues that language is linked to drives via jouissance. We ask for something in the field of the oral drive (for nourishment), the anal drive (for control), the scopic drive (for recognition), and the invocatory drive (for being heard). In this sense, one can argue that the paternal metaphor—the Lacanian Oedipus complex—can be rewritten as the Father's Name signifier (language itself) over the Mother's unconscious desire (Father's Name/Mother's Desire · Mother's Desire/?), which produces the Father's Name as the Other over the phallus that supplants the mother's unconscious desire with some interpretation of it. The product is the Other (of culture and representation) supposed as a *savoir* which is, at one level, repressed maternal desire. It is through such logical operations that biological sexuality becomes psychic sex. While the object (*a*) charts the pathways of drives—itself the cause of the dialectic underlying the drives insofar as desire is equal and respondent to the lack that is its inverse side—mind can be deduced from lack and loss supplemented by myths of the essential Woman who should exist; jouissance; the object (a); as well as the Φ representing language and law as a local (universal) reality.

Mind cannot be deduced from organs and their various displacements, as Freud thought, any more than one can readily see that the gap is itself a function *in* language and, as such, is an attribute of language. One gets to this in analysis through transference love that links desire to the drives whose structure is not only that of the signifier, but also the gaplike structure of the unconscious itself. Thus, the question of what determines sexuality is, for Lacan, desire, the partial drives, and love. That is, there is no genital drive per se that imposes itself on being as some blind, mechanistic id force. Love joins desire to the drives whose structure is that of the signifier and the unconscious. Woman, moreover, is not the drive object she is thought to be, but a signifier interpreting her fiction of the father. Between man and woman reside the asymmetries of their construction, as well as the particular Otherness of the unconscious of each. One cannot say, then, as do object-relations theorists, that identification is with objects rather than with a biological psyche. Identification is with signifiers, whose structure is already dialectical. Between being and meaning, the object (a) is the subject that is recoverable from the structure of separation.

Furthermore, there is no equation between a reproductive instinct and the sexual drive. Drives are constituted as a montage of signifiers and images, while produced as a residue of what is left over of cuts from the objects that first caused desire for lost objects, and what remains after the oedipal drama. Put another way, Thanatos *cum* alienation spoils a would-be "universal" Eros. Thus, the object (a) is not only not nothing, it is, indeed, one's cause. Furthermore, there is no inscription for man or woman in the unconscious; there is no signifier for sex there. This places confusion, illusion, myth, and mysticism at the heart of sexual "relations," not peace, love, harmony, and bliss. Sexuality is replaced by the object (a) of fantasy on the side of loss and by the other as partner on the side of lack.

Lacan gives a new theory of the place to look for sexuality. Going in the opposite direction of the imaginary pinups of the month, he situates sexuality in the master signifiers that make up one's singular jouissance marks. Not only do these compose thought, they also dictate "the particular conditions of love." In this sense, jouissance sublimates all human relations, making them automatically erotic and libidinal. To try to eliminate the threat of the real that this poses, the masculine in discourse, knowledge, and logic impose the One signifier whose nickname could well be the "superego." On the feminine side, the woman exposes the real void place in the symbolic set of ensembles, thus pulling the rug from under anyone's feet who thinks The Woman exists as a guarantee for wholeness and stability, given that the Father's Name does not. The goal of sex becomes twofold: to fill up the void with as many identifications and objects as possible and to capture the other's—the beloved one's—*agalma* (that in one that is more than one). *Agalma* would be a point where desire joins itself to jouissance to show that beyond the man and woman, beyond the masculine and the feminine, lies the phallus and its lack, creating symbols of difference that are themselves the pivot around which all things turn.

Whereas Aristotle settled for a universalist picture of the *All* when he could not see his way out of impasses such as how movement begins, Lacan made a subtle distinction between totality and the *all.* Taking up a point of slippage between Aristotle's and Frege's formulas, Lacan points out that the notion of a totality is opposed to an ensemble <> which evokes an open relation based on supplementarity, not complimentarity. There is no *all,* Lacan argues, except as empty, or as a propositional function of contingency, Thus, the logic by which one inscribes oneself as *all* within the phallic function is already based on a sham whose truth is given by the *not all* of the sexual masquerade. Male sexuality is *all* enclosed in a logic of difference from the mother, while female sexuality is *not all* enclosed in this logic of difference, for the girl resides in the phallic camp as well as outside it. What Lacan is doing, then, is using negativity, or its lack, as philosophical values which demonstrate how one moves in language.

Insofar as a child assumes his or her sexuation in reference to the asymmetrical relation of Man <> Woman, he or she learns that he or she is *not all* one sex, nor is he or she the mother's only treasure. The Father's Name imposes itself between the infant and the mother, claiming her as *his* at the level of desire. This "no" teaches males and females alike that they are castrated or lacking-in-being. Indeed, any male—despite being all identified with the symbolic—learns castration in reference to the group which accepts to defer to a leader. Such deferral, paradoxically, places a tendency toward masculine openness at the site of his thrust toward encompassing the *all,* being *all* identified with the law of the group, while the feminine position within knowledge is based on the closed set that need not aim for infinity since she already knows she is *not all* subjected to the signifier One of masculine castration logic. One can say that oedipal identifications as *all* or *not all* begin around age five or six, along with the acqustion of secondary-process language. Meanwhile, the feminine bedrock of language is laid down as the famous discovery of a feminine pre-Oedipus—*la lalangue*—that fixes the life of desire and the drives during the first four years. Afterward, primary jouissance and secondary representations will struggle with this war in each person's breast. That is, the primary imaginary opposes the secondary symbolic, the first seeking the consistency of jouissance and the second seeking to fill the lack in the Other.

The $ —the subject lacking in being a whole essence—*is spoken by* language. Lacan defined the subject as a gap in the signifying chain by going back to reconsider Aristotle's own impasse. Never having separated logic from language—that is, grammar from language—his propositions begin from the universal and proceed to a particular negation that is, erroneously, presupposed positivistically. Lacan, rather, approached the negative/positive divide of the subject residing in language, as a function of language. Moreover, it is created primarily by the loss of the object *a* and secondarily by the traumatic assimilation of sexual difference. During the primordial period, infants depend on the object that causes desire and the mother's love, but once the first oedipal moment is experienced identificatorily, the phallus takes on a $+/-$ value that ignores all physical, mental, and social attributes of the person and simply works to valorize difference ($+$) and to devalue sameness ($-$). Such a structural logic pushes men and women toward telling each other who and what they "are" at the level of attributes with a near disregard for gender, Lacan claimed, thus, constructing the battle between the sexes.

In assessing what is particular to the feminine and not to the masculine, Lacan's work on the paternal metaphor (Freud's Oedipus complex) is crucial. The incest taboo is a function that is coequivalent with castration. It not only gives birth to the possibility for metaphor (substitutions) and dialectic, it affects both sexes differently. At one level, Lacan says, the *cause* of mentality is to cover over the real and to negotiate desire. This occurs through identifications with the paternal metaphor that produce particular *sinthomes* that represent something like a wholeness of one's being. *Lacan developed his sexuation tables to insist that existence claims demand material proof.* The masculine logic of the whole or all is an epistemological position based on a logic of contradiction. That is, identification with the *all*, immediately implies its own limit which, Lacan says, is to be found in jouissance. Identification with the *not all* on the feminine side creates a double negative that is much like the number 2 in number theory. Two cannot be inscribed as a rational number because it consists of mirror-stage illusions flowing in and out of a pseudo-one. Rather than speak of a double negative, however, Lacan called the feminine—based on the idea that there is no exception to the rule of castration—a discordential logic.

Still, how does sexuation explain Freud's quandaries about the sexual difference? Freud uncovered in 1931 and 1932 that girls reject their mothers at the second oedipal stage. Lacan maintained that this is because they want to be defined by the symbolic, not the real. Based on the hypothesis that there is no pregiven genital drive, the nonrapport between the sexes will stem not only from a radical difference, but from different solutions in identity as well. The interplay goes back and forth between a $\sqrt{1+1}$ and a $\sqrt{-1+1}$ such that masculine closed sets evolve the following two logics, both against the Aristotelian universal: For Lacan there is a concrete universal based on a negative. That is, there is an exception to the rule, one who is supposed as not castrated, $\exists x$; the consequence is that all who are not this exception are castrated in reference to him or her. The two feminine logics work differently. Lacan says that a concrete universal based on a negative—the no exception to the rule of castration on the feminine side—means that there is not one who is not defined by this lack. The paradox is that this double negative ends up creating a positive: There is not one who is not all castrated. Thus, there is one part of the feminine that is free from the obligations of a given symbolic law. Women, thus, belong to closed sets, sets with limits, while men belong to open sets, trying, paradoxically, to break out of the strictures in which they are enclosed in the symbolic. The woman, having one foot already outside the symbolic, belongs to a closed set. The major point Lacan is making here is that the primacy of the phallus is correlated—not with jouissance, but—with the castration complex, with the identification of having or not having of the phallic imaginary partial object.

Lacan takes up what he means by sexuality, showing the consequences for gender studies when masculine (psychic) sex is formed as an asymmetrical veering to the side from feminine (psychic) sex. That does not mean that "man" and "woman" are *not* constituted as signifiers in a combinatory of language. It means, simply, that while a man *may* be preponderantly identified with the feminine, and a woman with the masculine, cultural mores try to tally biological gender to psychic identification. One can thereby understand the revolutionary character of Lacan's ethical stance which argues that one can only face oneself in the truth of desire by not giving up on it. Lacan wanted to be clear about the lack of equation between jouissance and sexuality. While sexuality is fixed in fantasy, jouissance is lost in alienation into language and separation from the primary objects that first caused desire. For this reason, Lacan equated the unconscious with sexuality, whose dual language is that of secondary-process repressions and denials and primary-process *la lalangue* of fantasy and desire. Mind is deduced from loss and supplemented by Woman, jouissance, the (a), as well as the Φ for the Father's Name signifier. All these letters denote psychic realities that are, in Lacan's teaching, formal properties of language that can be disengaged from language and studied as such. Moreover, they add up to a logic of desire, fantasy, and jouissance. Given these premises, it should not be so shocking to think of the subject as an actual gap in language, as well as a function in it.

This brings us back to the question of what sexuality is. Arguing that there is no sexual drive per se, no reproductive instinct, Lacan says Freud shows us where sexuality is in his work on the drives which, on closer scrutiny, appear as a montage of all the identifications particular to one. But what does this have to do with the sexual difference? A woman is a signifier who interprets the fiction of the father, Lacan maintains, while man is a fiction who believes in the myth of the essential Woman. These are not natural descriptions, nor are they harmonious within their own terms. People love one another by identification with signifiers and objects. Yet, since there is no signifier for sex in the unconscious, one must make do with substituting the object (a). Thus, at the level where meaning joins being, one's cause is one's cause as an object (a). Insofar as each subject depends on the imaginary other and the symbolic Other to verify/reify who he or she is (or is not) as an Ideal in the fields of the scopic, invocatory, oral, and anal partial drives, one must say that sexuality is hooked to a lack of being *all* and the loss of the objects that cause desire.

What this means—that there is no signifier for the sexual difference in the unconscious—is that we must take our self-believed descriptions from the signifiers that make up our thought out of traces of jouissance. This places all human relations—not just art—under the sublimation of the jouissance that Lacan finally equates with the Father's Name signifier, as it becomes the knot in the real he calls the *sinthome*. The master signifier, on the side of the Father's Name, is what Lacan called the One signifier, or an identification with the *all*, while the feminine signifier for ~~The Woman~~ who does not exist refers to the void place in the Other that marks a real emptiness there. The goal of sex, then, is to fill the void with the object (*a*) and to capture the other's *agalma*.

Sexuality starts, then, as a response to the real, symbolic, and imaginary at the level where the jouissance engaged is experienced as active or passive. One either actively seeks to fill the void place in the Other ($\varnothing$), or one lets oneself be used passively as the filler. Beloved or lover—these labels mark us all and take the moralistic tone out of Freud's description of active (i.e., successful) boys and passive (i.e., long-suffering) girls. The first separations from the object (*a*) create a hole in the Other which, in turn, is filled by an identification (an S_1, a master signifier). This produces jouissance which can be described as the object (*a*) that sutures the void: $\varnothing/a$. Everything that has to do with language, concept, proposition, or hypothesis is undergirded by and held in the cusp of primordial givens that, in turn, connect desire to love and love to language.

Drives, then, are a meaningful substance of jouissance that fill the void, not a mythology as Freud thought. Indeed, says Lacan, *Beyond the Pleasure Principle* proves that all drives are death drives. Another way to say this is that we are our own *sinthomes*. What trips us up are the repetitions that are ours and, thus, serve as our limits. "Sexuality is the desire for jouissance," Lacan says, and it is never separate from language. Its causes are as innumerable as are fantasies. The point is that sex is not the issue but that one repeat, rather, the particular, singular conditions that constitute one's jouissance. In Lacan's teaching, the object (*a*) is no myth. Freud spoke of the myth of the drives, while Lacan, finally, depicted the object (*a*) as real. Jean-Paul Gilson calls this an (*a*) spheric knowledge. This (*a*)-spherical writing begins with the object (*a*) that is lost and then returns in other forms to fill the hole its loss has created. In the usage of language, he says, the *aspheric* is creative, constructionist. This renders language living and means that what one can invent as new will always contain a small piece of the real which forges the paths of rememoration—or repression—rather than those of reminiscence. While reminiscence is not a *savoir* but a relived ideation belonging to the imaginary, rememoration belongs to the signifying chain and to the knot that makes something—unconscious—enter into our knowledge as a *savoir* that was already there. This theory of knowledge is nothing less than a new writing that symbolizes the chain that it, in turn, represents.

While the jouissance that maintains the status quo, or the ups and downs of affective life, has a plus or minus value in reference to the phallic signifier, one proof that the subject is a nonbiological subject at the level of meaning lies in the interplay between jouissance and desire. While desire is structured by the dialectic of the Ideal ego and the ego ideals referring themselves to the Father's Name signifier, the limit of jouissance that can be brought forth by the subject concerns the interplay between the *all* (the phallic signifier) of jouissance and the *not all* of fantasy and desire. Lacan's point is that the prime mover is neither Plato's Form nor Aristotle's thought. The prime mover is the (a) as lost. Since the (a) cannot be pinned down because it is always disappearing, imaginary lures, language, and law must supplement it, stand in for it. Indeed, this makes representation seem more substantial than libido. One begins to see how the drives can materialize entire meaning fields—invocatory, scopic, oral, and anal—with jouissance given that the human drive par excellence is to replicate oneself as Ideal. The drive is to be whole, to fill the void presupposed by the demand which, for Lacan, is the drive. In sex and in love, we think we are incorporating the (a), while we are actually incorporating the other's soul as a filler to our own lack. While love aims at the soul, sex aims at an organ. But neither satisfaction can make any one of us whole once and for all. Indeed, the gap from which love comes is the demand for more love which, by definition, is an insatiable, even narcissistic, demand. Desire, meanwhile, splits love between sex and the soul, which Lacan defines as the likeness between individuals.

Lacan's theory does not allow for any innate hetero- or homosexuality in man or woman. Nor is there a pre-oedipal mother who can fill the void with satiation. There is the symbolic mother, the infant's drives, and, in between, the gifts she has to offer. It is not that Lacan in any way minimalizes the importance of sexuality in relations of desire and love. It is, instead, that he sees that the stakes are so much larger than pleasure. After orgasm, after fulfillment, one is left with a oneness +, with the search (*encore*) for the *agalma*, one's greatest good as lost, missing, just missed. In his sexuation graph, the tables interpret the modal conditions of jouissance, its positive and negative features. If one chooses to reside on the feminine side, be it a biological man or a woman, one's subject choice is a being-for-the-other. If one chooses from the masculine side, one's choice is for reifying self and filling lack.

Insofar as the masculine identifies with the lack-in-being ($\$$) and the positivized phallus (Φ) and the feminine identifies with the object a and the void place in the Other ($\varnothing$), one can say the male identifies with castration ($\$$/lack), while the female identifies with the void ($\varnothing$/loss). Moreover, four fundamental concepts are regularly at play in structuring the interwoven mind/body of Lacanian thought—the unconscious, repetition, transference, and the drives—while three kinds of negation bear on the jouissance of being: the Φ, the $-\phi$ and the $\varnothing$. With these strictures, we use language to get the jouissance we can, showing that identity and sexuation are one and the same. Indeed, the unconscious is a secondary formation, erected in the assumption of sexuation. Lacan's logical tables show that instead of "being sexual" in one way or another, we are sexuated in taking a stance toward lack of the phallus (or not as in psychosis). Thus, there is no binary of a biological sexuality opposed to a masculine or feminine identity. Rather, masculine and feminine link the active and passive around power and desire as they negotiate the *all* of symbolic of knowledge, or the *not all* of another kind of knowledge, the real.

Insofar as certain *sinthomes*—identificatory *sinthomes* that are real knots—create the "self" as a series of knots concerning the mother's unconscious desire and the place of the Father's Name signifier in the social realm, they can be undone. Lacan called this "using the symbolic to work on the real." And *sinthomes* always concern one's place in the masculine or feminine. Indeed, Lacan goes so far as to say that the symbolic and imaginary orders arise as interpretations of sexual difference. He calls this principle of difference the phallic differential, or the oedipal cut. This signifier both creates lack and denies it, all the while joining jouissance (to be recuperated) to castration. Indeed, Lacan argues nothing less than that knowledge itself defends against castration and, in the process, founds social law. We have gone from Freud's organ- and content-based explanations to Lacan's topology in which a boy is opposed to a girl in reference to a tertiary term, the phallus. The result of the interplay between castration and jouissance in language is that we speak symbolically and imaginarily, but in real time.

Lacan's arguments will necessarily lead him to a new definition of the distinction that serves as the criterion for subject/object disalignment. Not only is the object not the image as the-thing-in-itself, as Lacan suggested in the seventies, the object is most present in its insignia of lack: anxiety, doubt, fear, panic. This is the level at which the object is real and makes use of the imaginary to cover over the real. In this sense, the imaginary is doubled, imagines wholes, and is marked by repetitions, in antithetical distinction to the discrete differences and partial qualities of the symbolic. Further, insofar as the oedipal axis is the differential that both causes and permits desire, as well as delimiting jouissance, difference from the mother will be comparable to distance from the object (a). There is real privation of the object, symbolic castration of it, and imaginary frustration by it. Further, one finds that subject/object instability proves that the object is external, bringing temporal tension into any quest of realizing desire and into any effort to reify or maintain jouissance.

It is to make new points about the object that Lacan reinterprets Freud's Little Hans case in which Hans's effort to solve the oedipal riddle shows three different ways in which the object can be lacking: Φ, $-\phi$, $\varnothing$. And, although it may seem that castration fear is what Lacan is all about, his concern is not to map out *why* the self suffers, but *how*. At the very least, one sees that there is no developmental theory of stages in Lacan. Rather, the emotions and intellect mature together in reference to $-\phi \rightarrow \$$, linked to the (a) (the formula for fantasy), and to the three jouissances. These functions bring logical time (the time of desire and lack) into language, making them attributes or properties of language. Turning Freud on his head, Lacan reveals conflict as a result of subject structuration, not the cause of tension between a preexisting id and superego. The real is there, in language, in present time, not regressed to some unknown, repressed past. Indeed, repression of castration concerns lack, loss, and negation; not only sexuality. Moreover, when repression is revisited, one finds the object as lacking and thus cognizable only insofar as it produces positive unary traits. Male repression of castration both gives a man a place in the social group and a double task in affirming his masculinity. Females need not repress castration to the degree the male does because they always already have one foot in the real.

Practically nothing is innate, Lacan teaches. There is no mind versus body, nor any inner versus outer. Rather, experience is rooted in the pre-oedipal mother Lacan calls *la lalangue* and that Miller defines as the primordial symbolic mother, giver of the first gifts and the first "givens." Thereby, Miller gives a new twist to Lacan's axiom that *The* generic (essential) Woman does not exist. Woman ex-sists at the level of the (a) and in the space of the real where love and Eros join in the symbolic, giving her a quality of being both there and beyond.

NOTES

Chapter I. "On the Signification of the Phallus" (1958) According to Lacan

1. Geneviève Morel, *La différence des sexes*, course given at the University of Lille, France (1996–1997), in the department of psychoanalysis, p. 17, unedited course.

2. Sigmund Freud, *The Standard Edition of the Complete Psychological Works of Sigmund Freud*, trans. and ed. James Strachey, in collaboration with Anna Freud, assist. Alex Strachey and Alan Tyson (London: The Hogarth Press and the Institute of Psycho-Analysis, 1974), vols. 1–24. Hereafter referred to as *SE*. "Some Psychical Consequences of the Anatomical Distinction between the Sexes" (1925), *SE*, 19: 248–58; "Female Sexuality" (1931), *SE*, 21: 225–43; "Femininity" (1932), *SE*, 22: 112–35.

3. Ernest Jones, *"Sigmund Freud" Life and Work* (3 vols) (London: Hogarth, 1953–1957), vol. I, pp. 1–33.

4. Ana Martinez Westerhausen, *"Le phallus, Pierre de touche de la question de la réalité de Freud,"* *La lettre mensuelle*, no. 97 (March 1991): 34–36.

5. Sigmund Freud, "The Project of a Scientific Psychology" (1950[1895]), *SE*, I: 294–397.

6. Sigmund Freud, *The Interpretation of Dreams* (1900), *SE*, 4 and 5.

7. Jeanne Granon-Lafont, *Topologie lacanienne et clinique analytique* (Cahors: Point Hors Ligne, 1990), p. 18.

8. David Macey, "Phallus: Definitions," *Feminism and Psychoanalysis: A Critical Dictionary*, ed. Elizabeth Wright (Oxford: Blackwell, 1992), p. 11; cf. also reference to Elizabeth Grosz, pp. 318–20.

9. Sigmund Freud, "The Infantile Genital Organization" (1923), *SE*, 19: 139–45.

10. Jacques Lacan, "The Function and Field of Speech and Language in Psychoanalysis" (1953), "The Rome Discourse" *Ecrits: A Selection*, trans. and ed. Alan Sheridan (New York: Norton, 1977), pp. 50–53.

11. Jacques Lacan, *Le séminaire, livre XIII: L'objet de la psychanalyse* (1956–1966), unpublished seminar; cf. also Gerard Wajcman, "Painting" *Critical Essays on Jacques Lacan*, ed. Ellie Ragland (New York: Hall, 1999), pp. 142–48.

12. Jacques Lacan, *Le séminaire, livre IX: L'identification* (1961–1962), *mai et juin*, 1962, unedited seminar.

13. Jacques Lacan, "The Signification of the Phallus" (1958), *Ecrits: A Selection*, trans., and ed. Alan Sheridan (New York: Norton, 1977), pp. 280–91; cf. p. 287.

14. Jacques Lacan, "*La troisième jouissance*," *Lettres de l'école freudienne*, no. 16 (1975): 178–203.

15. Ellie Ragland-Sullivan, "The Paternal Metaphor: A Lacanian Theory of Language," *Revue internationale de philosophie*, vol. 46, no. 1 (1992); cf. also chapter 6 of Ragland, *Essays on the Pleasures of Death: From Freud to Lacan* (New York: Routledge, 1995).

16. Jacques-Alain Miller, "*Le sinthome: un mixte de symptôme et fantasme*," *La cause Freudienne, Revue de la psychanalyse: Les maladies du nom propre*, no. 39 (mai 1998), p. 11.

17. Ellie Ragland-Sullivan, "Lacan Seminars on James Joyce: Writing as Symptom and 'Singular Solution'," *Psychoanalysis and . . .* , ed. Richard Feldstein and Henry Sussman (New York: Routledge, 1990), pp. 67–86; cf. also Jacques Lacan, *Le séminaire, livre XXIII* (1975–1976): *Le sinthome* (1975–1976), unpublished seminar.

18. Jacques Lacan, "The Subversion of the Subject and the Dialectic of Desire in the Freudian Unconscious" (1960), trans. and ed. Alan Sheridan, *Ecrits: A Selection* (New York: Norton, 1977), p. 317.

19. *The Seminar of Jacques Lacan: Encore, Book XX* (1972–1973), ed. Jacques-Alain Miller, trans. with Jacques Lacan, with notes by Bruce Fink (New York: Norton, 1998), p. 133. *Seminar* hereafter referred to in parenthical references as *S*.

20. Sigmund Freud, "The Ego and the Id" (1923), *SE*, 19: 3–66.

21. Jacques Lacan, *Le séminaire, livre V: Les formations de l'inconscient* (1957–1958), ed. Jacques-Alain Miller (Paris: Seuil, 1994), p 511.

22. Sigmund Freud, "Group Psychology and the Analysis of the Ego" (1921), *SE*, 18: 67–143.

23. Elizabeth Grosz, "Phallus: Feminist Implications," *Feminism and Psychoanalysis: A Critical Dictionary*, ed. Elizabeth Wright (Oxford: Blackwell, 1992), pp. 320–23.

24. Jacques Lacan, "*Desire and the Interpretation of Desire in 'Hamlet'*" (1959), trans. Jeffrey Mehlman, *Yale French Studies*, nos. 55–56 (1977): 11–52.

25. Jacques Lacan, "The Mirror Stage as Formative of the Function of the I as Revealed in Psychoanalytic Experience" (1949), *Ecrits: A Selection*, trans. and ed. Alan Sheridan (New York: Norton, 1977), pp. 4–5.

26. Stuart Schneiderman, *Jacques Lacan: The Death of an Intellectual Hero* (Cambridge: Harvard University Press, 1983), pp. 4–5.

27. Jacques-Alain Miller, "Suture (Elements of the Logic of the Signifier)," *Screen*, vol. 18, no. 4 (Winter 1977–1978): 24–34; cf. p. 25.

28. John Holland, "*Le Nom Propre et la Nomination: Russell et Gardiner Avec Lacan*," *Mémoir* pour Obtention du DEA "Concepts et clinique" (Sept. 1998); cf. also Jacques Lacan, "*Of structure as an Immixing of an Otherness Prerequisite to Any Subject Whatever*." *The Structuralist Controversy: The Sciences of Man*, ed. by Richard Macksey and Eugenio Donato (Baltimore: Johns Hopkins University Press, 1975).

29. Tim Dean, "The Germs of Empire: Heart of Darkness," *Colonial Trauma and the Historiography of Aids," The Psychoanalysis of Race*, ed. Christopher Lane (New York: Columbia University Press, 1998), p. 309; cf. also Louis Althusser, "Ideology and Ideological State Apparatuses," in *Lenin in Philosophy and Other Essays*, trans. Ben Brewster (New York: Monthly Review, 1971), 162.

30. Cathy Caruth, "Introduction," *Trauma: Explorations in Memory*, ed. with intro. Cathy Caruth (Baltimore: Johns Hopkins University Press, 1995), cf. pp. 91–92.

31. Immanuel Kant, *The Critique of Judgment*, trans. with intro. Werner S. Pluhar, with foreword by Mary J. Gregor (Indianapolis, Ind.: Hackett, 1987), *Book II,* "Analytic of the Sublime," 97–141.

32. Jacques-Alain Miller, *Ce qui fait insigne*, course given in the department of psychoanalysis, Paris VIII, Saint Denis, 1986-1987, unedited course.

33. Jacques Lacan, *Seminar XI: The Four Fundamental Concepts of Psycho-Analysis* (1964), ed. Jacques-Alain Miller, trans. with notes by Alan Sheridan (New York: Norton, 1977); cf. also Ellie Ragland, "Lacan, the Death Drive, and the Dream of the Burning Child," ed. Sarah Goodwin, *Death and Representation* (Baltimore: Johns Hopkins University Press, 1994), pp. 80–102.

34. Elizabeth Bronfen, "Castration Complex," *Feminism and Psychoanalysis: A Critical Dictionary*, ed. Elizabeth Wright (Oxford: Blackwell, 1992), pp. 41–45; cf. also Hélène Cixous, "Portrait of Dora," *Diacritics* 13 (I): 2–32.

35. Jacques Lacan, *Le séminaire, livre* IV: *La relation d'objet* (1956–1957), ed. Jacques-Alain Miller (Paris: Seuil, 1994), p. 46.

36. Gérard Wajcman, "Painting," *Critical Essays on Jacques Lacan*, ed. Ellie Ragland (New York: Hall, 1999), p. 143.

37. Charles Pyle, "Lacan's Theory of Language: The Symbolic Gap," unpublished ms. All rights reserved to the author.

38. Ellie Ragland-Sullivan, *Jacques Lacan and the Philosophy of Psychoanalysis* (Urbana & Chicago: University of Illinois Press, 1986); cf. ch I.

39. Jacques Lacan, *Seminar III: The Psychoses* (1955–1956), ed. Jacques-Alain Miller, trans. with notes by Russell Grigg (New York: Norton, 1993); cf. also Sigmund Freud, *Psycho-Analytic Notes on an Autobiographical Account of a Case of Paranoia (Dementia Paranoides)* (1911), *SE,* 12: 2–82.

40. Jacques Lacan, *Television: A Challenge to the Psychoanalytic Establishment*, ed. Joan Copjec, trans. Denis Holier, Rosalind Krauss and Annette Michelson and Jeffrey Mehlman (New York: Norton, 1990).

41. Luce Irigaray, *Speculum of the Other Woman*, trans. Gillian C. Gill (Ithaca, N.Y.: Cornell University Press, 1977 [1985]).

42. Ellie Ragland-Sullivan, "Seeking the Third Term: Desire, the Phallus and the Materiality of Language," *Feminism and Psychoanalysis*, ed. Richard Feldstein and Judith Roof (Ithaca, N.Y.: Cornell University Press, 1989), pp. 40–64.

43. Jacques-Alain Miller, *Silet*, course given in the department of psychoanalysis, University of Paris VIII, Saint Denis, 1994–1995, unpublished course.

Chapter 2. Freud's "Female Sexuality" (1931) and "Femininity" (1932)

1. Jacques Lacan, *The Seminar, Book II: The Ego in Freud's Technique of Psychoanalysis* (1954–1955), ed. Jacques-Alain Miller, trans. Sylvana Tomaselli, with notes by John Forrester (New York: Norton, 1991), p. 109.

2. Daniel Machado, "Phobia and Perversion," *Journal of the Centre for Freudian Analysis and Research*, no. 2 (Summer 1993), p. 24.

3. Jacques-Alain Miller, "To Interpret the Cause: From Freud to Lacan, *Newsletter of the Freudian Field*, vol. 3, nos. 1 & 2 (Sping/Fall 1989): 30–50.

4. *Le séminaire de Jacques Lacan, livre IX: L'identification* (1960–1961), unedited seminar.

5. Geneviève Morel, *Lacan et la différence des sexes*, course given in the ACT (*Association de la Cause freudienne*)—Lille, *Séminaie des Echanges* (1996–1997).

6. *The Seminar of Jacques Lacan, Book III: The Psychoses* (1955–1956), ed. Jacques-Alain Miller, trans. with notes by Russell Grigg (New York: Norton, 1993).

7. Sigmund Freud, "Female Sexuality (1931), *SE*, 21: 223–43. Joan Rivière also translated this essay from the German *"Uber die Weibliche Sexualität."*

8. *The Seminar of Jacques Lacan, Book XX: Encore* (1972–1973), ed. Jacques-Alain Miller, trans. Bruce Fink (New York: Norton, 1998), cf. ch. 1.

9. Jacques Lacan, *Le séminaire, livre IV: La relation d'objet* (1955–1956), ed. Jacques-Alain Miller (Paris: Seuil, 1994), cf. p. 269.

10. Jacques Lacan, *"L'étourdit"* (1972), *Scilicet*, no. 4 (Paris: Seuil, 1994); "Stunned," trans. into English, Jack Stone.

11. Ellie Ragland, *Essays on the Pleasures of Death: From Freud to Lacan* (New York: Routledge, 1995), cf. ch. 6.

12. Jacques Lacan, "The Subversion of the Subject and the Dialectic of Desire in the Freudian Unconscious" (1960), *Ecrits: A Selection*, trans. Alan Sheridan (New York: Norton, 1977), p. 315.

13. Jacques Lacan, *Le séminaire, livre XVIII: D'un discours qui ne serait pas du semblant* (1970–1971), unedited seminar.

14. Jacques Lacan, "On a Question Preliminary to Any Possible Treatment of Psychosis" (1957–1958), *Ecrits: A Selection*, trans. Alan Sheridan (New York: Norton, 1977).

15. Jacques Lacan, *De la psychose paranoïaque dans ses rapports avec la presonnalité, suivi de Premiers écrits sur la paranoïa* (Paris: Seuil, 1975).

16. Serena Smith, "The Structure of Hysteria—Discussion of Three Elements," *A-nalysis: The Australian Centre for Psychoanalysis in the Freudian Field*, no. 7 (1996), p. 109; Ragland, *Essays on the Pleasures of Death*, ch. 6, notes 1–18. Cf. also Elizabeth Newman, "The Sexuation Forumlas and Love," *A-nalysis*, no. 7 (1996), p. 61; cf. *Seminar XX*, ch. 2, "To Jakobson."

17. Sigmund Freud, "Instincts and Their Vicissitudes" (1915), *SE*, 14: 111–40, cf. p. 126.

18. Ellie Ragland, "The Structure of the Drives: Where Body and Mind Join," *On the Drives*, ed. Dan Collins, forthcoming as an *Umbr(a)* book.

19. Gilles Chatenay, "Real of Interpretaion," *A-nalysis: The Australian Centre for Psychoanalysis in the Freudian Field*, no. 7 (1996), p. 109.

20. Sigmund Freud, *Totem and Taboo* (1912–1913), *SE*, 13: ix–162.

21. Leonardo Rodriguez, "The Family and the Subject: A Lacanian Perspective," *A-nalysis: The Australian Centre for Psychoanalysis in the Freudian Field*, no. 7 (1996): 21–33, cf., p. 23.

22. Sigmund Freud, "Group Psychology and the Analysis of the Ego," (1921), *SE*, 18: 67–143.

23. *The Seminar of Jacques Lacan, Book VII: The Ethics of Psychoanalysis* (1959–1960), ed. Jacques-Alain Miller, trans. with notes by Dennis Porter (New York: Norton, 1992), pp. 12, 187, and 228.

24. Joel Dor, *"Idenification,"* *Umbr(a): Identity/Identification*, no. 1 (1998): 63–70; cf. p. 68 where he cites *Jacques Lacan, Le séminaire, livre IX: L'identification*, April 4, 1952, unedited seminar.

25. Jacques Damourette, *Des mots à la pensée; essais de la grammaire de la langue française*, tome 6 (Paris: Collection des linguistes contemporains, 1930), p. 172.

26. Jacques Lacan, *Le séminaire, livre XXI: Les non-dupes errent* (1972–1974), unedited seminar.

27. Jacques Lacan, *Le séminaire, livre XVIII: D'un discours qui ne serait pas du semblant* (1970–1971), unedited seminar.

28. Jacques Lacan, *"La troisième," Lettres de l'école freudienne*, no. 16 (1975): 178–203; cf. also *"L'étourdit,"* note #10.

29. John Holland, "Russell, *"Les noms propres, et l'ameublement dernier du monde,"* *DESU* thesis, p. 51; cf. also Jacqes-Alain Miller, *Extimité* (1985–1986), unedited course, Jan. 22, 29, and Feb. 6, 1986.

30. Kirsten Hyldegaard, "Sex as Fantasy and Sex as Symptom," *Umbr(a): Identification/Identity*, no. 1 (1998): 43–52, cf. esp. p. 48.

31. Jeanne Granon-Lafont, *Topologie lacanienne et clinique analytique* (Cahors: Point Hors Ligne, 1990), p. 14.

32. Jeanne-Granon Lafont, *La topologie ordinaire de Jacques Lacan* (Cahors: Point Hors Ligne, 1986, p. 106; cf. also *Le séminaire IX* and *Le séminaire XXIII* (1975–1976): *Le sinthome*. In *Le sinthome*, an unpublished Seminar, Lacan reintroduces the tripartite logic of the torus.

33. Jean-Jacques Bouquier, *"Retournements de Tores et Identifications." Analytica*, vol. 46 (1986): 9–18, cf. pp. 10–11; cf. also *Le séminaire IX* and *Le séminaire XXIII* (1975–1976): *Le sinthome*.

34. Geneviève Morel, "The Hypothesis of Compacity in Chapter 1 of *Encore: Seminar XX* (1972–1973)," *Critical Essays* on Jacques Lacan, ed. Ellie Ragland, G. K. Hall World Author Series (New York: MacMillan, 1999), pp. 149–60.

35. Sigmund Freud, "On Transformations of Instinct Exemplified in Anal Eroticism" (1971), *SE*, 17: 126–33.

36. Jacques Lacan, *Le séminaire, livre VIII* (1960–1961): *Le transfert*, ed. Jacques-Alain Miller (Paris: Seuil, 1991).

37. Jacques Lacan, *"Remarque sur le rapport de Daniel Lagache: 'Psychoanalyse et structure de la personnalité"* (1960), *Ecrits* (Paris: Seuil, 1966), pp. 647–84.

38. Geneviève Morel, *La Jouissance Sexuelle dans les Ecrits et le Séminaire ENCORE de Jacques, Lacan.* Course given in the *Association de la Cause freudienne*—Bordeaux, *Séminaire des Echanges* (November 1992 to June 1993).

Chapter 3. Feminine Sexuality, or Why the Sexual Difference Makes All the Difference

1. Jacques Lacan, "Propos directifs pour un Congres sur la sexualité féminine" (1960), *Ecrits* (Paris: Seuil, 1966), p. 725; See the translation in *Feminine Sexuality: Jacques Lacan and the Ecole freudienne* (New York: Norton, 1985).

2. Cf. Jean-Paul Gilson, "La sexualité, Ça s'extrait," *Actes de l'Ecole de la Cause freudienne: La sexualité dans les défilés du signifiant*, vol. 17 (October 1989), p. 133.

3. Guy Trobas, "Topologie de la réalité sexuelle, conditions du choix d'objet," *Actes de l'Ecole de la Cause freudienne: La sexualité dans les défilés du signifiant* vol. 17 (October 1989), p. 125.

4. Sigmund Freud, "Beyond the Pleasure Principle" (1920): *SE*, 18: 1–64.

5. Jacques Lacan, *De la psychose paranoïaque dans ses rapports avec la personnalité suivi de Premiers écrits sur la paranoïa* (Paris: Seuil, 1975); *The Seminar, Book III* (1955–1956), ed. Jacques-Alain Miller, trans. with Notes by Russell Grigg (New York: Norton, 1993); cf. also *Le séminaire, livre XXIII* (1975–1976): *Le sinthome*, unedited seminar.

6. Russell Grigg, "Lacan's Four Discourses," *Analysis*, no. 4 (1993): 35.

7. Jacques Lacan, "A Jakobson," *The Seminar, Book XX* (1972–73): *Encore*, text ed. Jacques-Alain Miller, trans. with notes by Bruce Fink (Paris, Seuil, 1975), p. 17.

8. Ellie Ragland, *Essays on the Pleasures of Death: From Freud to Lacan* (New York: Routledge, 1994), see chapter 6 on the Oedipus myth or paternal metaphor.

9. Jacques-Alain Miller, "Les divins details," course (1989) in the department of psychoanalysis, University of Paris VIII, Saint-Denis, May 3, 1989, unedited course; cf. also Jacques Lacan, "The Subversion of the Subject and the Dialectic of Desire in the Freudian Unconscious," trans. Alan Sheridan, *Ecrits: A Selection* (New York: Norton, 1977), p. 315.

10. Jacques Lacan, *The Seminar, Book VII: The Ethics of Psychoanalysis*, text ed. Jacques Alain Miller, trans. with notes by Dennis Porter (New York: Norton, 1992), ch. 9.

11. Jacques-Alain Miller, "To Interpret the Cause: From Freud to Lacan," *Newsletter of the Freudian Field*, vol. 3, nos. 1 & 2 (Spring/Fall 1989): 46.

12. Jacques-Alain Miller, "A Reading of Some Details in *Television* in Dialogue with the Audience," *Newsletter of the Freudian Field*, vol. 4, Nos. 1 & 2 (Spring/Fall 1990): 4–30.

13. Jacques Lacan, cf. Ch. 16, "The Subject and the Other: Alienation," *The Four Fundamental Concepts of Psycho-Analysis*, text ed. Jacques-Alain Miller, trans. Alan Sheridan (New York: Norton, 1978).

14. Marc Du Ry, "Desire in Dreams," *Journal of the Centre for Freudian Analysis and Research (JCFAR)*, no. 1 (Winter 1992–1993), pp. 32–33.

15. Jacques Lacan, "Subversion of the Subject and the Dialectic of Desire in the Freudian Unconscious" (1960), *Ecrits: A Selection*, trans. Alan Sheridan (New York: Norton, 1977), p. 315; cf. Sigmund Freud, "Fragment of an Analysis of a Case of Hysteria" (1905 [1901]), *SE*, 7: 3–122.

16. Jacques Lacan, "Hommage faite à Marguerite Duras," du ravissement de Lol V. Stein, *Ornicar? Revue du champ freudien* no. 34 (Autumn 1985): 7–13; cf. p. 9.

17. Jacques Lacan, *Seminar XI* (1964): *The Four Fundamental Concepts of Psycho-Analysis*, trans. Alan Sheridan, ed. Jacques-Alain Miller (New York: Norton, 1978).

18. Ellie Ragland-Sullivan, "Seeking the Third Term: Desire, the Phallus and the Materiality of Language," *Feminism and Psychoanalysis*, ed. Judith Roof and Richard Feldstein (Ithaca, N.Y.: Cornell University Press, 1989), pp. 40–64.

19. Sigmund Freud, "On the Psychological Consequences of the Anatomical Distinction between the Sexes," *SE*, 19: 243–60.

20. Jacques Lacan, *Le séminaire, Livre XXIII* (1975–1961): *Le sinthome*, unedited seminar.

21. Sigmund Freud, "Analysis Terminable and Interminable," *SE*, 23: 211–53.

22. Jacques Lacan, *Le séminaire, Livre VIII* (1960–1961): *Le transfert*, text ed. Jacques-Alain Miller (Paris: Seuil, 1991), p. 185.

23. Jacques Lacan, *Television: A Challenge to the Psychoanalytic Establishment*, text ed. Jacques-Alain Miller, trans. Annette Michaelson, Rosalind Krauss, Dennis Hollier and Joan Copjec (New York: Norton, 1990).

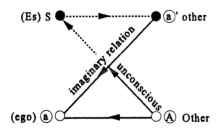

24. Ellie Ragland, chapter 5, "Lacan and the Ethics of Desire," in *Essays on the Pleasures of Death: From Freud to Lacan* (New York: Routledge, 1995).

25. Sigmund Freud, "Inhibitions, Symptoms and Anxiety," *SE*, 20: 75–176.

26. Jacques-Alain Miller, *Sur André Gide*, course for 1989–1990 in the department of psychoanalysis, University of Paris VIII, Saint-Denis, unedited course.

27. Jacques-Alain Miller, "De la nature des semblants," course for 1991–1992 in the department of psychoanalysis, University of Paris VIII, Saint-Denis, unedited course, February 5, 1992.

28. Jacques-Alain Miller, *Donc*, course for 1993–1994 in the department of psychoanalysis, University of Paris VIII, Saint-Denis, unedited course.

29. Jacques Lacan, "The Signification of the Phallus" (1958), *Ecrits: A Selection*, trans. Alan Sheridan (New York: Norton, 1977).

30. Jacques Lacan, *The Seminar, Book II: The Ego in Freud's Theory and in the Technique of Psychoanalysis*, 1954–1955, ed. Jacques-Alain Miller, trans. Sylvana Tomaselli (New York: Norton, 1988), p. 243.

31. Jacques-Alain Miller, "Duty and the Drives," *Newsletter of the Freudian Field*, vol. 6, nos. 1 & 2 (Spring/Fall 1992): 5–15.

32. Geneviève Morel, *La jouissance sexuelle dans les Ecrits et le Séminaire de Jacques LACAN*, ACF-BORDEAUX *Séminaire d' échange*, Nov. 1992–June 1993, pp. 27–31.

33. Carmen Gallano, *"De la femme aimée à la femme désirante," La cause freudienne: La revue de psychoanalyse: L'Autre sexe*, no. 24 (June 1993), p. 92.

34. Eric Laurent, "Positions féminines de l'être," *La Cause freudienne: La revue de psychoanalyse; L'Autre sexe*, no. 24 (June 1993), p. 107.

35. Silvia Tendlarz, "The Dream of Being the Most Beautiful," article in *Ms.*

36. Jacques Lacan, "The Direction of the Treatment and the Principles of Its Power" (1958), *Ecrits: A Selection*, trans. Alan Sheridan (New York: Norton, 1977), p. 256.

Chapter 4. A Rereading of Freud's 1925 Essay

1. Jacques Lacan, "A Love Letter" (*Une lettre d'âmour*), *The Seminar of Jacques Lacan, Book XX: Encore on Feminine Sexuality, The Limits of Love and Knowledge* (1972–1973), ed. Jacques-Alain Miller, trans. with notes by Bruce Fink (New York: Norton, 1998): 78–89, esp. sexuation graph on p. 78.

2. Marie-Hélène Brousse, "Feminism with Lacan," *Newsletter of the Freudian Field (NFF)*, vol. 5, nos. 1&2 (Spring/Fall, 1991): 113.

3. Sigmund Freud, "Analysis of a Phobia in a Five-Year-Old Boy" (1909), *SE*, 10: 3–149.

4. Sigmund Freud, "Analysis Terminable and Interminable" (1937), *SE*, 23: 211–53.

5. Sigmund Freud, "Some Psychical Consequences of the Anatomical Difference between the Sexes" (1925), *SE*, 19: 243–58.

6. Sigmund Freud, "Female Sexuality" (1931), *SE*, 21: 223–243; cf. also lecture 33 "Femininity" (1932) [from *the New Introductory Lectures to Psychoanalysis*] *SE*, 22: 112–35.

7. Aristotle, "On Interpretation," in *The Complete Works*, rev. Oxford translation, ed. Jonathan Barnes in two vols. (Princeton, N.J.: Princeton University Press, 1984); cf. also Jean-Paul Gilson, *La Topologie de Lacan: une articulation de la cure psychanalytique* (Cap-Saint-Ignace, Québec: Editions Balzac), p. 68.

8. Sigmund Freud, *Beyond the Pleasure Principle* (1920), *SE*, 18: 3–64.; cf. also Ellie Ragland, *Essays on the Pleasures of Death: From Freud to Lacan* (New York: Routledge, 1995).

9. Geneviève Morel. "The Hypothesis of Compacity in Chapter I of *Encore: Seminar XX* (1972–1973)," *Critical Essays on Jacques Lacan*, ed. Ellie Ragland (New York: G. K. Hall, 1999), pp. 149–60; cf. also Pierre-Gilles Gueguen, "Un trait de perversion: remarques sur un cas de Lacan," *Quarto: Traits de perversion*, no. 43 (mai 1991): 40–42; cf. p. 41.

10. Jacques Lacan, *Seminar, Book XI: The Four Fundamental Concepts of Psychoanalysis*, ed. Jacques-Alain Miller, trans. Alan Sheridan (New York; Norton, 1977), p. 43.

11. Jacques Lacan, *L'angoisse, livre X* (1962–1963), unedited seminar; cf. also Michel Bousseyroux, *Les séries de la découverte freudienne: a-bords de la père-version*, vol. 6 (July 1990): 120.

12. Jacques-Alain Miller, *Les noms-du-père et les semblants* (1991–1992), course given in the department of psychoanalysis at the University of Paris VIII, Saint Denis, unedited course.

13. Jean-Paul Gilson, *La Topologie de Lacan: Une articulation de la cure psychanalytique* (Cap-Saint-Ignace, Québec: Les Editions Balzac, 1994), p. 15. Cf. Sigmund Freud's efforts to evolve an account of an energetics, as, for example, in "Project for a Scientific Psychology" (1950 [1895]), *SE*, 1: 281–397.

14. *The Seminar of Jacques Lacan, Book III: The Psychoses* (1955–1956), ed. Jacques-Alain Miller, trans. with notes by Russell Grigg (New York: Norton, 1993).

15. Jacques Lacan, *L'étourdit, Scilicet*, vol. 4 (1973): 5–52.

16. Jacques Lacan, *Le sinthome:* livre XXIII (1975–1976), Unpublished seminar.

17. Jacques Lacan, *D'un discours qui ne serait pas du semblant* (1970–1971): *livre XVIII*, unpublished seminar.

18. *Joyce avec Lacan*, ed. Jacques Aubert (Paris: Navarin, 1987), p. 332.

19. Jacques Lacan, . . . *Ou pire, livre XIX* (1971–1972), unpublished seminar.

20. Jack Stone, *The Fantasy, Le Sinthome, and the "Babbling Pumpt of Platinism": From Geometry, to Topology, to Joyce*, a dissertation presented to the University of Missouri-Columbia Graduate School in partial fulfillment of the requirements for the degree, Doctor of Philosophy, May 1998.

21. Jacques Lacan, *Le séminaire, livre V: Les formations de l'inconscient* (1957–1958), ed. Jacques-Alain Miller (Paris: Seuil, 1995), p. 511.

22. Sigmund Freud, "Three Essays on the Theory of Sexuality" (1905), *SE*, 7: 125–245.

23. Sigmund Freud, "The Question of Lay Analysis" (1926), *SE*, 20: 179–258, cf. p. 212.

24. Sigmund Freud, *The Interpretation of Dreams* (1900), *SE*, 4 and 5.

25. Sigmund Freud, *Fragment of an Analysis of a Case of Hysteria* (1901 [1905]), *SE*, 7: 3–122.

26. Sigmund Freud, "The Development of the Libido and the Sexual Orientations," no. 21 in *Introductory Lectures in Psycho-Analysis* (Part III), *SE*, 16 (1916–1917): 320–38.

27. Jacques Lacan, *Le séminaire, livre IV: La relation d'objet* (1955–1956), ed. Jacques-Alain Miller (Paris: Seuil, 1994), p. 269.

28. Jacques Lacan, *Le séminaire, livre XXII: R. [real] S. [symbolic] I. [imaginary]* (1974–1975), unpublished seminar.

29. Sigmund Freud, "'A Child Is Being Beaten': A Contribution to the Study of the Origin of Sexual Perversions" (1919), *SE*, 17: 177–204.

30. Sigmund Freud, "The Infantile Genital Organization" (1923), *SE*, 19: 141–45

31. Sigmund Freud, "The Ego and the Super-Ego" (1923), *SE*, 19: 28–39; cf. also "The Dissolution of the Oedipus Complex" (1924), *SE*, 19: 173–79.

32. Cf also Sigmund Freud, "Femininity," lecture 33 of *The New Introductory Lectures* (1932), *SE*, 12: 112–35.

33. Sigmund Freud, "An Outline of Psycho-Analysis" (1940 [1938]). *SE*, 23: 141–207.

34. Jacques Lacan, "Seminar of 21 January 1975, *Feminine Sexuality: Jacques Lacan and the école freudienne,*" ed. Juliet Mitchell and Jacqueline Rose, trans. J. Rose (New York: Norton, 1982), pp. 162–71; cf. p. 170.

35. Ellie Ragland-Sullivan, "The Sexual Masquerade: A Lacanian Theory of Sexual Difference," *Lacan and the Subject of Language,* ed. Ellie Ragland-Sullivan and Mark Bracher (New York: Routledge, 1991), pp. 49–80.

36. Jacques Lacan, *Le séminaire, livre VIII* (1960–1961): *Le transfert,* ed. Jacques-Alain Miller (Paris: Seuil, 1991), pp. 278, 281, and 284

37. James M. Mellard, "Lacan and the New Lacanians: Josephine Hart's *Damage,* Lacanian Tragedy and the Ethics of Jouissance," *PMLA,* vol. 113, no. 3 (May 1998), p. 395.

38. Sigmund Freud, *Totem and Taboo* (1913), *SE*, 13: 1–164.

39. Jacques Lacan, *Les Complexes Familiaux dans la Formation de l'individu: Essai d'analyse d'une fonction en psychologie* (Paris: Navarin Editeur, 1984), pp. 40–73.

40. Jacques Lacan, *Le séminaire, livre IX* (1961–1962): *L'identification,* unpublished seminar.

41. Gerard Wajcman, "Painting," *Critical Essays on Jacques Lacan* ed. Ellie Ragland

(New York: Simon & Schuster/G. K. Hall, 1999), Twayne Critical World Author Series, pp. 142–48.

42. Jacques Lacan, *The Seminar, Book II* (1954–1055): *The Ego in Freud's Theory and in the Technique of Psychoanalysis,* trans. Sylvana Tomaselli, with notes by John Forrester (New York: Norton, 1991), pp. 109–243.

43. Bruno Bettleheim, *Freud and Man's Soul* (New York: Knopf, 1982).

44. Helena Schultz-Keil, *Review of Freud and Man's Soul* by Bruno Bettleheim, *Lacan Study Notes,* special issue, *Hystoria* 6–0 (1988): 262–66, cf. p. 260.

45. Sigmund Freud, "The Ego and the Id" (1923 [1927]), *SE,* 19: 3–63.

46. Jacques-Alain Miller, "*Le Sinthome: un mixte de symptôme et fantasme,*" *Revue de la psychanalyse: Ecole de la Cause Freudienne: Les maladies du nom propre,* no. 39 (mai 1998), p. 11; cf. also the course *Ce qui fait insigne,* given in 1986–1987, in the department of psychoanalysis at the University of Paris VIII, Saint Denis, unedited course.

47. Jacques-Alain Miller, *First Course,* given in 1981–1982, in the department of psychoanalysis at the University of Paris VIII, Saint Denis, unedited course.

48. Jacques Lacan, *Le séminaire, livre XVII: L'envers de la psychanqalyse* (1969–1970), ed. Jacques-Alain Miller (Paris: Seuil, 1991), cf. ch. 8.

49. Jacques Lacan, "*La troisième jouissance,*" *Lettres de l'école freudienne,* no. 16 (1975): 178–203.

50. Marc du Ry, "Desire in Dreams," *Journal of the Center for Freudian Analysis and Research,* vol. I (Winter 1992–1993): 28–44, cf. p. 34.

51. Ellie Ragland, *Essays on the Pleasures of Death* (New York: Routledge, 1995) cf. ch. 6 on the paternal metaphor.

52. Sigmund Freud, "Group Psychology and the Analysis of the Ego" (1921), *SE,* 18: 67–143.

53. Charles Pyle, *Logic, Markedness and Language Universals,* chapters 8 ("The Law of Marks") and 9 ("On the Mark"), July 11, 1991, Unpublished Ms. All rights reserved to the author; cf. also "Toward a Buddhist Theory of Language," *The Proceedings of the First International Conference on Tai Studies,* July 29–31, 1998 (Mahidol: Mahidol University Press, forthcoming).

54. Marc Darmon, *Essais sur la Topologie lacanienne* (Paris: Editions de l'Association Freudienne, 1990).

55. Jacques Lacan, "On a Question Preliminary to Any Possible Treatment of Psychosis" (1957–1958), *Ecrits: A Selection,* trans, with notes by Alan Sheridan (New York: Norton, 1977), p. 189.

56. Geneviève Morel, *La différence des sexes,* course given in the department of psychoanalysis, the University of Lille (1996–1997), p. 20, unpublished course.

57. Jacques Lacan, "Guiding Remarks for a Congress on Feminine Sexuality" (1960), *Feminine Sexuality: Jacques Lacan and the école freudienne,* ed. Juliet Mitchell and Jacqueline Rose (New York: Norton, 1982).

58. Sigmund Freud, "Inhibitions, Symptoms, Anxieties" (1926), *SE*, 20: 77–175.

59. Sigmund Freud, "The Taboo of Virginity" (1917), *SE*, 11: 192–208; cf. also . . . *Ou pire* (1971–1972).

60. Jacques Lacan, *Le séminaire, livre VI* (1958–1959): *Le désir et son son interprétation*, unpublished seminar. "*Hamlet*" (seminar of April 29), trans. James Hulbert, *Yale French Studies*, nos. 55/56 (1977): 11–52; "Desire and the Interpretation of Desire in *Hamlet*," ed. and trans. Shoshana Felman in *Literature and Psychoanalysis: The Question of Reading Otherwise* (Baltimore, Md.: Johns Hopkins University Press, 1982).

61. Sol Aparicio, "*Le désir au féminin*," *La cause freudienne, la revue de psychanalysis: L'autre sexe*, no. 24 (June 1993), p. 26.

62. Pierre Naveau, "*La Querelle du Phallus*," *La cause freudienne: Revue de psychanalyse*, no. 24 (June 1993), pp. 15–16.

63. Sandor Ferenczi, "Thalassa, A Theory of Genitality" (1924), (New York: Norton, 1968).

64. Dorion Sagan, "Gender Specifics: Why Women Aren't Men," *The New York Times*, section 15, Sunday, June 21, 1998, pp. 1 and 20.

65. Jacques-Alain Miller, "Commentary on a Fragment of 'Spring Awakening' by Jacques Lacan," *Analysis* 6 (1995): 35–39.

Chapter 5. The Place of the Mother in Lacanian Analysis

1. Jacques Lacan, *Le Séminaire, livre IV: La relation d'objet* (1956–1957), ed. Jacques-Alain Miller, (Paris: Seuil, 1994).

2. Steven A. Mitchell, "Gender and Sexual Orientation in the Age of Postmoderism: The Plight of the Perplexed Clinician," *Gender & Psychoanalysis: An Interdisciplinary Journal*, vol. 1, no. 1 (Jan. 1996): 45–73.

3. Jacques Lacan, *The Seminar, Book XI: The Four Fundamental Concepts of Psycho-Analysis* (1964), ed. Jacques-Alain Miller, trans. Alan Sheridan (New York: Norton, 1981).

4. Jacques Lacan, *Le séminaire, livre XXVI: La topologie et le temps* (1977–1978), unedited Seminar; seminar of November 10, 1978.

5. Jacques Lacan, *Le séminaire, livre XXIII: Le sinthome* (1975–1976), unedited seminar; partially published in *Ornicar?*, nos. 6 to 11.

6. Jacques Lacan, *Les complexes familiaux dans la Formation de l'individu: Essai d'analyse d'une fonction en psychologie* (Paris: Navarin, 1984). The text was written for vol. 7 of *l'Encyclopédie française* for the part on "mental life" and was placed under the section on "The Family" (1938).

7. Ellie Ragland, *Essays on the Pleasures of Death: From Freud to Lacan* (New York: Routledge, 1995), cf. chapter 6.

8. See Lacan's simplification of his schema L where he shows the *subject* as stretched over the four corners of the schema:

$$\begin{array}{l} \text{S(ubject)} \longrightarrow \text{o(ther) [ego ideal]} \\ \text{o'[ideal ego]} \longleftarrow \text{O(ther)} \end{array}$$

in "On a Question Preliminary to Any Possible Treatment of Psychosis" (Dec. 1957– Jan. 1958), trans. Alan Sheridan (New York: Norton, 1977), p. 193.

9. Jacques Lacan, *The Seminar Book XX: Encore* (1972–1973), ed. Jacques-Alain Miller, trans. with notes by Bruce Fink (New York: Norton, 1998) (Paris: Seuil, 1975), p. 78; cf. "A Love Letter."

10. Jacques Lacan, *The Seminar, Book III: The Psychoses* (1955–1956), ed. Jacques-Alain Miller, trans. with notes by Russell Grigg, (New York: Norton, 1994).

11. Nancy Chodorow, *The Reproduction of Mothering: Psychoanalysis and the Sociology of Gender* (Berkeley: University of California Press, 1978); Carol Gilligan, *In a Different Voice: Psychological Theory and Women's Development* (Cambridge, Mass.: Harvard University Press, 1982).

12. Lacan's first rewriting of Freud's concept of the Oedipus complex is to be found in "On a Question Preliminary to Any Possible Treatment of Psychosis" in *Ecrits: A Selection* (p. 200):

$$\frac{\text{Name-of-the-Father.}}{\text{Desire of the Mother,}} \quad \frac{\text{Desire of the Mother}}{\text{Signified to the subject}} \rightarrow \text{Name-of-the-Father}$$
$$\left(\frac{\text{Other}}{\text{Phallus}}\right)$$

See also Lacan's completed graph of desire in "The Subversion of the Subject and Dialectic of Desire in the Freudian Unconscious" (1960) in *Ecrits: A Selection*, where the base is constituted of the I(O), Lacan's matheme for the ideal ego, and the $\not{S}$, or the lack-in-being that marks a split in the ego between one's own Ideal formation and the role of others and the Other in constituting it on an imaginary axis (p. 315).

13. Luce Irigaray, *Speculum of the Other Woman*, trans. Gillian C. Gill (Ithaca, N.Y.: Cornell University Press, 1985); Elizabeth Grosz, *Jacques Lacan: A Feminist Introduction* (New York: Routledge, 1990).

14. Geneviève Morel, *La jouissance sexuelle dans les Ecrits et le Séminaire Encore de Jacques Lacan, Associates cause Freudienne, Séminaire des Echanges—Bordeaux*, course given in Nov. 1992 to June 1993: "The 'feminine' symbols have no grip except an imaginary one. That's because these images are, in fact, subjected to other symbols in the unconscious. That's what Freud meant or understood in attacking femininity in a surrealist manner (how does one speak of a castrated woman?) to a complex of castration and a castrated mother" (p. 27).

15. Jacques Lacan, "On a Question Preliminary to Any Possible Treatment of Psychosis," cf. Schema I, p. 212 of *Ecrits: A Selection.*

16. Sigmund Freud, "Splitting of the Ego in the Process of Defence" (1937), *SE,* 23: 275–78; cf. also pages 201–204 in Freud's discussion of the phenomenon of ego splitting under pressure from the external world as applicable to the neuroses, as well as the psychoses, and cases of fetishism in "An Outline of Psycho-Analysis" (1940 [1938]), *SE,* 23: 138–207.

17. Jacques-Alain Miller, "To Interpret the Cause: From Freud to Lacan," *Newsletter of the Freudian Field,* vol. 3, nos. 1 & 2 (Fall–Spring 1989): 30–50. Jacques Lacan "The Function and Field of Speech and Language in Psychoanalysis" (1953) *Ecrits: A Selection,* trans and ed. Alan Sheridan (New York: Norton, 1974).

18. Jacques-Alain Miller, *De la nature des semblants,* course given in the department of psychoanalysis 1991–1992, University of Paris VIII, Saint-Denis, unedited course.

19. Jacques Lacan, *Le séminaire, livre X* (1962–1963): *L'angoisse,* unedited seminar.

20. Ellie Ragland, "Lacan," *Feminism and Psychoanalysis: A Critical Dictionary,* ed. Elizabeth Wright (Oxford: Blackwell, 1992), p. 203.

21. Jacques-Alain Miller, *Extimité.* Course given in the department of psycho-analysis in 1985–1986, University of Paris VIII, Saint-Denis, unedited course.

22. Jacques Lacan, *Television: A Challenge to the Psychoanalytic Establishment,* ed. Joan Copjec, trans. D.Holier, R. Krauss, A. Michelson, and J. Mehlman (New York: Norton, 1990). In *Television* (1974), Lacan solidifies the third phase of his teaching, which elaborates the real and jouissance, a phase clearly ennunciated in *Encore* (1972–1973).

23. Jacques Lacan, "The Subversion of the Subject and the Dialectic of Desire in the Freudian Unconscious" (1960), *Ecrits: A Selection,* trans. with notes by Alan Sheridan (New York: Norton, 1978), pp. 149–61.

24. Jacques Lacan, "The Signification of the Phallus," *Ecrits: A Selection,* trans. with notes by Alan Sheridan (New York: Norton, 1977), pp. 281–91.

25. A classic example can be found in the case of Judge Daniel Paul Schreber's *Memoirs of My Nervous Illness,* trans. Ida Macalpine and Richard A. Hunter, with a new intro. by Samuel M. Weber (Cambridge, Mass.: Harvard University Press, 1988). Schreber solves the dilemma brought on by his psychotic break concerning whether he is a man or woman, not at the level of organ reality, but by a delusory reorganization of his subjective worldview such that he becomes the wife of God, identifying both as God and as God's wife; cf. also Louis A. Sass, *The Paradoxes of Delusion: Wittgenstein, Schreber, and the Schizophrenic Mind* (Ithaca, N.Y.: Cornell University Press, 1994). Sass stresses that schizophrenia is not concomitant with poor reality testing, nor is delusion. Lacan taught that delusion is a strange use of language that tries to impose a lack where there is none, tries to answer the question of sexual difference where difference has been foreclosed.

26. Robert Groome, "Towards a Topology of the Subject," *Umbr(a): Aesthetics and Sublimation* (1999): 83–92; cf. pp. 83 and 86.

27. Jacques-Alain Miller, *Divine Details* (1989), course given in the department of psychoanalysis, University of Paris VIII, Saint-Denis, unedited course.

28. Nancy Chodorow, "Heterosexuality as a Compromise Formation: Reflections on the Psychoanalytic Theory of Sexual Development," *Psychoanalysis and Contemporary Thought*, vol. 15: 267–304, p. 273.

29. Jacques Lacan, *Le séminaire, livre XXIII* (1975–1976): *Le sinthome*, unedited seminar, partially published in *Ornicar?*, nos. 6 to 11. In this seminar, Lacan depicted James Joyce as manifesting a kind of schizophrenic language. This study led him to his third theory of psychosis in which he argued that the void in the Other—the hole in the symbolic ($\varnothing$)—is filled by objects rather than signifiers. The object takes preponderence over the dialectical interaction of signifiers (S1→S2). The object, unlike the signifiers, is absolute, non-dialectical, and stabilizes the schizophrenic's universe when he or she is not in an episode which is marked by being plagued by the objects, such as the gaze or the voice, experienced as separated from the body.

30. Jacques Lacan, *Le séminaire, livre XXII* (1974–1975): *R.S.I.*, seminar of March 18, 1975, unedited seminar.

31. Jacques Alain Miller, *Donc* (1993–1994), course given in the department of psychoanalysis, University of Paris VIII, Saint-Denis, unedited course.

32. Rosine Lefort, in collaboration with Robert Lefort, *Birth of the Other* (Urbana & Chicago: University of Illinois Press, 1994): "The essential character of the object relation [is]—its being a relation with the lack of object—which found[s] desire" (pp. 276–77).

33. Ellie Ragland, "The Psychical Nature of Trauma: Freud's Dora, The Young Homosexual Woman, and the *Fort! Da!* Paradigm," *Topologies of Memory: Essays on the Limit of Knowledge and Memory*, ed. Linda Belau and Peter Ramadanovic (New York: Other Press, 2002), pp. 75–100.

34. Sigmund Freud, "The Dissolution of the Oedipus Complex" (1924), *SE*, 19: 171–87; "Some Psychical Consequences of the Anatomical Distinction between the Sexes" (1925), *SE*, 19: 243–60.

35. Alexander Stevens, "Two Destinies for the Subject: Neurotic Identifications and Psychotic Petrifications," *Newsletter of the Freudian Field*, vol. 5, nos. 1/2 (Spring/Fall 1991): 96–112.

36. Sigmund Freud, *Totem and Taboo* (1913): *SE*, 13: 1–161.

37. Jacques-Alain Miller, *Silet* (1994–1995), course given in the department of psychoanalysis, University of Paris VIII, Saint Denis, unedited course.

38. Ellie Ragland, "Lacan and the Subject of Law: Sexuation and Discourse in the Mapping of *Subject* Positions That Give the Ur-Form of Law," *Washington and Lee Law Review*, vol. 54, no. 3 (Summer 1997): 1091–1118.

39. Jacques Lacan, *Le séminaire, livre VI* (1958–1959): *Le désir et l'interprétation du désir*, unedited seminar; cf. "Desire and the Interpretation of Desire in *Hamlet*," trans. James Hulbert, *Yale French Studies*, nos. 55 & 56 (1977).

40. Jacques Lacan, "*La troisième jouissance,*" *Lettres de l'école freudienne,* no. 16 (1975): 178–203.

41. Jacques Lacan, *Le séminaire, livre XVII* (1970–1971): *L'envers de la psychanalyse,* ed. Jacques-Alain Miller (Paris: Seuil, 1991).

42. Jacques Lacan, "The Agency of the Letter in the Unconscious or Reason since Freud" (1957–1958), *Ecrits: A Selection,* trans. with notes by Alan Sheridan (New York: Norton, 1977), p. 146–78.

43. Ellie Ragland, "An Overview of the Real," *Reading Seminars I and II,* ed. R. Feldstein, B. Fink, and M. Jaanus (Albany: State University of New York Press, 1995); cf. also Sigmund Freud, *From the History of an Infantile Neurosis* (1918 [1914]), SE, 17: 2–122.

44. Jean-Paul Gilson, *La topologie de Lacan: Une articulation de la cure psychanalytique* (Cap. Saint-Ignace, Québec: Les Editions Balzac, 1994), p. 194.

45. Jacques-Alan Miller, *First Course* (1981–1982), course given in the department of psychoanalysis, University of Paris VIII, Saint-Denis, unedited course.

46. Jacques-Alain Miller, "Matrice," *Ornicar?* no. 4 (1975); cf. also "Matrix," trans. Daniel Collins, *lacanian ink,* no. 12 (Fall 1997): 44–51.

Conclusion

1. *The Seminar of Jacques Lacan, On Feminine Sexuality, The Limits of Love and Knowledge: Book XX: Encore,* 1972–1973, ed. Jacques-Alain Miller, trans. with notes by Bruce Fink (New York: Norton, 1998), p. 125.

2. Geneviève Morel, "The Hypothesis of Compacity" in chapter 1 of *Encore: Seminar XX* (1972–1973), *Critical Essays on Jacques Lacan,* ed. Ellie Ragland (New York: Macmillan, in the G. K. Hall Twayne series on World Authors, 1999), pp. 149–60.

3. Jean-Paul Gilson, *La Topologie de Lacan: Une articulation de la cure psychanalytique* (Cap-Saint-Ignace, Québec: Editions Balzac, 1994), p. 194.

Index